I0576141

TRUE NORTH

CANADIAN COOKING FROM
COAST TO COAST

TRUE
NORTH

True North

Copyright © 2015 by Derek Dammann and Chris Johns.

Foreword © 2015 by Jamie Oliver.

All rights reserved.

Published by HarperCollins Publishers Ltd

First edition

No part of this book may be used or reproduced in any manner whatsoever
without the prior written permission of the publisher, except in the case
of brief quotations embodied in reviews.

HarperCollins books may be purchased for educational, business, or
sales promotional use through our Special Markets Department.

HarperCollins Publishers Ltd
2 Bloor Street East, 20th Floor
Toronto, Ontario, Canada
M4W 1A8

www.harpercollins.ca

Food photography by Farah Khan; scenic photography by Farah Khan and Alison Slattery

Library and Archives Canada Cataloguing in Publication information is available

ISBN 978-1-44343-173-6

Printed and bound in China

IMA 9 8 7 6 5 4 3 2 1

To my son and best friend, Felix.
—DD

For Harper, Jillian and Suzanne.
—CJ

CONTENTS

FOREWORD BY JAMIE OLIVER ix

INTRODUCTION BY CHRIS JOHNS xiii

ATLANTIC 1

FOREST 35

Freshwater 62

FIELD 73

Tundra 92

Charcuterie 100

FARM 115

Foie Gras 138

Prairies 146

ORCHARD & VINEYARD 157

Canadian Plateau de Fruits de Mer 176

PACIFIC 183

HOME 213

FUNDAMENTALS 233

ACKNOWLEDGEMENTS FROM DEREK 249

ACKNOWLEDGEMENTS FROM CHRIS 251

INDEX 255

✗

FOREWORD

by JAMIE OLIVER

It's with great pleasure that I'm writing this foreword for Derek's book, as we've been good friends for over a decade now and—most importantly—damn, that boy can cook. I really think he's up there with some of the absolute best chefs in the world.

If you're a regular customer at his restaurant Maison Publique you'll know exactly what I'm talking about when I say that Derek has a brilliant ability to surprise you with his food, yet at the same time make you feel you're in a really homely place. He's an interesting chef because his cooking is incredibly rustic and real, but he's a bit zany and punky in his approach. You'll definitely get that vibe in this book. What you won't get quite as much is that he can also do that clever, molecular, high-end technique and camp, pretty presentation, and I think that deep down he loves that level of detail (he's probably showing off . . . or maybe I'm just jealous). For me, he really cooks the perfect modern Canadian food, steeped in heritage. What he's achieved at Maison Publique is spectacular.

Although I don't see him enough these days, I definitely consider Derek to be one of my best friends. He's a good guy with a dark, dark sense of humour and makes me laugh more than anyone I know. I think he may have been a drag queen in a previous life, but I'll leave that aside for the moment.

INTRODUCTION
by CHRIS JOHNS

This is a book about Canadian food. About the people and places that give this country its distinct flavour. About the ingredients and ideas that inspire us every day.

Over the past year Derek and I, along with our trusty, motion-sickness-prone photographer, Farah, traversed the country from sea to shining sea, meeting with farmers, winemakers, chefs and fishermen. We travelled by planes, trains and automobiles, by fishing boat, ferry and snowmobile. We cooked on beaches and on boats, in vineyards and backyards, at home and at large, and we had a blast doing it.

Derek and I are both West Coast kids who, after various adventures across the country and abroad, settled in Eastern Canada: Montreal and Toronto respectively. My work as a food and travel writer has taken me across Canada many times to pretty much all of our great restaurants, and Derek's cooking draws on the best ingredients our country has to offer.

I probably first tasted Derek's food many years ago, long before we ever met, when he was working in Victoria at the great Zambri's restaurant—then and today easily among the best Italian restaurants in the country. Years later, when he was the chef at Montreal's DNA, I reviewed the restaurant for the *Globe and Mail* and was thrilled to discover a chef who was cooking personal, sophisticated food that was approachable, fun and,

above all, utterly delicious. A couple of years after that we finally met and discovered that we shared not only similar palates and ideas about what makes great food, but similar backgrounds and attitudes. When the opportunity to collaborate on a book came up, it seemed like a natural fit.

At its most basic, Derek's food can be described as regionally inspired, seasonally driven nose-to-tail cooking, but that only scratches the surface. Although his cooking is inspired by Italian, British and Quebec traditions, he is fundamentally a pan-Canadian chef.

That's why we've chosen to structure the book the way we have. *True North*'s recipes are divided into chapters that are arranged not by season or dish but by the ingredients from the locations that inspired them: Atlantic, Forest, Tundra, Orchard & Vineyard, etc. Ours is a massive country, and by breaking the book down this way we are able to highlight the specific areas and ingredients that give Canada its culinary identity.

The recipes are laid out in such a way that they evolve from dead simple to more complex. While the more involved creations might present a challenge to all but the most dedicated of home cooks, we offer shortcuts and detours that make even the most advanced recipes accessible to everyone. Besides, anyone who challenges themselves to cooking through the entire book will gain enough knowledge and technique through the simpler recipes that they will be able to tackle the more involved ones with ease.

Canada is in the midst of a culinary revolution. Our ingredients are the envy of the world, our chefs are drawing on varied backgrounds to use those ingredients in exciting ways and our great national melting pot is growing more delicious every year.

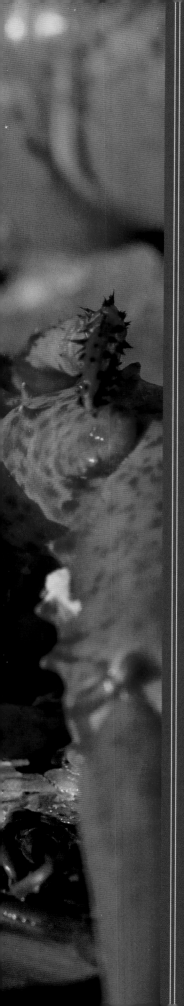

⚔ ATLANTIC

"You see that point of land out there?" asks Captain Frankie, pointing to a hazy grey shape hovering between the slate-grey ocean and the steel-grey sky. "That's Cape Spear, the farthest point east in North America." It's a sight as rugged and dramatic as anyone could hope for out here on the edge of the continent, and it marks, in some ways, the launch of our trip across the country.

Derek and I had arrived in Newfoundland a couple of days before, but this moment, out here on the water at the edge of the continent, it feels like our trip has really begun. We had picked Newfoundland and Labrador as the first stop on our cross-country tour not only because it's as far east as we can go but also because the food coming out of here right now is some of the best and most exciting anywhere.

Our first stop in the province was the town of Elliston, for the Roots, Rants and Roars Festival, an annual celebration of

Newfoundland and Labrador culinary traditions. Elliston is best known as the root cellar capital of the world, and seeing all those ancient, mysterious-looking structures built into the earth—"like hobbit houses," Derek said—was a reminder of how deep the food traditions run in this part of the world. Refrigeration and modern shipping methods mean that people in Elliston no longer have to rely on their root cellars to survive the winters, but most houses still maintain lush vegetable gardens, and the great cod-drying racks known as flakes still line the seashore.

Despite, or maybe because of, its remoteness, the festival in Elliston is one of the most coveted invitations a chef in Canada can receive, and it's a great opportunity to check out what the locals are up to. The pristine quality of the ingredients available around Newfoundland and the surrounding Maritime provinces is astounding. Shellfish, of course, with names as romantic as they are delicious: Raspberry Point, Lovers Creek, Malpeque, Black Point and Beausoleil oysters; fat, bright clams; massive libidinous mussels; but also grass-fed beef from PEI, grain-fed pork from Point Leamington, Newfoundland, and oil-black Acadian caviar from New Brunswick. Not to mention the wild game—moose, grouse, seal—that local chefs are incorporating into their menus.

No resource, however, has been more central to the culinary history of Newfoundland and Labrador than cod. For centuries the rich waters of the Atlantic delivered hundreds of thousands of tonnes of these fish. So much, in fact, that advances in fishing technology resulted in overfishing, and the cod stocks were depleted to the point of collapse. In 1992 the federal government imposed a moratorium that had a deep and dramatic impact on the region, both economically and socially.

It has taken more than twenty years, but there are signs that the stocks are beginning to recover, and Newfoundland itself has entered a new era of prosperity thanks to increased oil production and resource development. There's even the start of a recreational cod fishery.

That's how we find ourselves bobbing along in a small fishing vessel early one morning outside the Quidi Vidi Gut beside the dramatic cliffs of Logy Bay. We're here with Captain Frankie; his silent first mate whose name we never learn; Alex Cruz from Société-Orignal; and our host, Todd Perrin, owner of Mallard Cottage and one of Newfoundland's greatest proponents, hauling in cod in the cold and drizzle. Cod, it turns out, are ridiculously easy to catch. "That's part of the reason they got so overfished," Perrin tells us. "They'll bite at just about anything."

"We could catch them with a bent knife with a hook on it," Captain Frankie claims. "We don't even need bait!" Our setup today is a little more sophisticated, but only a little. Dozens of hooks are strung along a long line that's wound around a large spindle. As soon as we drop the line into the water and start lowering it, we can feel the hooks bumping into fish on the way down. Seconds after that they start biting. Then it's just a question of pulling up the line and seeing how many of the sluggish, leopard-skinned fish are on it. Within an hour we've reached our quota.

This kind of bounty is only one of the reasons Newfoundland and Labrador is such a phenomenal source of great food, as Perrin explains back at his restaurant, where the bones from the day's catch are simmering on the stove. "The economy of the city has changed a lot in the past ten years," he says. "Chefs who have been away and seen some things are coming back home and putting their own stamp on Newfoundland food. We have access to game, which we're able to use and sell, and that's a big advantage for us. Plus it's a clean, pristine rural environment. I pick my chanterelles a ten-minute drive from Costco."

Just then, one of those chefs who went away and came back home with new ideas walks in the door. Jeremy Charles, the chef and co-owner of Raymonds Restaurant, with his soft-spoken demeanour and prospector's beard, is easily one of the best chefs Canada has ever produced. Charles spent a decade traversing the continent as a private cook, moving from remotest Quebec to Los Angeles and Chicago before returning to Newfoundland. I first tasted his food when he was cooking at Atlantica Restaurant in Portugal Cove. At the time I was seeking out Canada's best new restaurants for a magazine story, and Atlantica was my last stop. After one bite I suspected I'd found a winner. By the end of dessert—the best carrot cake ever made—it was decided. When Raymonds won that same award in 2011, Charles became the only chef to ever receive the honour twice.

No sooner is Charles offered a beer than there's a knock at the back door. A hunter friend of Perrin's arrives with a bag of ptarmigan he's just caught, their impossibly soft feathers barely ruffled. Perrin will hang the birds for a few days before serving them on his menu. This kind of "barrens to table" cooking doesn't happen anywhere else in the country and is incredibly rare the world over. Derek can barely believe his eyes.

"Chefs across Canada look at what's happening in Newfoundland with envy," he says. "Having these resources right here is incredible. A lot of the things these guys can do because of where they're located, because they're sort of off the grid. Everyone just seems to let them do their own thing. They have an advantage by being able to catch the fish themselves—cod like we did today, but also steelhead or arctic char—process it and serve it that same day. Same with hunting. If you have the licence you can do it or you can get a hunter to shoot it for you: moose, deer, caribou. Sure, there's government regulations they have to go through, but chefs here can get their moose and age it exactly how they want it and butcher it exactly how they want to, and that gives them a huge advantage over everybody else."

That advantage is more than evident on the plates that the chefs start putting up family style, everyone helping themselves from platters laid out on the bar. Perrin has taken the offal from the cod—an act that caused quite a stir earlier in the day when we were cleaning the fish on the dock and some of the older locals were incredulous that anyone would want to keep the guts—and cooked them to an almost creamy consistency in a rich tomato gravy.

Derek's working with the cod fillets—"the freshest I've ever cooked," he says—and has gently poached them in a fish fumet he made from the bones and heads. There's a barley risotto studded with those same chanterelles Todd forages out past Costco, and tempura-batter capelin (a kind of smelt) with fresh aïoli to dip them in, and a big water-cress salad dressed with some of Cruz's sunflower oil and late-harvest apple vinegar.

Perrin's business partner and the restaurant's sommelier, Stephen Lee, is mixing up cocktails and pouring wine for friends and family who stop by throughout the evening. Someone lights the fireplace, the music gets turned up and the tales get taller as the hours pass. It's an authentic Newfoundland kitchen party, and it might just be the best thing happening in food in this country.

Société-Orignal

You'll see the name Société-Orignal cropping up a lot in this book. The Moose Society, as its name directly translates, is the brainchild of Alex Cruz and Cyril Gonzales and is one of the coolest culinary projects not just in Canada but in the world.

Working closely with small independent farmers, fishermen and food producers from remote regions in Quebec and across Canada, Cruz and Gonzales seek out the finest, nearly forgotten or underutilized ingredients and give them the attention they deserve. We're talking about things like goat milk jam, sea urchin bottarga, raw-honeydew-and-maple syrup, as well as sustainable fish, a whole line of small family dairy products, and wild game birds.

Alex and Derek worked together at the restaurant DNA, where Alex was sommelier. In its early days, Société-Orignal ran its office out of Maison Publique space. Derek was one of their first supporters, but today the company attracts the attention of some of the best chefs in the world, from Thomas Keller to Daniel Boulud. The passion and dedication of Alex and Cyril and the quality of Société-Orignal's products are emblematic of everything good that's happening in Canada's food scene today.

Salt and Pepper Squid

This classic is an absolute pleasure to include on your playoff platter. Man, I love squid.

Serves 4 as a snack

¾ lb (340 g) fresh squid, cleaned
  (see page 20 for cleaning
  technique)
½ tsp (2 mL) black peppercorns
½ tsp (2 mL) Szechuan peppercorns
1 tsp (5 mL) flaky sea salt, plus more
  to finish
1 tbsp (15 mL) cornstarch
Oil for deep-frying
Lime wedges

Cut each cluster of tentacles in half lengthwise. Slice each squid body in half lengthwise and score the inside in a criss-cross pattern using a sharp knife. Cut the scored bodies into pieces about 2½ inches (6 cm) square and pat dry with paper towels.

Toast the black and Szechuan peppercorns in a dry pan until fragrant. Transfer to a spice grinder, add the salt and grind to a powder. Transfer to a large bowl and stir in the cornstarch.

Heat the oil in a deep-fryer or deep, heavy pot to 365°F (185°C). Toss the squid in the spice mixture to lightly coat, then fry in batches for about 45 seconds, until they just start to turn golden. Drain the squid on paper towels and season with flaky sea salt. Serve hot with the lime wedges.

Almost-Raw and Cooked Lobster with Butter and Mayonnaise

"We all cracked open Dick Nixon's giant pincher claws and enjoyed some of his sweet, sweet hand meat."
—Will Sasso as Elvis

There are loads of lobster recipes out there, so you probably don't need to hear another one from me. Instead I'll share how I like my lobster cooked, and then you can choose where to take it from there. I cook the claws completely and just quickly blanch the tail so it is just shy of raw. Personally, I like my lobster cold, with either some warmed butter or a nice mayonnaise. Maybe I'm a purist that way.

Kill the lobster by plunging your knife straight into the head, right between its eyes. Twist off the claws and the knuckles and set aside. Twist off the tail and insert a bamboo skewer lengthwise through the tail, just under the shell. This will keep the tail straight when you cook it so it slices nicely.

Drop the lobster claws and knuckles into boiling court bouillon (see page 64) and cook for 5 minutes. Then drop in the tail and cook for 1 minute. Using tongs, immediately transfer the lobster parts to an ice bath to cool completely.

Serve with drawn butter and homemade mayonnaise (see page 236).

Cod à la Nage

This is a classic technique that works beautifully with all kinds of fish. Working with impeccably fresh cod, like we did in Newfoundland, is a rare treat, so I wanted to treat it simply. This delicious method came immediately to mind. Whatever fish I use, I like to take the centre cut from the fillets and gently poach them in chicken stock until they are just set. Then I glaze them in a fumet made from their bones and infused with fresh herbs. It makes for a stunning plate of white on white, and it really lets the fish sing. Extra sauce can be frozen.

Serves 4

FOR THE FISH FUMET

2 lb (900 g) halibut bones
3 tbsp (45 mL) canola oil
6 white button mushrooms, thinly sliced
3 stalks celery, thinly sliced
½ cup (125 mL) thinly sliced shallots
¼ cup (60 mL) peeled and diced celery root
2 sprigs fresh thyme
1 fresh bay leaf
½ cup (125 mL) white wine
¼ cup (60 mL) dry vermouth
4 cups (1 L) ice cubes
6 cups (1.5 L) cold water

FOR THE SAUCE

1 cup (250 mL) whipping cream
3 sprigs fresh tarragon
3 sprigs fresh mint
2 sprigs fresh chervil
1 sprig Italian parsley
1 strip lemon peel
Sea salt
A pinch of cayenne pepper
Lemon juice
2 tbsp (30 mL) cold butter
2 tbsp (30 mL) crème fraîche (see page 241), lightly whipped

TO FINISH THE DISH

4 skin-on cod fillets
 (8 oz/225 g each)
3 cups (750 mL) chicken stock
 (see basic stock, page 238)
4 sprigs fresh thyme
2 cloves garlic, lightly crushed
1 tbsp (15 mL) cornstarch
1 tbsp (15 mL) cold water
Kosher salt
Flaky sea salt

FOR THE FISH FUMET

Cut the halibut bones into 2- to 3-inch (5 to 8 cm) pieces and rinse well under cold water. In a large, heavy pot, heat the oil over medium heat until it just begins to smoke. Add the halibut bones and gently sauté until they are cooked and start to fall apart, taking care that they don't take on any colour.

Remove the bones from the pot and reserve them. Add the mushrooms, celery, shallots, celery root, thyme and bay leaf, stirring to coat the vegetables completely. Turn down the heat to low and cover with a round of parchment paper. Cook the vegetables, stirring every so often and making sure they do not take on any colour, until they are tender, 35 to 40 minutes. If they start to catch, just pull the pot off the heat and let it rest for a minute.

Discard the parchment paper. Add the reserved bones, the wine and vermouth. Slowly reduce until the pot is almost dry. Add the ice cubes and the water and bring to a simmer, skimming any impurities that come to the surface. Gently simmer the fumet for 1 hour.

Strain through a colander and then strain through a fine-mesh sieve into a medium saucepan. Fumet can be made a day or two in advance and refrigerated.

FOR THE SAUCE

Add the cream to the fumet and bring to a simmer over medium heat. Simmer until the liquid is reduced by one-third, or until it is your desired sauce consistency, making sure the sauce does not take on any colour.

Turn off the heat and add the tarragon, mint, chervil and parsley sprigs and the lemon peel. Allow to steep for 10 minutes. Strain through a fine-mesh sieve and return to the saucepan. Season with the sea salt, cayenne and a few drops of lemon juice. Whisk in the cold butter gradually, then stir in the crème fraîche.

TO FINISH THE DISH

Remove the cod from the fridge 30 minutes before you are ready to cook it.

Bring the chicken stock, thyme and garlic to a gentle simmer. After 5 minutes, discard garlic and thyme. Make a slurry with the cornstarch and water, and whisk this into the stock. Cook for 3 minutes, whisking occasionally, until thickened slightly. Season with kosher salt.

Gently lower in the cod. Bring the stock back up to the lightest simmer, then turn off the heat and allow the fish to finish cooking in the residual heat of the stock, about 3 more minutes.

Using a fish slice, transfer the cod skin side up to a paper-towel-lined plate and allow to rest for 2 minutes. Carefully peel away the skin and turn the fish over.

Pool the fumet sauce onto four warmed dinner plates, season the fish with a few flakes of sea salt and place one portion on each plate.

Snow Crab Toast

Crab toast is nothing short of a pure pleasure to eat. When the little guys start appearing from the Gulf of St. Lawrence, you'll see them on menus everywhere around Quebec. They're a treat no matter if you prepare them simply (cracked with lemon) or dressed to the nines, like here.

You can buy fresh cooked snow crab clusters in season from your fish purveyor, or substitute Dungeness if you are on the West Coast. If you plan on cooking your own snow crab, be sure to separate the bodies from the legs and discard the bodies before you boil or steam the legs. The body contains toxins that are released from the innards, turning the meat slightly green and making it inedible.

Serves 6

FOR THE CRAB
3 live snow crabs (2 lb/900 g each)
 or 6 cooked snow crab clusters

TO DRESS THE CRAB
6 slices sourdough rye bread, sliced
 ½-inch (1 cm) thick
1 clove garlic
¼ cup (60 mL) mayonnaise
 (see page 236)
1½ tbsp (20 mL) crème fraîche
 (see page 241), lightly whipped
Kosher salt and black pepper
2 tbsp (30 mL) finely chopped
 Italian parsley
2 tbsp (30 mL) finely minced shallot
1 tbsp (15 mL) finely minced
 jalapeño pepper, seeds intact
1 tbsp (15 mL) thinly sliced fresh
 red chili pepper
2 tsp (10 mL) lemon vinaigrette
 (see page 240)
2 tbsp (30 mL) fresh mint leaves,
 torn
½ cup (125 mL) pangritata
 (see page 88)
Finely grated zest of 1 lemon
Good sea salt
Good-quality extra virgin olive oil

FOR THE CRAB
Bring a large pot of heavily salted water to a boil over high heat.

Meanwhile, dispatch the live crabs by splitting them in half lengthwise through the underside of the shell. Remove the top portion of the shell and carefully remove all the innards and the gills (the "dead man's fingers"), leaving the legs and body meat attached.

Drop the crabs into the boiling water and simmer for 8 minutes. Scoop the crabs out of the pot and immediately transfer to a large bowl of salted ice water. Allow to cool completely.

Set a medium bowl into a larger bowl of ice. Remove the crab legs from the body. Using sharp scissors, split the leg sections lengthwise. Carefully remove the meat in one piece, adding the meat to the chilled bowl. Using tweezers, remove the tendon that runs through the middle of each piece of leg meat. With the back of a large knife, crack the claws right above the joint but below the "thumb" and remove the sweet, sweet claw meat, adding it to the leg meat. Using a crab fork or a skewer, remove all of the white meat from the body of the crab. Carefully feel the meat with the tips of your fingers to check for any missed pieces of shell. Cover and refrigerate the crab if not using it soon.

TO DRESS THE CRAB
You could toast the bread in the oven, but it's much better done over charcoal. With the coals glowing on your grill, toast the bread a little more than golden. If it gets a bit too much colour on the edges, that's fine. Immediately rub each side of the toast with the garlic clove. Keep the toast warm.

In a small bowl, stir together the mayonnaise and the crème fraîche. Season with kosher salt and black pepper.

To the crab in the cold bowl, add the parsley, shallot, jalapeño and red chili. Drizzle with the lemon vinaigrette, then fold in the mayonnaise mixture and torn mint. Season with kosher salt and pepper.

Divide the crab meat among the pieces of toast. Shower the crab with some of the pangritata and a small sprinkling of lemon zest per toast. Sprinkle with a touch of good sea salt and a generous drizzle of good olive oil.

Clam Chowder

I use three types of clams in this recipe. The cherrystones add a deep briny flavour to the base, while the little-necks and Manilas bring sweetness.

Serves 6 to 8

FOR THE SOUP BASE
½ lb (225 g) bacon (see page 239)
   cut into lardons
2 cups (500 mL) diced leeks, white
   and light green parts only
2 cups (500 mL) diced yellow onions
5 cloves garlic, chopped
Kosher salt

FOR THE POTATOES
Bouquet garni (3 sprigs fresh thyme,
   3 sprigs parsley, 1 fresh bay leaf,
   10 coarsely cracked black peppercorns, 1 clove garlic)
2 lb (900 g) russet potatoes, peeled
   and cut into ½-inch (1 cm) cubes

FOR THE CLAMS
4 lb (1.8 kg) cherrystone clams
2 lb (900 g) littleneck clams
2 lb (900 g) Manila clams
1½ cups (375 mL) kosher salt
10 cups (2.4 L) water
2 tbsp (30 mL) unsalted butter
½ cup (125 mL) diced shallots
3 sprigs fresh thyme
¾ cup (175 mL) white wine

FOR THE BÉCHAMEL BASE
4 tbsp (60 mL) unsalted butter
¼ cup (60 mL) all-purpose flour
3 cups (750 mL) whole milk
3 cups (750 mL) whipping cream
Kosher salt and black pepper
A pinch of cayenne pepper

FOR THE SOUP BASE
Heat a few tablespoons of water in a stockpot over medium-low heat. Add the bacon and cook gently, stirring occasionally, until the fat has rendered and the bacon has coloured but isn't crisp, 15 to 20 minutes. Using a slotted spoon, remove the bacon from the pot and drain on paper towels.

Stir the leeks, onions and garlic into the bacon fat and season with kosher salt. Turn down the heat to low and cover the vegetables with a round of parchment paper. Sweat the mixture, stirring occasionally, for about 45 minutes, until the vegetables are melted and very forgiving, taking care not to let them colour or catch on the bottom of the pot.

FOR THE POTATOES
While the soup base sweats, add the bouquet garni to a large pot of heavily salted water and bring to a boil. Add the potatoes and simmer for 8 minutes or until just shy of tender. Drain the potatoes, spread them evenly on a baking sheet and allow to cool.

FOR THE CLAMS
Scrub the clams under cold running water to remove any grit. Combine the kosher salt and the water, stirring to dissolve the salt. Place the clams in a large bowl and pour over enough salt water to cover them (save the remaining water). Let them sit for 30 minutes to purge any interior sand. Drain the clams, return them to the bowl and repeat the process. Drain the clams again and give them a good rinse.

Heat a large, heavy saucepan with a tight-fitting lid over medium-high heat. Melt the butter, then add the shallots and thyme. Cook, stirring frequently, for 2 to 3 minutes, until the shallots are tender. Add the wine and simmer for 2 minutes to cook off most of the alcohol. Add the clams, cover the pan and cook for 4 minutes. Then start to remove the clams as they open, transferring them to a bowl. Discard any clams that don't open. Strain the clam liquid through a fine-mesh sieve lined with a coffee filter into a bowl. Set aside for use in the béchamel base. Remove the clam meat from the shells, discarding the shells.

FOR THE BÉCHAMEL BASE
Remove the parchment paper from the vegetables, turn up the heat to medium and add the butter. Once the butter has melted, add the flour and cook, stirring constantly, until it smells like biscuits, about 5 minutes. Whisk in the milk and cream, season with kosher salt and pepper and bring to a gentle simmer. Simmer for 15 minutes or until thickened, stirring occasionally.

Stir the clam liquid and cayenne into the béchamel. Adjust the seasoning.

HOW TO CLEAN CLAMS

Fill a bowl with cold water and stir in some salt to mimic their natural environment. Add the clams and leave them in the water for about 30 minutes. The clams will filter the water and push out any sand trapped inside their shells. Do this twice to ensure they are completely purged. Lift the clams out of the water and scrub the shells with a brush under cold running water.

TO FINISH THE DISH

¼ cup (60 mL) very finely chopped chives

2 tbsp (30 mL) finely chopped Italian parsley

FOR THE OYSTER CRACKERS

1 cup (250 mL) all-purpose flour

1 tsp (5 mL) kosher salt

1 tsp (5 mL) sugar

1 tsp (5 mL) baking powder

2 tbsp (30 mL) cold unsalted butter, cubed

¼ cup (60 mL) cold water

Flaky sea salt to garnish

TO FINISH THE DISH

In a small frying pan, crisp the reserved bacon lardons.

Stir the potatoes and the clams into the chowder and cook for 3 minutes or until heated through. Stir in the chives and parsley.

Pour the chowder into bowls and garnish with the lardons. Serve with a bowl of oyster crackers.

FOR THE OYSTER CRACKERS

Preheat the oven to 375°F (190°C).

Sift the flour, kosher salt, sugar and baking powder together into a bowl. Add the cold butter. Using your fingertips, quickly rub the butter into the flour until the mixture resembles coarse sand. Add the cold water and lightly knead together until it forms a ball of dough; you may need a touch more water. Wrap tightly in plastic wrap and refrigerate for 30 minutes.

On a floured surface, roll out the dough to ⅛-inch (3 mm) thickness. Using cookie cutters (I like to use fish-shaped ones, but you can use a half-moon or a five-sided cutter for the classic shape), cut out crackers. If you are using a round cutter, give each cracker a couple of pokes with a skewer to keep it from puffing too much during baking.

Transfer the crackers to a parchment-lined baking sheet, spacing them out as much as possible. Bake until the crackers are showing colour around the edges, about 15 minutes. Turn off the oven, crack the oven door open and leave the crackers in the oven for 25 minutes to continue to crisp. Remove from the oven and season with the flaky sea salt. Allow to cool completely. (Crackers can be stored in an airtight container for up to 1 week.)

Whelks in Escabèche

This recipe came to life after a trip Chris and I took to Spain to eat canned fish. I originally made it with mussels, which you could also do, but I found that the final texture was even better with whelks. The combination of the two paprikas brings the dish into balance. I like to make my own paprika with the excess of peppers I get in the late summer from one of my farmers, but the store-bought ones will definitely work.

Serves 6

FOR THE WHELKS

48 whelks in the shell (or 1½ lb/
  675 g cooked meat)

TO FINISH THE DISH

1 cup (250 mL) extra virgin olive oil
5 cloves garlic, peeled and lightly
  crushed
1 lemon, peeled with a vegetable
  peeler and juiced
1 orange, peeled with a vegetable
  peeler and juiced
1 fresh red chili pepper, split in
  half lengthwise, seeds intact
2 sprigs fresh thyme
2 sprigs fresh rosemary
2 fresh bay leaves
½ cup (125 mL) sherry vinegar
1½ tbsp (20 mL) black peppercorns
1 tbsp (15 mL) sweet smoked
  paprika
1 tbsp (15 mL) hot smoked paprika
2 tbsp (30 mL) finely chopped
  Italian parsley

FOR THE WHELKS

Thoroughly rinse the whelks under cold running water, removing any seaweed, sand, barnacles and slime. This may take a few rinses.

In a large, heavy pot, bring 1 cup (250 mL) water to a simmer. Add enough whelks to cover the bottom in one layer and cover tightly with the lid. Turn down the heat to medium and gently braise the whelks until they are hot all the way through, 12 to 15 minutes. Transfer the whelks to a bowl and repeat with the remaining whelks.

Strain the liquor through a very fine sieve into a clean pot. Cook briefly over medium heat until reduced to ¼ cup (60 mL). Allow to cool.

Using a wooden skewer, pry the whelks out of their shells. With a sharp knife, trim off and discard the operculum (the hard, hornlike oval window protecting the opening of the shell). Trim off and discard the digestive tract.

TO FINISH THE DISH

Heat the olive oil over low heat. Add the garlic, lemon and orange peels, chili, thyme, rosemary and bay leaves. Gently sweat, stirring, until fragrant. Remove from the heat and stir in the reduced whelk liquor, lemon and orange juices, vinegar, peppercorns, sweet smoked paprika and hot smoked paprika. Allow to cool to room temperature.

Adjust the seasoning. Stir in the whelk meat and refrigerate, covered, for 10 hours.

Bring to room temperature. Stir in the parsley and serve with plenty of crusty bread and ice-cold beer.

"Boquerónes" and "Anchovies" on Toast

While writing this book, Chris and I were lucky enough to be invited on a food trip to Spain, to find and taste the best preserved and canned delicacies produced there. Many people think canned fish is a second-rate product, but I can tell you this doesn't have to be the case. At its best, canned fish has a mellow, soft texture and the great flavour of fresh fish caught and cooked at the peak of its season. Preserving your own is quite easy and gives you the chance to control every aspect of the quality.

At the famous Boqueria Market in Barcelona I had a simple piece of heavily grilled toast topped with both salted and brined anchovies that was just incredible. That snack is what inspired this recipe, but I use fish that are indigenous to Atlantic Canadian waters: smelts instead of anchovies, and capelin instead of boquerónes.

Serves 4 with leftovers

FOR THE SMELTS

2½ lb (1.125 kg) very fresh smelts, heads removed, gutted and rinsed
½ lb (225 g) coarse sea salt
Canola oil

FOR THE CAPELIN

1 tbsp (15 mL) kosher salt
2 tsp (10 mL) sugar
2 cups (500 mL) warm water
2½ lb (1.125 kg) very fresh capelin, heads removed, gutted and rinsed
Zest and juice of 2 lemons
1½ cups (375 mL) white wine vinegar
2 cloves garlic, finely minced
1 shallot, finely minced
2 tbsp (30 mL) finely chopped Italian parsley
1 tsp (5 mL) red chili flakes
½ cup (125 mL) canola oil

TO FINISH THE DISH

¼ cup (60 mL) finely chopped Italian parsley
2 cloves garlic, 1 whole and 1 finely minced
Zest of 1 lemon
Kosher salt and black pepper
4 slices sourdough bread
1 very ripe tomato, cut in half crosswise
Flaky sea salt
¼ cup (60 mL) good-quality olive oil

FOR THE SMELTS

Line the bottom of a nonreactive container with a single layer of smelts. Top with a layer of coarse sea salt. Repeat layering with the rest of the smelts and salt. Cover with plastic wrap, then cover with a flat object that sits just inside the top of the container, such as a pot lid or piece of cardboard. Place a brick or a couple of cans on top and refrigerate for 1 month.

Remove the smelts from the cure, rinse them well and pat dry. Fillet the smelts and remove the pin bones.

Place the fish in a small nonreactive dish and cover with canola oil. Cover with plastic wrap and refrigerate for 24 hours. The smelts are now ready to use. They will keep in the oil for up to 3 weeks.

FOR THE CAPELIN

Stir the salt and sugar into the warm water until dissolved. Allow the brine to cool completely.

Place the capelin in a nonreactive container large enough to hold them snugly. Pour the brine over the capelin—the fish should be submerged. Cover and refrigerate for 4 hours.

Drain the capelin and rinse them well. Return them to the cleaned nonreactive container. Combine the lemon juice and vinegar. Pour over the capelin—the fish should be submerged. Cover and refrigerate overnight.

Drain the capelin and fillet the fish carefully. Arrange the fillets in a single layer in a baking dish. Evenly scatter the garlic, shallot, lemon zest, parsley and chili flakes over the fish. Cover completely with the canola oil. Cover with plastic wrap and refrigerate for 4 hours. The capelin are now ready to use. They will keep in the oil for up to 3 weeks.

TO FINISH THE DISH

Bring the smelts and capelin to room temperature.

Combine the parsley, minced garlic and lemon zest in a small bowl. Season with kosher salt and pepper.

Grill the bread, preferably over a charcoal grill, until it is a little charred around the edges. Rub one side of the grilled bread liberally with the whole garlic clove, then with the cut side of the tomato, squeezing the tomato to massage the juices into the toast. Season with the flaky sea salt.

Arrange 2 smelts and 2 capelin on each toast and garnish with the parsley mixture. Generously drizzle each toast with good olive oil.

Swordfish Bresaola and Celery Root Salad

There is this beautiful harpoon-caught swordfish out of Nova Scotia, and because cold-water fish is the best, naturally it's delicious. This recipe showcases a great way to make a cured fish other than gravlax. Since swordfish usually starts showing up as fall approaches, the celery root salad is a nice complement. You can exchange the fish for a filet of beef or venison, using the same technique.

Makes 1 lb (450 g) of bresaola and 8 salads

FOR THE BRESAOLA
1 clove garlic, crushed
¼ cup (60 mL) kosher salt
A pinch of cinnamon
A pinch of ground cloves
¼ tsp (1 mL) freshly cracked
  black pepper
1 centre-cut swordfish loin
  (1½ lb/675 g), bloodline removed

FOR THE CELERY ROOT SALAD
1 celery root, peeled
Juice of 1 lemon
¼ cup (60 mL) crème fraîche
  (see page 241)
1½ tbsp (20 mL) Dijon mustard
Sea salt and black pepper
2 tbsp (30 mL) chopped fresh chervil

TO FINISH THE DISH
Good-quality olive oil

FOR THE BRESAOLA
Combine the garlic, kosher salt, cinnamon, cloves and pepper in a bowl large enough to fit the piece of fish. Rub the spice mix all over the swordfish and massage it into the meat. Place the swordfish on a wire rack set over a baking sheet and let rest at room temperature for 48 hours.

Rinse the fish under cold water and pat dry. Vacuum-seal the fish and refrigerate for 4 days to complete the curing process.

FOR THE CELERY ROOT SALAD
Using a mandoline, slice the celery root as thick as a matchstick. Stack the slices and, using a sharp knife, cut the celery root into matchstick strips. In a medium bowl, toss the celery root with the lemon juice to keep it from browning.

Fold together the crème fraîche and the mustard. Season with sea salt and pepper. Add to the celery root with the chopped chervil and mix together.

TO FINISH THE DISH
Using a wet, sharp knife, slice the swordfish as thinly as possible against the grain (think carpaccio). Arrange the fish on 8 plates and mound the celery root in the centre of each. Finish each dish with a drizzle of good olive oil.

Mortadella-Stuffed Squid

This dish came about after I had an abundance of mortadella ends on my hands. Being a pork-centric cook who hates waste, and who stuffed who knows how many squid at Zambri's, this just seemed like a good idea.

Serves 6

FOR THE STUFFED SQUID
12 fresh squid, 6 to 8 inches (15 to 20 cm) long, cleaned (see below for cleaning technique)
2 oz (55 g) fatty pork scraps or boneless pork shoulder
2 oz (55 g) flat pancetta (see page 110)
2 oz (55 g) mortadella (see page 96, or store-bought)
2 tbsp (30 mL) finely chopped shallot
1 tbsp (15 mL) dry white bread crumbs
1 egg, lightly beaten
Sea salt and white pepper
2 tbsp (30 mL) olive oil
½ cup (125 mL) white wine

FOR THE SAUCE
1 tbsp (15 mL) olive oil
1 oz (28 g) flat pancetta (see page 110), finely diced
1 cup (250 mL) white wine
2 Roma tomatoes, peeled, seeded, juice reserved and tomatoes finely diced
1 cup (250 mL) frozen peas
Sea salt and black pepper
Good-quality olive oil
2 tbsp (30 mL) finely chopped Italian parsley

TO FINISH THE DISH
A few sprigs of fresh chervil
A few of the inside baby leaves of fresh mint

FOR THE STUFFED SQUID
Cut the wings off the squid; reserve the squid and tentacles, refrigerated. Cut the pork, pancetta and mortadella into 1-inch (2.5 cm) cubes. Spread the meat cubes and the squid wings on a baking sheet and freeze for 1 hour. Chill a large bowl.

Fit a meat grinder with the small die and grind the meats and squid wings, catching them in the chilled bowl. Stir in the shallot, bread crumbs and egg, then season with salt and white pepper.

Spoon the stuffing into a pastry bag fitted with a ½-inch (1 cm) plain tip. Pipe the stuffing into the squid bodies, filling them just over halfway. (The stuffing will expand during cooking.) Attach one set of tentacles to each squid body with a toothpick, taking care that the body opening is securely closed.

Heat the olive oil in a large, heavy sauté pan or frying pan over medium-high heat. Season the squid with salt and white pepper and brown the squid on all sides. Pour in the wine, turn down the heat to medium, cover and cook for 12 minutes. Transfer the squid to a warm plate and allow to rest for 7 minutes.

FOR THE SAUCE
Heat the oil in a frying pan over medium heat. Add the pancetta and cook for 2 to 3 minutes, until it is starting to go translucent (do not let it brown). Add the wine and cook until reduced by one-quarter.

Add the tomatoes and their juice and cook until the liquid is reduced by three-quarters. Stir in the peas and season with salt and black pepper. Swirl in a drizzle of olive oil and the parsley. Remove from the heat.

TO FINISH THE DISH
Remove the toothpicks from the squid and, with a sharp knife, slice each squid into 5 even rounds. Arrange the squid and tentacles neatly on six warmed plates. Swirl any squid resting juices into the sauce and spoon the sauce over and around the slices. Garnish with the chervil and mint.

HOW TO CLEAN SQUID
Pull the head and tentacles away from the body, then reach inside the body and pull out the innards and the quill, taking care not to puncture the body. Cut off the tentacles just below the eyes and discard the head. Squeeze the base of the tentacles to push out the beak. Rinse everything under cold running water while peeling the grey membrane off the outside of the body.

Pork and Clams

This recipe is a bit of an investment in time, but if you prepare the dish in stages, there isn't much work to do on the day you're serving it. This recipe grew out of many late-night conversations with Alex Cruz of Société-Orignal about the dishes his mother made for him when he was growing up. To enrich the broth, I add some spicy sausage, and I use a pork shoulder that is cooked confit, so that the end result is crispy-fatty morsels of goodness.

When cooking the clams, make sure to remove each one as it starts to open. You will reheat them in the sauce at the end, and it's important not to overcook the shellfish after you've worked so hard on the other components. Nobody likes a lousy clam.

Serves 8

FOR THE BRINED PORK
2 tbsp (30 mL) allspice berries
2 tbsp (30 mL) juniper berries
1 tbsp (15 mL) fennel seeds
½ cup (125 mL) kosher salt
½ cup (125 mL) sugar
1 onion, sliced
1 fennel bulb, sliced
2 jalapeño peppers, cut in half
  lengthwise, seeds intact
1 head garlic, separated into
  unpeeled cloves and smashed
Peel of 1 lemon
6 sprigs fresh thyme
6 sprigs Italian parsley
2 sprigs fresh savory
4 fresh bay leaves
2 whole cloves
14 cups (3.5 L) cold water
1 boneless pork shoulder
  (2 lb/900 g), tied at even
  intervals with butcher's string

FOR THE PORK CONFIT
10 cups (2.4 L) rendered pork
  or duck fat

FOR THE AÏOLI
1 clove garlic
Kosher salt and black pepper
1 large egg yolk
½ cup (125 mL) canola oil
½ cup (125 mL) extra virgin
  olive oil
Juice of ½ lemon
A pinch of cayenne pepper

FOR THE BRINED PORK
Crush the allspice, juniper berries and fennel seeds with a mortar and pestle. In a large saucepan, combine the spice mixture, kosher salt, sugar, onion, fennel, jalapeños, garlic, lemon peel, thyme, parsley, savory, bay leaves, cloves and 2 cups (500 mL) of the cold water. Bring to a simmer, stirring occasionally to dissolve the salt and sugar. Pour into a large nonreactive container and add the remaining 12 cups (3 L) cold water. Place the pork in the brine, weighting it with a plate if needed so the meat is submerged. Refrigerate for 48 hours.

FOR THE PORK CONFIT
Preheat the oven to 300°F (150°C).

Drain the pork and pat dry. Melt the fat in a large Dutch oven over medium heat. Lower in the pork, cover, transfer to the oven and cook for 6 hours or until the meat yields easily to the poke of a paring knife. Check the pot from time to time—you do not want the fat to boil. Remove the pot from the oven, uncover and allow the meat to cool to room temperature in the fat. Remove the pork from the fat. Strain the fat, reserving it. Refrigerate the pork, wrapped in plastic, overnight.

Alternatively, prepare the confit using an immersion circulator or water bath. (This will significantly reduce the amount of fat you need.) Place the pork in a vacuum bag with 1 cup (250 mL) rendered fat and seal. Cook at 180°F (82°C) for 12 hours. Remove the bag from the water and allow the pork to rest for 15 minutes before removing it from the bag and straining and reserving the fat. Refrigerate the pork and the fat overnight.

FOR THE AÏOLI
Place a mortar and pestle in the refrigerator an hour before you plan to make the aïoli. Using the cold mortar and pestle, smash the garlic to a paste with a pinch of kosher salt. Add the egg yolk and stir to combine. Drop by drop, drizzle in the canola oil and the olive oil, stirring furiously with the pestle until an emulsion forms. Keep going until all the oil has been added. Season with lemon juice, cayenne, salt and pepper. Cover and refrigerate if not using soon.

FOR THE ROASTED POTATOES

2 lb (900 g) russet potatoes

¼ cup (60 mL) canola oil

1 head garlic, separated into
  unpeeled cloves and smashed

1 fresh bay leaf, julienned

6 sprigs fresh thyme

1 tbsp (15 mL) kosher salt

TO FRY THE POTATOES

1 clove garlic, minced

½ chile de árbol, crumbled

1 tbsp (15 mL) finely diced shallot

1 tbsp (15 mL) finely chopped
  Italian parsley

1 tsp (5 mL) finely chopped
  fresh thyme

Kosher salt to taste

1 cup (250 mL) reserved pork
  confit fat or duck fat

TO FINISH THE DISH

3 tbsp (45 mL) reserved pork
  confit fat or duck fat

1½ lb (675 g) pork confit, cut
  into 1-inch (2.5 cm) cubes

Sea salt and black pepper

2 tbsp (30 mL) canola oil

¾ lb (340 g) spicy sausage
  (see page 222), removed from
  the casing and crumbled

1 chile de árbol, crumbled

½ cup (125 mL) finely diced shallots

2 tbsp (30 mL) finely chopped garlic

1 tbsp (15 mL) chopped fresh thyme

3 lb (1.35 kg) littleneck clams,
  purged (see page 15)

6 oven-dried tomatoes
  (see page 234), finely chopped

1 cup (250 mL) dry vermouth

½ cup (125 mL) white wine

1 cup (250 mL) chicken and pork
  stock (see basic stock, page 238)

2 tbsp (30 mL) unsalted butter

3 tbsp (45 mL) finely chopped
  Italian parsley

1 tbsp (15 mL) lemon juice

FOR THE ROASTED POTATOES

Preheat the oven to 425°F (220°C).

Toss the potatoes in a large bowl with the oil, garlic, bay leaf, thyme and kosher salt. Transfer to a large cast-iron pan, cover with foil and roast for 1½ hours or until tender when pierced with a paring knife. Allow to cool in the pan to room temperature. Discard the garlic and herbs. Peel the potatoes and break them into chunks with your hands. (Potatoes can be roasted a few hours ahead of time and refrigerated, covered.)

TO FRY THE POTATOES

In a large bowl, combine the garlic, chile, shallot, parsley, thyme and kosher salt; set aside. Heat the fat in a large cast-iron pan over medium-high heat until just before the smoking point. Add the potato chunks and fry, turning every couple of minutes, until golden on all sides. Remove with a slotted spoon and transfer to the bowl with the seasonings; toss to combine. Keep warm.

TO FINISH THE DISH

In a large cast-iron pan, heat the reserved fat over medium-high heat until almost smoking. Working in batches if necessary, add the pork cubes and fry them until golden and crispy on all sides. Drain on paper towels. Season with sea salt and keep warm.

In a large, heavy saucepan over medium-high heat, heat the canola oil until almost smoking. Add the spicy sausage and sauté until it starts to get crispy and has rendered some of the fat, 3 to 5 minutes. Add the chile, shallots, garlic and thyme, and quickly sauté them.

Add the clams and tomatoes and cook for 2 minutes, stirring them in the fat. Pour in the vermouth and wine, cover the pot and cook for 2 minutes. Peek under the lid and start to remove the clams as they open, transferring them to a warmed bowl. Discard any clams that don't open.

Once you've removed all the clams, turn up the heat. Add the stock and boil until the sauce is reduced by half. Remove from the heat and swirl in the butter until emulsified. Adjust the seasoning. Add the parsley, lemon juice, 2 tbsp (30 mL) of the aïoli and all the clams and the liquor that has gathered in the bowl; toss to combine everything. Don't worry if there are streaks of aïoli—it's a good thing not to fully blend it.

Transfer the clams and sauce to a large serving bowl. Garnish with the crispy confit and potatoes. Dot the whole lot with some aïoli, serving the rest on the side at the table.

Salt Cod Gratin

I thought about this dish (pictured on pages 26 and 27) when we were out in Newfoundland for the Roots, Rants and Roars Festival. Our station on the food hike was right on the ocean, with old salt cod stands as the background. It was stunning, and despite getting hit by a rogue wave in my clogs, it was one of the best events I've ever done. It was September 19 and it actually snowed that night, which gives you an idea how far north we were. So in the light snow, with a huge soaker, the North Atlantic, and the salt cod stands right there, I thought of how rewarding a big baked fish pie would be.

Serves 8

FOR THE BRANDADE
2 lb (900 g) salt cod
8 cups (2 L) whole milk
½ cup (125 mL) peeled garlic cloves
Bouquet garni (6 sprigs fresh thyme,
  6 sprigs Italian parsley, 2 fresh
  bay leaves, 1 tbsp/15 mL lightly
  cracked black peppercorns)
1 onion, peeled
6 whole cloves

FOR THE POTATO SLICES
2 lb (900 g) russet potatoes
  (unpeeled)
2 tbsp (30 mL) olive oil
6 cloves garlic (unpeeled)
6 sprigs fresh thyme
1½ tsp (7 mL) kosher salt

FOR THE BÉCHAMEL
2 tbsp (30 mL) unsalted butter
2 tbsp (30 mL) all-purpose flour
3 cups (750 mL) whole milk
3 whole cloves
1 fresh bay leaf
½ onion, peeled
Kosher salt and white pepper
A few gratings of nutmeg

FOR THE BRANDADE
Soak the cod in cold water in the refrigerator for 48 hours, changing the water every 12 hours.

Drain the cod, pat it dry and transfer it to a wire rack set over a baking sheet. Allow it to dry under the fan in the fridge for 4 hours.

Place the cod in a large, heavy saucepan (cutting it to fit if necessary) and add the milk, garlic cloves and bouquet garni. Stud the onion with the cloves and add this to the milk as well. Simmer over medium heat for 45 minutes or until the cod and garlic are tender. Cool the cod in the milk until it is cool enough to handle.

Drain the cod, discarding the onion and bouquet garni. Flake the cod with your fingers into a medium bowl. Mash the garlic cloves to a paste with a mortar and pestle and stir into the cod.

FOR THE POTATO SLICES
Preheat the oven to 400°F (200°C).

In a large roasting pan, toss the potatoes with the olive oil, garlic, thyme and kosher salt. Cover the pan with foil and roast for 1½ hours or until the potatoes are tender when pierced with a paring knife. Allow to cool.

Peel the potatoes and cut them into ¼-inch (5 mm) slices.

FOR THE BÉCHAMEL
In a medium saucepan, melt the butter over medium heat. Add the flour and cook, stirring with a wooden spoon, until the roux starts to smell nutty and is on the edge of turning golden brown. Whisk in the milk a little at a time, whisking until there are no lumps. Bring to a simmer. Using the cloves, stud the bay leaf to the onion and add to the pot. Turn down the heat to medium-low and gently simmer the sauce for 35 minutes, stirring occasionally.

Remove the béchamel from the heat and discard the onion. Season with the kosher salt, white pepper and nutmeg. Strain through a fine-mesh sieve.

FOR THE POTATO PURÉE

4 lb (1.8 kg) russet potatoes
2 tsp (10 mL) kosher salt
1 cup (250 mL) cold unsalted butter,
  cut into pieces
¾ cup (175 mL) whipping cream
¾ cup (175 mL) whole milk
1 clove garlic, mashed to a paste
A few gratings of nutmeg
Kosher salt and white pepper

TO FINISH THE DISH

¼ cup (60 mL) Thompson raisins
¼ cup (60 mL) apple vinegar
  (see page 163)
½ lb (225 g) Avonlea Clothbound or
  other aged artisanal cheddar, grated
Sea salt and black pepper
¾ cup (175 mL) roasted red peppers
  torn into 1-inch (2.5 cm) pieces
½ cup (125 mL) Italian parsley
  leaves, lightly disciplined with
  a knife
¼ cup (60 mL) fresh mint leaves,
  treated the same
1 tsp (5 mL) lemon vinaigrette
  (see page 240)

FOR THE POTATO PURÉE

Peel the potatoes and cut each lengthwise into 4 wedges. Place them in a large pot with the salt and cover with cold water. Simmer until they are tender. Drain the potatoes and leave them to steam in the colander for 10 minutes.

Pass the potatoes through a ricer or a sturdy fine-mesh strainer using a rubber spatula. (You can also use a food mill or mash them with a masher, but they won't be as smooth.) Return them to the cleaned pot.

Over medium-low heat, add the butter, cream and milk, gently folding with the spatula until everything is incorporated. Fold in the garlic and season with nutmeg, kosher salt and white pepper.

TO FINISH THE DISH

Soak the raisins in the vinegar for 4 hours.

Preheat the oven to 425°F (220°C).

Spread one-quarter of the potato purée evenly in the bottom of a 9-inch (23 cm) casserole dish. Top with one-quarter of the cod brandade, spreading evenly, then one-quarter of the potato slices, one-quarter of the béchamel and finally one-quarter of the grated cheese. Season with sea salt and black pepper. Repeat the layering three more times.

Bake the gratin for 45 minutes or until it is golden and bubbly on top. Allow it to rest for 20 minutes before serving.

Meanwhile, prepare the salad. Drain the raisins and, in a medium bowl, toss them with the roasted peppers, parsley, mint and lemon vinaigrette. Season with sea salt and black pepper. Mound the salad on top of the gratin just before you take it to the table.

Bouillabaisse

A really well made bouillabaisse (pictured on pages 30 and 31) is a thing of beauty. Yes, it's an all-day affair, but it's a labour of love, and if you're willing to put in the time, the payoff is huge. A few things to remember: don't skimp on the quality of the fish—it must be pristine and fresh—and add the pieces in the order stated in the recipe. You'll probably have to pull some pieces out if they're done a little early, then return them to the finished dish. This recipe makes a lot, because if you're going to go to the effort of making a proper bouillabaisse, you might as well share it. And show off a bit.

Serves 10

FOR THE MARINATED FISH
1 whole fresh snapper, sea bass or halibut (8 lb/3.5 kg)
1 whole fresh cod (8 lb/3.5 kg)
¼ cup (60 mL) Italian parsley leaves
1 tbsp (15 mL) fresh thyme leaves
1 tbsp (15 mL) chopped fennel fronds
2 cloves garlic
A pinch of sea salt
1 cup (250 mL) white wine
½ cup (125 mL) extra virgin olive oil
2 tbsp (30 mL) Pernod
A pinch of saffron

FOR THE FUMET
¼ cup (60 mL) extra virgin olive oil
2 carrots, peeled and coarsely but evenly chopped
2 leeks, washed and cut into 1-inch (2.5 cm) rings
1 onion, peeled and coarsely but evenly chopped
2 Roma tomatoes, quartered
10 button mushrooms, quartered
4 cloves garlic, lightly crushed
12 mussels
12 clams
Bouquet garni (6 sprigs curly parsley, 4 sprigs fresh tarragon, 4 sprigs fresh thyme, 2 fresh bay leaves, 12 lightly crushed black peppercorns, 12 lightly crushed coriander seeds, 1 tbsp/15 mL fennel seeds)
Peel of 1 orange, removed with a vegetable peeler
A pinch of saffron
A pinch of cayenne pepper
2 cups (500 mL) white wine
2 tbsp (30 mL) Pernod

FOR THE MARINATED FISH
Fillet the fish. Cut away and discard the gills, then thoroughly rinse the fish bones and pat dry. Reserve the bones and heads for the fumet. Cut the fillets into 2-inch (5 cm) pieces about 1 inch (2.5 cm) thick and place in a large bowl. Add the trim and scraps to the bones.

Using a mortar and pestle, pound the parsley, thyme, fennel, garlic and sea salt to a smooth paste. Add the wine, olive oil, Pernod and saffron; stir to combine thoroughly.

Toss the fish pieces with the marinade. Cover and refrigerate for 2 hours.

FOR THE FUMET
In a stockpot, heat the olive oil over medium-high heat. Add the reserved fish bones, trim and heads, the carrots, leeks, onion, tomatoes, mushrooms and garlic. Stir for 1 minute or so, then turn down the heat and gently sweat the mixture for 10 minutes, until the fish starts to break down. Do not let the mixture boil. Cover with a round of parchment paper, turn down the heat to medium and continue to sweat the vegetables and fish for 25 minutes, stirring occasionally and making sure that they do not colour or catch on the bottom of the pot. Discard the parchment paper.

Add the mussels, clams, bouquet garni, orange peel, saffron, cayenne, wine, Pernod and enough cold water to cover the ingredients. Bring to a boil. Turn down the heat to a simmer and skim off any impurities that rise to the top. Simmer, uncovered and without stirring, for 45 minutes, skimming as required. Remove from the heat and allow the fumet to stand for an additional 45 minutes.

Strain the fumet through a fine-mesh sieve, discarding the solids.

FOR THE ROUILLE

1 sweet red pepper
1 tomato
A pinch of saffron
A pinch of cayenne pepper
¼ cup (60 mL) fumet
1 slice white bread, crust removed
4 egg yolks
6 cloves garlic, mashed to a paste
¾ cup (175 mL) extra virgin olive oil
¾ cup (175 mL) canola oil
Kosher salt and black pepper

FOR THE CROUTONS, AND
TO FINISH THE DISH

2 leeks, white part only, very
  finely diced
2 onions, very finely diced
¼ cup (60 mL) + ⅓ cup (75 mL)
  extra virgin olive oil
A pinch of saffron
Kosher salt and black pepper
6 Roma tomatoes, peeled, seeded
  and very finely diced
3 cloves garlic, minced
1 fresh bay leaf
Peel of ½ orange, removed with
  a vegetable peeler
1 cup (250 mL) white wine
Pernod to taste
20 or so slices baguette
3 cloves garlic, peeled
50 Manila clams, scrubbed
30 mussels, scrubbed
¼ cup (60 mL) finely chopped
  curly parsley
10 fresh basil leaves
Nice olive oil to finish

FOR THE ROUILLE

Blacken the red pepper and tomato over a flame or under the broiler. Place them in a small bowl, cover with plastic wrap and leave until they are cool enough to handle. Peel and seed them.

In a shallow dish, whisk the saffron and cayenne into the fumet. Add the bread and let soak until it has absorbed all the liquid.

In a blender, blend the bread, yolks and mashed garlic. With the motor running, slowly drizzle in the olive oil and the canola oil until emulsified. Transfer the mayonnaise to a bowl.

Pound the red pepper and tomato to a paste with a mortar and pestle. Stir into the mayonnaise. Season the rouille with kosher salt, black pepper and some additional saffron.

FOR THE CROUTONS, AND TO FINISH THE DISH

Preheat the oven to 425°F (220°C).

Reheat the fumet. In a pot big enough to hold the marinated fish without crowding, sauté the leeks and onions in ¼ cup (60 mL) olive oil with the pinch of saffron for 10 to 12 minutes. Season with kosher salt and black pepper.

Add the tomatoes, garlic, bay leaf, orange peel, fumet, wine and Pernod. Simmer gently for 10 minutes.

Meanwhile, brush both sides of the baguette slices with ⅓ cup (75 mL) olive oil and arrange on a baking sheet. Bake until they are golden, just a few minutes. Immediately rub them with the garlic cloves.

Add the clams to the soup and simmer for 2 minutes. Add the mussels and simmer for 1 minute. Add the marinated fish and simmer, without stirring, for 3 to 4 minutes, until the fish just starts to firm up. Discard any mussels or clams that do not open.

Divide the fish and shellfish among warmed serving bowls. Bring the broth to a boil and adjust the seasoning if necessary with kosher salt, black pepper, saffron or Pernod. Ladle the broth over the fish. Garnish with the parsley, basil, a dollop of rouille and the croutons. Drizzle a bit of nice olive oil into each bowl.

FOREST

Shortly after we started working on this book, Derek and I travelled to London, England, where we met up with his old pal and business partner Jamie Oliver, toured some of the city's food markets and visited some of the pubs that inspired Maison Publique. It was high hunting season when we were there, and it seemed like just about every menu we came across proudly displayed the warning "Game may contain shot."

"I love seeing that on a menu," Derek said one afternoon.

"There's something so ruthless about it," I replied. "But I've never actually come across a pellet in anything. Have you?"

"No," he said, "but if I did, it would be like finding a pearl in an oyster."

Outside of a few places in Newfoundland and Labrador and a handful now in Quebec, including Maison Publique, you don't see those words very often on Canadian menus. In most of the country, chefs aren't allowed to serve wild game in their restaurants.

Derek, having got used to serving wild game while working in London, found this frustrating. It bothered him so much, in fact, that he's working to change the laws in Quebec and would like to do so for the rest of the country too.

"My family are big hunters," he explains, "so the meat we had growing up was always moose, deer, grouse or whatever the hunting season brought. A lot of chefs around the world are completely envious of the quality of our wild game—it's some of the best in the world. I'm really hoping that for the first time we're going to be allowed to serve wild game in the restaurant, and I would love to see it happen in more places."

Of course, Canada's vast forests offer a lot more than just moose, grouse and deer. Maple syrup is probably our most famous forest product, and we couldn't very well write a book about Canadian food without including it. The syrup that's coming out of Quebec right now is far and away the best in the world. It's incredible on pancakes, obviously, but it's just as delicious drizzled over pork and beans or glazing some potatoes.

The varied climates across the country mean that we have a beautiful long season when wild mushrooms are available. Wandering around in the forest looking out for fresh mushrooms is an absolutely excellent way to spend your time. It's always a special day at Maison Publique when the first morels come in from BC or when those first fresh porcini arrive from Gaspésie. The cap on a big fresh porcini is like foie gras, and when you dry it you get an incredible, chewy texture in a sauce and an extra-delicious smell that you just can't get from fresh mushrooms. Grating raw pine mushrooms over a bowl of pan-roasted pheasants is the Canadian equivalent of grating white truffles over a bowl of pasta in Piedmont.

Recently, Derek and Alex Cruz from Société-Orignal started working on a honey in collaboration with Thierry Trigaux, a beekeeper in Gaspésie. They placed their hives an equal distance from the estuary of the St. Lawrence River and the forest, the idea being that in the morning there's more humidity on the estuary and the flowers don't open up as quickly, so the bees go to the forest first, pollinate there, take the pollen back to the hives, and in the afternoon go to the river and gather pollen from those flowers.

The honey turned out better than anyone expected. It has an almost salty component to it, probably because the flowers are so close to the ocean that they get the salt on them, but it also has a kind of saffron flavour that comes from some mysterious thing the bees are doing in the forest. It's delicious spread on some of the best, most herbaceous multigrain bread you can get your hands on.

The following recipes highlight these and a few more of the best ingredients found in Canada's forests.

Wild Garlic Pasta

Wild garlic, bear leeks, ramps or whatever hip word they are being called are quite possibly my favourite vegetable. They grow in deciduous woodlands with moist, acidic soil. In Quebec they are a protected species, so there's a moratorium on picking them and they can't be used commercially. Individuals are permitted to pick a limited amount for personal consumption. That said, there is a grey area that I've been known to tread in. If a person was to selectively pick the leaves and leave the bulb behind, there'd still be plenty of wild garlic growing again next year. I'm just saying. No matter what, people should pick them responsibly and never take an entire patch. Also, pick only the plants with two flat leaves. The third one that grows in the middle will be the flower and eventually go to seed, giving you a new plant to pick next year.

In my opinion, the best way to eat this green pasta is with chopped wild garlic leaves warmed in salted butter and a splash of the pasta water, or with wild garlic purée (see page 40). A few shavings of a hard goat cheese would be a crowning touch.

Makes 1 lb (450 g)

1 cup (250 mL) wild garlic leaves
5 large eggs
3½ cups (875 mL) all-purpose flour

Bring a large pot of salted water to a rolling boil and have a bowl of salted ice water on standby. Plunge the garlic leaves into the boiling water and cook for 30 seconds. Immediately transfer them to the ice water. Once cool, drain them and squeeze out any excess water with your hands.

THERE ARE TWO PATHS TO TAKE HERE:
For evenly green dough (my preference): Coarsely chop the garlic leaves. Crack the eggs into a blender and add the leaves. Purée until you have a smooth, bright green liquid. Give the blender jug a few good taps on the counter to knock some of the air out of the mix.

For speckled green dough: Finely chop the blanched garlic leaves and whisk together with the eggs.

Mound the flour on the counter and make a well in the centre. Add the garlic/egg mixture to the well. Stirring with a fork, begin to incorporate the flour from the sides. Keep pushing the outside edge of the flour to maintain the well shape (don't worry if it looks messy). When about half of the flour is incorporated, the dough should begin to come together. Start to gently knead the dough with your hands to incorporate the rest of the flour. As soon as the dough comes together in a cohesive mass, scrape up and discard the leftover flour and any dried bits of dough.

Lightly flour the counter and knead the dough for about 10 minutes, dusting lightly with flour if the dough sticks to your hands or the counter. Scrape the counter from time to time, just to make sure any dried bits aren't being incorporated into the dough. The dough should be smooth and soft and just a touch tacky, but it should no longer be sticking to your hands or the counter. Wrap it in plastic wrap and allow it to rest at room temperature for 30 minutes before rolling it out.

This dough can be rolled into any pasta shape, whether lasagna noodles, pappardelle (pictured), fettuccine, ravioli—whatever you like.

Wild Garlic Purée

Wild garlic is one of the first things to come up in the spring, but only during a three- or four-week window, depending on the weather. Since the season is so short, I process as much of this delicious, vibrant green purée as I can and freeze it to enjoy the rest of the year.

There's nothing you could replace this with. Use it to make pasta dough, fold it into aïoli or mix it into softened butter to be rubbed under the skin of a chicken. And this emerald purée looks incredible swirled into a soup. Basically, use this on anything you want to make delicious.

Makes 1½ cups (375 mL)

6 oz (170 g) wild garlic leaves
1 cup (250 mL) vegetable oil

Bring a large pot of salted water to a rolling boil and have a bowl of salted ice water on standby. Add half of the leaves and cook for 30 seconds. Immediately transfer them to the ice water. Once cool, drain them and squeeze as much water out of them as you can. Coarsely chop them along with the raw leaves.

If you have a large blender you could do this all in one shot; if not, do it in batches. Place the raw and blanched garlic leaves in the blender with the oil and let it rip until you have a smooth, bright green purée.

Wild Boar and Rosemary Ragù

This is a workhorse ragù. You can leave out the boar if you can't find it and sub in lamb shank, venison or even beef shin—just double the cooking time if you're using the latter. My choice would be to serve this with pappardelle (the wild garlic pasta on page 39, for example, would be incredible) or gnocchi, but do whatever blows your hair back. Don't forget the last step: the finishing touch of the rosemary and orange zest brings the dish to life.

Makes 10 servings

¼ cup (60 mL) olive oil

1 lb (450 g) wild boar shoulder, cut into 1-inch (2.5 cm) chunks

Kosher salt and black pepper

1 medium onion, finely diced

1 carrot, peeled and grated

1 stalk celery, finely diced

6 cloves garlic, coarsely chopped

1 can (5½ oz/156 mL) tomato paste

2 cups (500 mL) red wine

2 cups (500 mL) chicken and pork stock (see basic stock, page 238)

Leaves from 3 sprigs fresh rosemary, finely chopped

Chopped Italian parsley to finish

Freshly grated Parmesan cheese to finish

Extra virgin olive oil to finish

1 tsp (5 mL) finely chopped fresh rosemary to finish

1 or 2 rasps of orange zest to finish (err on the side of less, as you don't want it to overpower)

In a large flameproof casserole dish, heat the olive oil over medium-high heat until it is smoking. Season the boar with salt and pepper and sear on all sides until nicely browned. Remove to a plate.

In the same pan, cook the onion, carrot, celery and garlic, stirring frequently, until lightly browned. Stir in the tomato paste and cook, stirring, until it is rust-coloured. Add the wine and simmer until reduced by one-third. Add the stock and rosemary and bring to a simmer once again. Return the boar and any juices to the pot and bring to a boil. Turn down the heat to a simmer, cover with a round of parchment paper and gently simmer until the meat is very tender, about 1½ hours.

Remove the meat from the liquid and shred it with a fork. Skim the fat from the surface of the broth. Return the meat to the broth and simmer gently over medium heat until the sauce is a thick ragù consistency, stirring every so often so it doesn't catch on the bottom of the pot. Season with salt and pepper.

Reheat the sauce while your pasta cooks. Finish the sauce with the parsley, Parmesan, a splash of the pasta cooking water and some extra virgin olive oil. Spoon the sauce over the pasta and sprinkle with the rosemary and orange zest.

Fried Smoked Rabbit

Rabbit: the noblest of meats. If you don't have easy access to a supplier of dried balsam fir tips, chopped rosemary will work, or save a branch of your Christmas tree for this recipe. This rabbit is lightly smoked and fried in cast iron. I imagine it is what rabbit would have tasted like when cooked over a campfire somewhere on the Canadian Shield. I like to serve this with a little foie gras parfait (see page 140) on toast.

Serves 2

FOR THE RABBIT
1 cup (250 mL) kosher salt
1 tbsp (15 mL) sugar
1 tbsp (15 mL) dried balsam fir tips
1 tbsp (15 mL) fennel seeds, toasted
1 tbsp (15 mL) black peppercorns, toasted
1 tsp (5 mL) crumbled chile de árbol
1 tsp (5 mL) sodium nitrate
1 clove garlic
1 rabbit

TO FINISH THE DISH
2 tbsp (30 mL) canola oil
1 cup (250 mL) all-purpose flour
1 cup (250 mL) cornmeal
¼ cup (60 mL) + 1 tbsp (15 mL) cold unsalted butter, cubed
4 sage leaves
2 tbsp (30 mL) chopped Italian parsley
Juice of ½ lemon
¼ cup (60 mL) chicken jus (see page 237)
A drop or two of apple vinegar (see page 163)
Sea salt and black pepper

FOR THE RABBIT

In a mortar, combine half of the kosher salt, the sugar, balsam fir tips, fennel seeds, peppercorns, chile, sodium nitrate and garlic. Pound with a pestle until you have a homogenous mixture. Stir in the rest of the salt and set aside.

Break the rabbit down into primary cuts: two front legs, two back legs, one rib cage/top loin, one saddle and two belly flaps, reserving the liver, kidneys and heart if you have them. Split the saddle in half with a cleaver and trim off the hip joints where the legs were connected. Bone out the rib cage/top loin and cut it in half. Roll the belly flap around each half and secure with butcher's string.

Place the rabbit on a parchment-lined baking sheet and season liberally with the salt cure. Refrigerate, uncovered, for 2 hours. Rinse the rabbit under cold water, pat dry and arrange on a wire rack set over a baking sheet. Refrigerate, uncovered, for 12 hours.

Prepare a smoker. Heat 4 cups (1 L) of maple wood chips in the heating pan until they start to smoke. Place large bowls or trays full of ice on the lower smoking rack. Place the rabbit on the upper rack. Cold-smoke the rabbit for 25 minutes, replenishing the ice halfway if necessary.

Remove the rabbit from the smoker and refrigerate, uncovered, for 2 hours.

TO FINISH THE DISH

Bring the smoked rabbit pieces to room temperature.

Heat the canola oil in a large cast-iron pan over medium heat until smoking. Stir together the flour and cornmeal, and dredge the rabbit pieces in the mixture. Gently sear the back legs and the saddle for 2 minutes. Don't be a high-heat cowboy—adjust the heat of the pan if necessary by removing it from the element a bit and turning the rabbit pieces. Add the remaining rabbit pieces and continue with turning and adjusting the heat until the rabbit is golden brown on all sides and just cooked past medium, 12 to 15 minutes.

Add ¼ cup (60 mL) butter and allow it to foam slightly and start to brown. Add the reserved offal and sage leaves and cook them in the browning butter, all the time turning and basting the rabbit pieces. When the butter has browned, add the parsley and lemon juice and toss to fully coat the meat. Turn out onto a warm plate and allow to rest for 7 to 10 minutes.

In a small saucepan, reduce the chicken jus until it lightly coats the back of a spoon. Turn off the heat and whisk in 1 tbsp (15 mL) cold butter and a drop or two of vinegar. Season with salt and pepper.

Remove the string from the belly rolls and slice diagonally into 3 or 4 pieces. Slice the liver and kidneys (and the heart, if you have it) in half. Flood two plates with the sauce and neatly arrange the rabbit pieces on the plate. Season with sea salt and a turn or two of pepper.

Wild Pheasant with Immature Juniper, Speck and Pine Mushrooms

In Piedmont, where this dish gets its inspiration, white truffle season starts in October. Here in Canada, that's when pine mushroom season starts. Back in the DNA days we started thinly slicing raw pine mushrooms over plated pheasant just the way you would a truffle. It smelled great, and people loved the theatre of it. The sauce is enriched at the end with cream and apple brandy (I use the phenomenal Michel Jodoin calijo brandy made with Cortland, Lobo and Empire apples).

When working with wild birds, it is best to let them hang for a week to develop the flavour. Dry the cavity thoroughly and season lightly with juniper salt (see sidebar below) and suspend from a rack at 40°F (4°C) for seven days. The meat will change a bit each day, but don't worry, it's getting better.

Serves 2

1 wild hen pheasant, cleaned
6 sprigs fresh thyme
2 cloves garlic, smashed and peeled
2 tbsp (30 mL) unsalted butter
Sea salt and black pepper
5 slices speck or other artisanal smoked fatty ham
½ cup (125 mL) white wine
1 tbsp (15 mL) Société-Orignal black immature juniper berries (or regular juniper berries)
4 sage leaves
¼ cup (60 mL) apple brandy
¼ cup (60 mL) whipping cream
2 tbsp (30 mL) Société-Orignal green immature juniper berries (or regular juniper berries)
1 tsp (5 mL) pickling liquid from Société-Orignal green immature juniper berries (or a few drops of apple vinegar, page 163)
Black pepper
4 button-size pine mushrooms
1 recipe rye berries with red wine (see page 48)

Preheat the oven to 420°F (215°C).

Wipe the cavity of the pheasant and remove any excess fat. Put the thyme, garlic and butter in the cavity and season generously with salt. Lay the speck over the breast, overlapping slightly to make a nice "blanket." Truss the bird with butcher's string, making sure to go over the speck to keep it in place. Put the pheasant breast side up in a Dutch oven that will just hold the bird. Add the wine, black juniper berries and sage leaves. Partially cover with the lid and place in the oven.

Roast for 30 minutes. Turn the bird onto its breast. Partially cover again and roast for 20 minutes. Turn the bird breast up again and roast, uncovered, for 10 minutes. By this time the legs should just pull away from the body and the juices should run clear.

Remove the pot from the oven and pour the apple brandy over and around the bird. Allow the bird to rest for 15 minutes.

Lift the bird from the pot and tip the buttery juices from the cavity into the sauce. Put the bird on a warmed platter and keep warm. Strain the cooking liquid and return it to the pot, discarding the solids. Reduce the sauce slightly over medium heat. Stir in the cream, green juniper berries and their liquid. Season with salt and pepper.

Remove the string from the pheasant. Remove the speck and coarsely chop it. Pour the sauce over the bird. Top with the crispy speck. Using a truffle slicer or a mandoline, shower over the raw pine mushrooms. Serve with the rye berries.

JUNIPER SALT

Juniper salt can be used to season any game meats with great success. To make, take 3 tablespoons (45 mL) toasted juniper berries and ½ cup (125 mL) sea salt. Using a mortar and pestle, pound the juniper berries with half of the sea salt until you have a smooth mixture. Stir in the remaining salt. (Juniper salt keeps well in an airtight container.)

Rye Berries with Red Wine

This very straightforward side dish can be eaten hot or cold, and is perfect as the base for a salad. Rye berries are a cereal grain. If you can't find them, you can substitute farro or lentils du Puy and follow the same method.

Makes 4 cups (1 L)

2 cups (500 mL) basic stock
 (see page 238), plus more as
 needed
Sea salt and black pepper
2 tbsp (30 mL) canola oil
1 medium red onion, finely chopped
2 small carrots, finely chopped
½ bunch celery, finely chopped
2 cloves garlic, finely chopped
1 tbsp (15 mL) finely chopped
 fresh sage
1 tbsp (15 mL) finely chopped
 fresh rosemary leaves
3½ oz (100 g) pancetta, finely
 chopped
9 oz (250 g) rye berries
1½ cups (375 mL) red wine
A swirl of good-quality olive oil
2 tbsp (30 mL) finely chopped
 Italian parsley

Heat the stock, season with salt and pepper if needed, and keep warm.

In a large saucepan, heat the oil over medium heat. Add the onion, carrots and celery and fry until soft. Turn down the heat to low and add the garlic, sage, rosemary and pancetta. Cook, stirring frequently so the pancetta does not crisp, for about 10 minutes.

Add the rye berries and stir to coat. Add the wine a ladleful at a time, stirring until the liquid is absorbed before you add any more. Add 1 cup (250 mL) of the stock and cook, stirring occasionally, until it is mostly absorbed. Add the remaining 1 cup (250 mL) and continue to cook, stirring occasionally, until the rye berries are tender, about 25 minutes, adding a little more stock if necessary.

Season with salt and pepper, swirl in some good olive oil and finish with the chopped parsley.

Hare Ravioli

The whole "wild game" thing in Canada, with the exception of in Newfoundland, is pretty strange. When people see venison or caribou on a menu, they assume it's wild. But in most of Canada, serving wild game is illegal. We can serve all the wild fish we want from any part of the world. In Quebec we are legally allowed to serve beaver, muskrat, squirrel, hare and seal. So why not deer or moose? It doesn't make any sense at all.

Serves 4

FOR THE BRAISED HARE
1 wild hare (2 lb/900 g), cut into
 8 pieces
Kosher salt and black pepper
3 tbsp (45 mL) olive oil
1 onion, finely and evenly chopped
1 carrot, finely and evenly chopped
½ stalk celery, finely and evenly
 chopped
2 cloves garlic, thinly sliced
1 cup (250 mL) red wine
1 cup (250 mL) canned tomatoes,
 chopped, with their juice
1 tbsp (15 mL) chopped fresh
 rosemary

FOR THE RAVIOLI FILLING
1 lb (450 g) braised hare mixture
½ cup (125 mL) freshly grated
 Parmesan cheese
1 tbsp (15 mL) red chili flakes
4 tbsp (60 mL) cold unsalted butter,
 cut into ¼-inch (5 mm) pieces
6 oz (170 g) foie gras terrine (see
 page 141), cut into ¼-inch (5 mm)
 pieces and chilled
Kosher salt and black pepper

**FOR THE PASTA DOUGH AND
THE RAVIOLI**
1 recipe basic pasta dough (see
 page 244)
1 tsp (5 mL) olive oil

TO FINISH THE DISH
½ cup (125 mL) unsalted butter
6 tbsp (90 mL) Balconville vinegar or
 good-quality balsamic vinegar
Kosher salt and black pepper
¼ cup (60 mL) Italian parsley, cut
 into chiffonade
Parmesan cheese for serving

FOR THE BRAISED HARE
Preheat the oven to 375°F (190°C).

Season the hare liberally with salt and pepper. In a large flameproof casserole dish with a lid, heat the olive oil over medium heat. Add the onion, carrot, celery and garlic and cook, stirring occasionally, until the vegetables are very soft but not browned.

Turn up the heat and add the hare pieces, in batches if necessary, and brown them on all sides. Deglaze with the wine, scraping the bottom of the pan to remove any caramelized bits. Simmer the wine until it is reduced by one-third.

Add the tomatoes with their juice and the rosemary. Bring to a simmer, cover and transfer to the oven. Braise for 1 hour or until the meat is very tender. Uncover and cool completely to room temperature.

Carefully pick the meat from the bones, discarding the bones. Transfer the meat and the vegetables to a food processor and pulse until almost but not quite smooth. You want to maintain a bit of texture.

FOR THE RAVIOLI FILLING
Place the hare mixture in a large bowl and stir in the Parmesan and chili flakes. Gently fold in the cold butter and foie gras terrine until evenly distributed. Season with salt and pepper. Refrigerate until needed.

FOR THE PASTA DOUGH AND THE RAVIOLI
Make pasta according to the recipe directions, adding the oil as indicated.

Roll the pasta dough to the thinnest setting on a pasta machine. Cut the sheets into 2-inch (5 cm) squares—you'll need at least 36. Place 1 tablespoon (15 mL) of the filling in the centres of half of the squares. Lightly brush the edges of the meat squares with water and top with another pasta square, pressing gently around the filling to push out any air. Press the edges to seal. Arrange the ravioli without overlapping on a floured baking sheet and cover with an ever so slightly damp kitchen towel until you are ready to cook them. The ravioli are best cooked right away but can be frozen; do not thaw before cooking.

TO FINISH THE DISH
Bring a large pot of salted water to a rolling boil.

In a large sauté pan, melt the butter over medium heat until the foam subsides. Add the vinegar and swirl the pan to incorporate. Season with salt and pepper. Keep warm.

Drop the ravioli into the boiling water and cook until they float, about 2 minutes. Add a splash of the cooking water to the butter/vinegar mixture, then drain the ravioli. Add the ravioli to the sauté pan, add the parsley and toss to combine.

Transfer ravioli to four warmed dinner plates and grate the cheese over top.

Mushroom Pappardelle

I'm not reinventing the wheel here: it's mushroom pasta, plain and simple. The key is finessing the ingredients: making sure the noodles are rolled just right and having just enough sauce to complement them. You can certainly make this with whatever mushrooms are readily available to you, but in the fall, if you can source a variety of wild mushrooms, they will take the dish to the next level. I get my supply through Société-Orignal and Gérard at Gaspésie Sauvage—they really get the best out East. To be honest, though, the range of wild mushrooms available all across the country is unbelievable and can't be beat.

Here's what I like to use in the pasta:
Chanterelles • Yellowfoot chanterelles • Lobster mushrooms • Pine mushrooms (matsutake) • Swollen-stalked cat mushrooms • Wild oyster mushrooms • Hedgehog mushrooms • Coral mushrooms • Cauliflower mushrooms • Any boletus or porcini

If you can get your hands on all of these, you're in a very good place. They are all in the same season and will make for a showstopper of a dish. What's nice is to decorate a basket full of your bounty and present it to the table. That way they know what they are in for.

Serves 4 handsomely

FOR THE PASTA DOUGH
1 cup (250 mL) Red Fife flour
2½ cups (625 mL) all-purpose flour
4 large eggs, plus another if needed
1 tbsp (15 mL) olive oil

FOR THE MUSHROOM RAGÙ
4 to 5 cups (1 to 1.25 L) any
   mixture of the above-mentioned
   wild mushrooms, cleaned
3 tbsp (45 mL) olive oil
Kosher salt and black pepper
6 tbsp (90 mL) cold unsalted
   butter, divided
3 cloves garlic, thinly sliced
   Goodfellas style
2 tbsp (30 mL) finely minced
   shallot
1 tbsp (15 mL) finely chopped
   fresh thyme
¼ cup (60 mL) white wine
Lemon juice to taste
¼ cup (60 mL) mascarpone cheese
   (see page 241)
3 tbsp (45 mL) freshly grated
   Parmesan cheese, plus more
   to finish
2 tbsp (30 mL) finely chopped
   Italian parsley
Very good olive oil to finish

FOR THE PASTA DOUGH
Preheat the oven to 350°F (180°C).

Spread the Red Fife flour on a small parchment-lined baking sheet. Roast, stirring every 15 minutes, until the flour has a nutty aroma and is dark brown, about 45 minutes. Allow to cool to room temperature, then stir into the all-purpose flour.

Mound the flour on the counter, make a well in the centre and add the eggs and oil. Using a fork, beat the eggs and then start to incorporate the flour from the sides. The dough will start to come together when about half of the flour has been incorporated. At this point, start kneading with your hands to make a cohesive mass. If the mixture is too dry, add a little more egg. If it is too wet, work in a little more flour.

Scrape up and discard any scraps of dough, then knead the dough for 10 minutes or until the dough is smooth and soft and just a touch tacky, but it should no longer be sticking to your hands or the counter. Wrap in plastic wrap and allow it to rest in the refrigerator for at least 2 hours before rolling.

Using a pasta machine and working down to the thinnest setting, roll out the dough into long, thin sheets. Cut the sheets into 10-inch (25 cm) lengths, dust liberally with flour and roll them up into cylinders. Turn each roll lengthwise in front of you and cut ribbons that are 1 inch (2.5 cm) wide. Unroll the noodles, dust again with flour and cover with an ever so slightly damp kitchen towel. The pasta can rest for up to 1 hour.

FOR THE MUSHROOM RAGÙ AND COOKING THE PAPPARDELLE
While the pasta rests, trim the mushrooms and set aside. Place all the mushroom trimmings in a saucepan and cover with water. Bring to a boil, then turn down the heat and simmer, uncovered, for 20 minutes. Remove from the heat and allow to steep, uncovered, for an additional 20 minutes. Strain the mushroom stock through a coffee filter, discarding the solids. Reserve ½ cup (125 mL) of the mushroom stock.

Bring a large pot of salted water to a boil.

Cut the mushrooms in half or quarters if large, maintaining their general shape. In a sauté pan big enough to hold the bounty of mushrooms without crowding, heat the olive oil over medium-high heat. Once it begins to smoke, add the mushrooms and sauté until they begin to colour around the edges.

Turn down the heat to medium and season the mushrooms with salt and pepper. Add half of the butter, the garlic, shallot and thyme. Continue to sauté until the garlic and shallot have started to melt away.

Deglaze with the wine and boil for 30 seconds. Add the reserved mushroom stock and cook until reduced by half. Adjust the acidity with the lemon juice. You want the sauce to be slightly on the acidic side, as the mushrooms, cheese and pasta dough are very rich.

Add the pasta to the boiling water and gently stir to ensure it doesn't clump together.

Add the remaining butter to the sauce and turn the heat down to low. Swirl the pan to emulsify the butter into the sauce. Add the mascarpone cheese and swirl the pan to start to incorporate the cheese. It's okay if it's not fully emulsified, as having nice swirls of the rich white cheese through the pasta is a good thing. Adjust the seasoning with salt, pepper and lemon juice.

Add 2 tablespoons (30 mL) of the pasta water to the sauce and drain the noodles. Add them to the sauce along with the Parmesan and parsley. Toss well to combine.

Divide the pasta among four warmed plates, drizzle with good olive oil and shower with more Parmesan.

CLEANING MUSHROOMS

Never submerge your mushrooms in water to clean them. Lightly wipe them with a dry pastry brush and trim off any dark spots or oxidized parts. I prefer not to slice wild mushrooms. Instead, tear them into organic shapes so your guests can see the different shapes and sizes. The contrasting textures of larger pieces will also add a great mouthfeel.

Devilled Venison Pluck

The pluck is essentially the mass of innards from the windpipe to the end of the intestines of an animal. Normally, you don't get everything, so I've just listed this with the heart, liver and kidneys. Don't be put off if you aren't the biggest fan of offal. The cumin, fennel and coriander in the marinade really tame down the iron, and the flavours from the charcoal grill round everything out. You can replace the venison innards with lamb meat, sweetbreads or chicken legs; the marinade is good for anything cooked over charcoal.

Serves 6

FOR THE DEVIL SPICE RUB
2 tbsp (30 mL) cumin seeds
1 tbsp (15 mL) coriander seeds
1 tbsp (15 mL) fennel seeds
1 tbsp (15 mL) black peppercorns
A pinch of saffron
1 tbsp (15 mL) dried oregano
1 tbsp (15 mL) dried thyme
1 tbsp (15 mL) sweet smoked
 paprika
1 tsp (5 mL) ground turmeric

FOR THE DEVIL SPICE PASTE
6 cloves garlic, peeled
1 tbsp (15 mL) kosher salt
¼ cup (60 mL) olive oil
¼ cup (60 mL) sherry vinegar
¼ cup (60 mL) water
2 tbsp (30 mL) sweet smoked
 paprika
1 tbsp (15 mL) dried oregano

TO FINISH THE DISH
8 oz (225 g) venison kidney,
 sinew, silverskin and adrenal
 gland removed
8 oz (225 g) venison liver,
 silverskin and veins removed
8 oz (225 g) venison heart, fat
 and sinew removed
1 yellow onion, thinly sliced
2 tbsp (30 mL) extra virgin olive oil
Flaky sea salt
Lemon wedges

FOR THE DEVIL SPICE RUB
In a dry pan over medium heat, toast the cumin seeds, coriander seeds, fennel seeds, peppercorns and saffron until fragrant. Pound the toasted spices with a mortar and pestle to a fine powder. Stir in the oregano, thyme, paprika and turmeric. (Spice rub will last for up to 6 months in an airtight container.)

FOR THE DEVIL SPICE PASTE
Pound the garlic and kosher salt together with a mortar and pestle to a smooth, emulsified paste.

Combine the oil, vinegar, water, paprika and oregano. Add to the garlic paste, mixing until you have a smooth red paste.

TO FINISH THE DISH
Soak 12 wooden skewers in water for 30 minutes.

Cut the kidney, liver and heart into pieces roughly the width of a quarter and place each organ in its own bowl.

In a separate bowl, combine the spice paste, 2 tbsp (30 mL) of the spice rub and the sliced onion; mix well. Add one-third of the marinade to each bowl of meat and massage well to coat each piece.

Thread the meats onto the skewers, making sure you get two pieces of each type on each skewer. Don't worry if some onions get caught up in the mix; they will char on the grill and bring a nice sweetness to the finished dish. Transfer the skewers to a nonreactive container and pour over the remaining marinade. Cover and refrigerate for 12 hours.

Prepare a charcoal grill. While the coals are getting ready, bring the skewers to room temperature. When the coals are broken down and glowing, grill the skewers in batches, rotating them every 2 minutes, for 8 to 10 minutes. The outsides should be nicely caramelized and the interior a blushing rose. Remove from the grill and allow to rest for 5 minutes.

Arrange the skewers on a platter. Stir the olive oil into the resting juices and drizzle over the skewers. Sprinkle a few flakes of sea salt on each skewer and garnish with lemon wedges.

Moose Tongue Smoked Meat

After visiting Newfoundland and being amazed at how the chefs there are able to serve game meats legally (pay attention, rest of Canada!), I got to thinking about how moose tongue and heart are such a true Canadian delicacy. The rest of the animal is a noble beast, don't get me wrong, but you are allowed to shoot only one moose per year—and that's if you're lucky enough to draw a tag. That means there's only one tongue and one heart every year, and the opportunity to use these parts should be celebrated. Use veal or beef tongue for this recipe if you aren't one of the fortunate few.

Makes 1 tongue

FOR THE BRINE AND TONGUE
5 cloves garlic, lightly crushed
1 fresh bay leaf
12 allspice berries
5 whole cloves
5 oz (150 g) kosher salt
1 oz (30 g) brown sugar
5 g sodium nitrate
5 g black peppercorns
5 g mustard seeds
5 g coriander seeds
2 g ground ginger
1 g celery seeds
1 g red chili flakes
10 cups (2.4 L) water
1 moose tongue (about
  2¾ lb/1.25 kg)

TO FINISH THE DISH
Dill pickles (see page 230), cut into
  whatever shape blows your
  hair back
Pickled onions, separated into leaves
maple mustard (1 cup/250 mL Dijon
  mustard mixed with 1/2 cup/125 mL
  maple syrup)

FOR THE BRINE AND TONGUE
In a large nonreactive container, combine the garlic, bay leaf, allspice, cloves, kosher salt, sugar, sodium nitrate, peppercorns, mustard seeds, coriander seeds, ginger, celery seeds and chili flakes.

Heat 2 cups (500 mL) of the water and pour over the spice mixture, stirring to dissolve the salt, sugar, sodium nitrate and ginger. Add the remaining 8 cups (2 L) water and the tongue, cover and refrigerate for 20 days.

Remove the tongue from the brine and place in a large vacuum bag. Strain 2 cups (500 mL) of the brine and add this to the bag, then vacuum-seal. Discard the remaining brine. Cook the tongue in a water bath or immersion circulator set at 162°F (72°C) for 24 hours.

Remove the bag from the water bath and cool completely in a bowl of ice water. Remove the tongue from the bag and pat dry. Peel the skin and membrane off the meat.

Prepare a smoker. Heat 4 cups (1 L) of maple wood chips in the heating pan until they start to smoke. Place the tongue on the upper smoking rack. Place large bowls or trays full of ice on the lower smoking rack. Cold-smoke the tongue for 30 minutes, replenishing the ice halfway if necessary. Turn off the smoker and allow the tongue to rest until the smoke subsides. Remove the tongue from the smoker and refrigerate, covered, until ready to use.

TO FINISH THE DISH
Slice the tongue lengthwise as thinly as possible with a meat slicer. Delicately gather the sliced meat into decorative yet natural bundles. Use a light touch to do this, as the more you manipulate things, often the worse they will look.

Garnish with pickles, onions and maple mustard.

Sucre à la Crème Pot de Crème

I was in a mall one day and came across a Laura Secord—a famous Canadian chocolate chain named, for some reason, after a heroine of the War of 1812. I hadn't been in one of these stores for eons. I figured they'd probably gone extinct. As a kid I would sometimes get some of her butterscotch pudding in my school lunch, and since we had just come back from tapping trees for maple syrup, this recipe came to me. Sucre à la crème hurts my teeth (in a good way), and pudding is awesome, so why not combine the two and get the best of both worlds?

Serves 6

½ cup (125 mL) unsalted butter
1 cup (250 mL) brown sugar
A pinch of kosher salt
1½ cups (375 mL) whipping cream
1 cup (250 mL) whole milk
8 egg yolks
Flaky sea salt to finish

Preheat the oven to 325°F (160°C). Have ready a bowl of ice water with another bowl set inside it.

In a medium, heavy saucepan over medium heat, melt the butter. Stir in the sugar and kosher salt. When the sugar has dissolved and the mixture is bubbling away, add the cream and milk. Bring to a simmer. Cook for 5 minutes, then remove from the heat.

Whisk the egg yolks in a heatproof bowl. Whisking constantly, slowly add a bit of the hot cream mixture to temper the yolks. Keep adding the hot cream a little at a time, whisking constantly, until the yolks have come up to temperature and won't scramble when you add them to the pot.

Pour the mixture back into the pot. Cook the custard over low heat, stirring constantly with a rubber spatula (making sure to get in the corners, as they scald first), for about 7 minutes, until the mixture thickens enough to coat the back of the spatula. Immediately pour the custard through a fine-mesh sieve into the cold bowl to stop the cooking. Stir the custard every couple of minutes to aid in the cooling. (Cooling the custard before baking it prevents overcooking.)

Pour the cooled custard into six 5-oz (150 mL) ramekins and place them in a roasting pan. Add enough warm water to come halfway up the sides of the ramekins. Cover the pan with foil and bake for 35 to 40 minutes, until the custard is just set and still has a slight wobble in the centre.

Remove the foil and allow the ramekins to cool in the water until it is tepid. Remove the ramekins from the water and refrigerate, uncovered, until set.

Top each pot de crème with a light sprinkle of flaky sea salt. Serve with a bowl of lightly whipped cream and a plate of cookies of your choice.

Honey Marshmallows

This recipe is a great opportunity to break out that single-variety artisanal honey you've got kicking around: thyme, clover, lavender. The one I use is from Thierry Trigaux in eastern Quebec, a unique seashore honey. Made from the pollen of wild seashore plants, it has a slightly salty taste and a saffron finish.

Marshmallows are fun to make, and homemade are light years better than the store-bought kind. They make great petits fours at the end of a meal. For something more fancy, pipe them (as in the photo) on top of a lemon tart and hit them quickly with a torch.

Makes 36 to 48 marshmallows

3 egg whites
1½ cups (375 mL) sugar
¾ cup (175 mL) artisanal honey
¼ cup + 1 tbsp (75 mL) glucose
½ cup (125 mL) water
10 sheets gelatin
Icing sugar
Bee pollen or maple sugar to garnish

Spray a 10-inch (25 cm) square baking pan with nonstick cooking spray. Place the egg whites in the bowl of a stand mixer fitted with the paddle attachment.

Combine the sugar, honey, glucose and water in a small, heavy saucepan and bring to a simmer over medium heat, stirring to dissolve the sugar. Cook without stirring until a candy thermometer reads 230°F (110°C).

Meanwhile, soften or "bloom" the gelatin in a bowl of ice water for 5 to 10 minutes, then gently squeeze out the excess water.

When the sugar syrup reaches 230°F (110°C), beat the egg whites on medium speed until you have soft peaks. As soon as the syrup reaches 240°F (116°C), with the mixer running, slowly pour the syrup into the whites, avoiding the beater as much as you can. Increase the speed to high and add the bloomed gelatin. Continue to beat at high speed until the mixture is cool to the touch, increases in volume and starts to thicken, 12 to 15 minutes.

Immediately scrape the marshmallow into the prepared pan. Smooth the top with a damp spatula, dust lightly with icing sugar and cover with plastic wrap. Leave at room temperature overnight.

Heavily dust a cutting board with icing sugar and tip the marshmallow onto it. Using a knife sprayed with nonstick cooking spray, and spraying the knife between cuts, slice into desired shapes. Gently toss or roll each marshmallow in icing sugar to coat, and garnish with either the bee pollen or maple sugar.

⚔ Freshwater

Like all good Canadian boys, Derek and I were both fishing from the time we could bait a hook. Growing up in the Northwest Territories, I had access to some of the best freshwater fishing in the world: Great Slave Lake, Sparrow Lake, Bighill Lake, lakes that no one even knows the name of. That part of the world is riddled with fresh water, and those cold, deep lakes produce incredible fish, fat trout, massive, colourful arctic char and monstrous pike so big they're scary. In Yellowknife we had a family friend with an old Cessna 182 on floats, an old bush plane even back then, and I remember being allowed to take the controls sometimes when we'd fly out to Hidden Lake for special occasions.

Gutting and cleaning the fish that we caught was probably the first proper cooking I ever did, and I still love few things more than a freshly caught trout cooked in a cast-iron skillet over a fire. How lucky it was to be able to fish those lakes that avid fishermen the world over dream of visiting.

Derek would spend his summers fishing at a family cottage on Kootenay Lake in British Columbia. "I have great memories from that time," he recalls. "We'd fish for Kokanee all day every day like it was going out of style. That was the whole summer. We'd go to the Balfour Superette to buy maggots that they sold in sawdust. The Kokanee don't get huge, but it was always great to catch one that was two, two and a half pounds. Mostly we'd smoke it or fry them up at the cabin. It was the same routine every summer.

"In the winter, for Christmas, they had the opening of the season for the big rainbow trout, and those were 20 or 25 pounds. That was my big claim to fame as a kid, I think I was ten when I caught a 22½-pound rainbow trout. It's mounted on my parents' wall. I caught that one with my favourite lure: Old One-Eye. My uncle was an avid fisherman and he used to come to Campbell River every summer to go fishing. I remember going to River Sportsman with him once, and we found this lure that was just a piece of pink wool with a googly eye stuck on the back. It was the biggest piece-of-shit lure I've ever seen in my life, and it was a killing machine."

You'll hear stories like that across this country. The names of the lures might change and the types of fish, of course, will be different, but the thrill is the same. Kids in New Brunswick will brag about brook trout. In Abitibi they'll tell you about the pike that got away. And in Manitoba, fishing means doing battle with blackflies, whose bite is made less painful knowing that those same insects that feed on us also feed the fish that grow to legendary size.

Trout au Bleu

This dish traces back to nineteenth-century Switzerland and the French Alps, and it was held in high regard. It is said that this cooking method preserves the trout flavour better than almost any other way of cooking. You need live trout for this dish: for the fish to turn its namesake blue, the fresh slime has to be there, and it dries up in about an hour even if the fish is kept on ice. The vinegar bath needs to happen quickly to set the colour of the fish, and then it will stay blue throughout the poaching.

Serves 4

FOR THE COURT BOUILLON
1 cup (250 mL) diced onion
½ cup (125 mL) diced carrot
½ cup (125 mL) diced celery
6 sprigs fresh thyme
6 sprigs Italian parsley
2 fresh bay leaves
2 strips lemon peel
12 black peppercorns
1 tbsp (15 mL) yellow mustard
   seeds
6 cups (1.5 L) white wine
16 cups (3.8 L) water
Kosher salt

FOR THE TROUT
8 cups (2 L) white vinegar
2 live rainbow trout (2 lb/900 g
   each)
Flaky sea salt

FOR THE COURT BOUILLON
In a stockpot, combine the onion, carrot, celery, thyme, parsley, bay leaves, lemon peel, peppercorns, mustard seeds, wine and water. Season with kosher salt. Bring to a boil, then turn down the heat and gently simmer for 1 hour. Strain the stock into a clean pot large enough to hold the trout and keep warm. Discard the vegetables.

FOR THE TROUT
Bring the court bouillon to a gentle simmer. Pour the vinegar into a shallow dish large enough to hold the trout.

Grab a trout—taking care not to rub the layer of slime off the skin—and place it on a cutting board. Using a blunt object, give it a disciplined whack on the back of the head. Gut the fish, remove the gills, and immediately transfer the fish to the vinegar bath, turning to expose both sides to the vinegar.

Once the trout has turned blue, transfer it to the warm court bouillon and gently poach the fish until just cooked through, 8 to 10 minutes depending on the size.

Carefully lift the fish out of the court bouillon and allow it to drain. Transfer to warmed plates and fillet at the table. Season the flesh with the flaky sea salt.

This is nice served with cabbage glazed with butter and some of the court bouillon, and boiled potatoes with mustard and dill.

Fried Fermented Walleye

Fermenting the fish in rice gives the meat an addictive rich, nutty sourness. Some care is needed to make this safely: the fish needs to be rinsed very well, especially the stomach cavity. The Thai chilies and the ginger give this dish a real Southeast Asian flavour. This is about as Asian as my cooking gets.

Serves 8

2 cups (500 mL) wild rice
1 very fresh walleye (3 lb/1.35 kg), scaled and filleted
About 6 tbsp (90 mL) kosher salt
12 cloves garlic
2 inches (5 cm) fresh ginger, peeled and sliced
2 shallots, peeled
Canola oil for deep-frying
Flaky sea salt
4 Thai bird chilies, thinly sliced
Leaves from 6 sprigs fresh mint
Lime wedges

Soak the wild rice in water overnight. Drain the rice and steam it until it is completely puffed, 45 minutes to 1 hour. Allow to cool.

Score the skin of the fish fillets, taking care not to cut right through. Season the scored sides liberally with kosher salt. Place in a nonreactive container, cover with cold water and soak in the brine for 2 hours.

With a mortar and pestle, pound the garlic and ginger to a paste with some kosher salt. Working in batches if you have a smaller mortar, add the wild rice and massage it with the pestle until you have a coarse paste. Season with kosher salt.

Drain the fillets and dry them with paper towels. Dry the container. Rub the rice paste all over the fish and return it to the container. Cover loosely with plastic wrap and let the fish rest in a warm place for 30 hours.

Scrape off most of the rice paste, then wipe with a damp cloth to remove excess paste. Transfer the fish to a clean dish and refrigerate, covered, for 24 hours.

Slice the shallots into thin rings and soak in ice water for 10 minutes.

In a deep-fryer, or in a heavy pot at least 12 inches (30 cm) deep, heat 6 inches (15 cm) of canola oil to 375°F (190°C). Cut the fish into serving pieces and deep-fry, turning a few times, until crispy and golden all over. Drain on paper towels and season with flaky sea salt.

Arrange the fish on a decorative platter and scatter over the drained shallots and the chilies. Mound the mint up on the side of the plate with the lime wedges.

Trout Amandine

Everyone will benefit from knowing how to make this timeless bistro classic. I serve the fish with the head and skin on, but you could always remove those after it's cooked.

Serves 4

4 whole rainbow trout (1 lb/450 g
 each), cleaned
4 oz (115 g) haricots verts, trimmed
4 oz (115 g) yellow wax beans,
 trimmed and frenched
Kosher salt and white pepper
4 tbsp (60 mL) canola oil, divided
1 cup (250 mL) + 2 tbsp (30 mL)
 unsalted butter
¾ cup (175 mL) blanched almonds,
 toasted
1½ tbsp (20 mL) finely chopped
 Italian parsley
1 tbsp (15 mL) lemon juice

Using sharp scissors, cut the dorsal fin, pectoral fins and gills from each trout. Turn each fish on its back and, using a sharp knife, make a shallow incision down each side of the spine, being careful not to cut through the fish. Using the scissors, sever the spine just behind the head and just in front of the tail, then gently pull out the entire spine. Cut away the belly flaps and remove the pin bones. Finally, cut off the tail.

Bring a large pot of heavily salted water to a boil and prepare an ice bath. Blanch the haricots verts and wax beans for 2 minutes, then transfer to the ice bath until cool. Drain, then spread out on paper towels to dry.

Season the fish with the salt and pepper. Get two nonstick frying pans big enough to hold 2 trout each. In each pan, heat 2 tbsp (30 mL) of the canola oil over medium-high heat. When it is about to smoke, gently lay in the trout and fry for 4 minutes on one side only. (It's okay if the fish still looks undercooked; the hot beans and butter will finish the cooking.) Transfer the fish to a platter and keep warm.

In a sauté pan, sauté the beans with 2 tbsp (30 mL) butter and ¼ cup (60 mL) water until they are glazed. Season with salt and pepper.

Drain the oil from one of the fish pans and add 1 cup (250 mL) butter. Cook over medium heat until the butter is brown, 4 to 5 minutes. Stir in the almonds and parsley. Remove the pan from the heat, swirl in the lemon juice and season with salt and pepper.

Divide the beans into four and place them inside each fish. Spoon the almond brown butter over each trout and around the warmed plates.

Lake Fish Quenelles

The recipe for quenelle Lyonnaise is thought to have been created in 1830, so this dish has some staying power. I like to make these quenelles because they're so old school and delicious. Traditionally they are made with pike, a fish that, happily, is abundant in many of our remote lakes. If you aren't able to get your hands on northern pike, a walleye or several perch will do the trick. But in the end they're just dumplings, so you can make them with other fish, chicken or vegetables. To gild the lily, stud the quenelles with black truffles and serve them with a truffle purée.

Serves 8

FOR THE TRUFFLE PURÉE (OPTIONAL)
2½ tbsp (37 mL) cold unsalted butter, divided
1 tbsp (15 mL) finely chopped shallot
½ cup (125 mL) finely chopped brown button mushrooms
½ cup (125 mL) finely chopped black truffle
2 tbsp (30 mL) Madeira
½ cup (125 mL) canned truffle juice
Salt and sherry vinegar

FOR THE PIKE FUMET
5 lb (2.25 kg) pike or other white-fish bones
¼ cup (60 mL) canola oil
1 cup (250 mL) thinly sliced onions
½ cup (125 mL) diced carrots
½ cup (125 mL) diced celery
½ cup (125 mL) diced leeks
½ cup (125 mL) diced fennel
2 cloves garlic, lightly crushed
2 tbsp (30 mL) tomato paste
½ cup (125 mL) apple brandy
1 cup (250 mL) white wine
5 sprigs fresh thyme
5 sprigs fresh tarragon
2 fresh bay leaves
12 white peppercorns
20 cups (5 L) cold water
½ cup (125 mL) whipping cream

FOR THE TRUFFLE PURÉE (OPTIONAL)
In a heavy sauté pan over medium heat, melt 1½ tbsp (20 mL) of the butter. When it starts to foam, add the shallot and sweat, stirring frequently, until they are completely softened but not coloured. Add the mushrooms and truffle and sweat until they are tender, 12 to 15 minutes.

Add the Madeira and reduce until the liquid is almost evaporated, then add the truffle juice and cook until the liquid is reduced by half.

Immediately transfer the mixture to a blender and purée on high speed until completely smooth. Blend in the remaining 1 tbsp (15 mL) butter and season with the salt and vinegar. Strain through a fine-mesh sieve into a bowl. Chill in an ice bath, stirring occasionally. (Rapid chilling prevents the butter from separating.) Place in a squeeze bottle. (Purée keeps, refrigerated, for a couple of days.)

FOR THE PIKE FUMET
Preheat the oven to 350°F (180°C).

Rinse the fish bones well and pat dry with paper towels. Spread the bones in a roasting pan and roast, turning every so often, until they are golden brown, 40 to 45 minutes.

Heat the canola oil in a stockpot over medium-high heat. When it is almost smoking, add the onions, carrots, celery, leeks, fennel and garlic. Sauté until they are tender, 12 to 14 minutes. Add the tomato paste and cook, stirring, for 5 minutes. Add the apple brandy and cook until reduced to 2 tbsp (30 mL).

Add the fish bones to the pot, then deglaze the roasting pan with the wine, stirring to scrape up all the caramelized fish bits. Cook until the wine has reduced to ½ cup (125 mL). Add the thyme, tarragon, bay leaves, peppercorns and water. Bring to a simmer over medium heat, constantly skimming the surface of any impurities. Simmer, uncovered and without stirring, for 1 hour.

Strain the stock through a fine-mesh sieve into a clean pot, discarding the solids. Reserve 8 cups (2 L) of the stock for poaching the quenelles.

Reduce the remaining stock over medium heat to 4 cups (1 L). Add the cream and reduce to 2 cups (500 mL). The sauce should be thick enough to coat the back of a spoon. Strain the sauce again through a fine-mesh sieve into a small, clean saucepan and reserve.

recipe continues . . .

FOR THE PÂTE À CHOUX

1 cup (250 mL) water
4 tbsp (60 mL) unsalted butter
1 tsp (5 mL) kosher salt
¾ cup (175 mL) all-purpose flour
2 eggs
2 egg whites

FOR THE QUENELLES

1¼ lb (565 g) skinless, boneless
  pike, very cold
Pâte à choux, cold
½ tsp (2 mL) kosher salt
¼ tsp (1 mL) white pepper
6 tbsp (90 mL) cold whipping cream
3 tbsp (45 mL) grated Avonlea
  Clothbound or other aged
  artisanal cheddar
2 tbsp (30 mL) chopped black truffle
  (or a good pinch of nutmeg)

FOR FINISHING THE PIKE SAUCE

½ cup (125 mL) cold unsalted
  butter, cubed
1 tbsp (15 mL) lemon juice
Kosher salt

FOR THE PÂTE À CHOUX

In a medium, heavy saucepan over medium-high heat, bring the water to a boil with the butter and salt. Remove from the heat and add the flour all at once, stirring with a wooden spoon to combine.

Place the pot over medium heat and cook, beating constantly, until the mixture forms a smooth, cohesive mass that pulls away from the sides of the pan. Remove from the heat.

Add the eggs one at a time, beating vigorously after each addition, then beat in the egg whites until the dough is glossy and smooth. Set the saucepan in an ice bath and stir until cold. (Chilling the dough rapidly prevents the butter from separating out.)

FOR THE QUENELLES

Chill the bowl and blade of a food processor for about 1 hour.

Cut the fish into 1-inch (2.5 cm) strips. In the food processor, combine the fish, cold pâte à choux, salt, pepper and 4 tbsp (60 mL) of the cream. Process for 30 seconds, then scrape down the sides. If the mixture seems too stiff, add a little more cream.

Add the cheese and truffle and blend again until smooth, adding as much of the cream as you can without making the paste so loose that it won't hold its shape when formed.

FOR FINISHING THE PIKE SAUCE

Shortly before serving, bring the reduced pike sauce to a simmer. Remove from the heat and add the butter one cube at a time, whisking constantly until the butter is almost incorporated before adding more. Season with the lemon juice and salt. Keep warm.

TO FINISH THE DISH

Bring the reserved pike fumet to a bare simmer over medium heat. Scoop a small amount of the quenelle paste into the fumet. Poach for 4 to 5 minutes, then taste for seasoning. Add more cream if you think the mixture can take it.

With two wet spoons, scoop out a rounded mass of the quenelle paste with one spoon and smooth the sides of the paste with the second spoon to make a smooth, even quenelle. Drop the quenelle into the barely simmering fumet and repeat to make 7 more quenelles, adding them to the fumet as they're made. Gently poach until they have almost doubled in size and roll over easily, 12 to 15 minutes. Do not let the water come above a bare simmer. Remove the quenelles with a slotted spoon and drain on paper towels.

If using the truffle purée, pipe a thick circle just inside the edge of each of eight plates. Flood the inside of the purée with the warm pike sauce and place a quenelle in the centre of each plate. Sprinkle each quenelle with a couple of flakes of sea salt and finely grate any remaining truffle over each dish.

Watercress, Radishes and Pickerel Bottarga

This is an incredibly easy salad to make, and such a pleasure when you break the yolk and start mixing everything together. Bottarga, either homemade or store-bought, brings excitement to every party. Like anchovies, it has that potato-chip quality that makes you want to keep eating.

Serves 4 as a starter

FOR THE PICKEREL BOTTARGA
Pickerel roe sacs
Kosher salt

FOR THE SALAD
4 eggs
1 shallot, peeled
20 radishes (a mixture of varieties
  and colours), trimmed
Kosher salt
3 cups (750 mL) watercress,
  coarse stems removed
1 tbsp (15 mL) minced
  Italian parsley
3 tbsp (45 mL) lemon vinaigrette
  (see page 240)
2 inches (5 cm) pickerel bottarga
Flaky sea salt and black pepper

FOR THE PICKEREL BOTTARGA

In a nonreactive container, bury the roe sacs in the kosher salt and refrigerate for 8 hours.

Remove the sacs from the salt and rinse them under cold water. Pat dry with paper towels. Roll each roe sac in cheesecloth to form a fairly even log (this ensures that it cures evenly). Tie the ends of each log with butcher's string and hang in a cool, dark place—60°F (15°C) with 65% humidity—for 3 weeks or until they are firm enough to grate (think stale-fudge consistency). (Bottarga can be vacuum-sealed and frozen for up to 6 months.)

FOR THE SALAD

Place the eggs in a saucepan and cover with cold water. Bring to a simmer and cook for 5 minutes. Immediately transfer to ice water to cool. Peel the eggs and keep at room temperature.

Slice the shallot into thin rings and soak in ice water for 10 minutes.

Using a mandoline, slice the radishes as thinly as possible. Place the slices in a bowl, toss with kosher salt and let them sit for 5 minutes while you finish the dish.

Toss the watercress, parsley and drained shallots with the lemon vinaigrette. Season with the flaky sea salt and pepper.

Place an egg in each of four bowls and surround each egg with the salad, making a nest. Scatter the radishes over the salad and around the egg. Using a mandoline, shave the bottarga over each salad. Finish with a few flakes of salt and a little pepper.

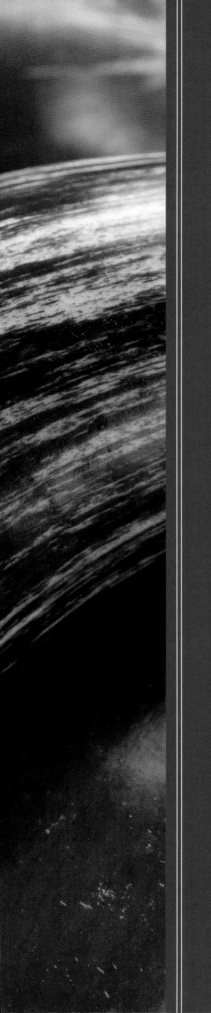

⚔

FIELD

Ever stop to think about how many delicious things come from Canadian fields? That fancy Dijon mustard that spices up your vinaigrette is almost certainly made with Canadian mustard seeds. Same with the bright yellow version that makes sports stadium hot dogs edible. Those comforting curried lentils? Probably from Saskatchewan. Ditto the chickpeas in that creamy, rich hummus. Peas, beans, sunflower, buckwheat—I wonder if people realize how important the Canadian field is to some of the most influential cuisines in the world. Our fields produce more than a third of all the world's pulses. We are the largest producer of lentils and dry peas and one of the largest exporters in the world: our farmers ship to more than 150 markets around the globe.

One of Derek's favourite things is working directly with small, local farmers. A lot more chefs are doing this because they can work with farmers to grow specific things for their restaurant.

"There's something really special about going and finding seeds and doing little test batches to see what kind of produce grows well in different places," he says.

At the restaurant, Derek works mainly with two farmers: Jocelyn and Pascale at Jardins Bio-Santé in Howick. "Every year they give me seed books," Derek explains. "They tell me to go through them to pick out what I want and they tell me if they can do it or not. Some things they just flat out refuse. Once I saw these peas that looked interesting and I asked Pascale to grow some for me and he said, "I'm not growing peas. Why would you want me to grow peas? Just go buy frozen peas, they're better than anything anyone could grow." And you know what? He's right. I've never bought fresh peas since. You have to shuck them, they're all starchy, and they're never as good as they're supposed to be. Buy frozen for a fraction of the cost. They're sweet, they're green, they're great."

The restaurant also has a dedicated potato guy, Lowek, who grows nothing but one type of potato. He grows German butter potatoes and he grows them very, very well. One day Derek asked him why he grew only one type of potato. "I'm not going to try to do anything fancy," Lowek said. "Why would I? I've got the right soil and the right location to grow this kind of potato really well, so I'm not going to try to do purple Peruvian fingerlings or Russian bananas. I know these are great, my life isn't complicated, people buy them and that's the way it is. I just focus on doing one thing properly instead of doing ten things half-assed."

You can learn a lot from Canadian farmers.

Slow-Roasted Shoulder of Pig

This is roast pork in all its glory. I like it with the salsa verde, but if you choose to take the applesauce route it will be just as good. The key to this dish is to score the skin with a heavy hand and generously salt it, then leave the shoulder out on the counter overnight. Don't worry, you're not going to die. Besides, if this big cut of meat went in the oven cold, it would lower the temperature and create steam, which means you wouldn't get the desired crackling. The best way to get that crackling is to start with quality pork, give it the 30-minute sizzle, then turn down the heat and forget about it. Don't even baste it, just leave it alone. You really have to try hard to mess this dish up. Err on the side of it being done early. You can turn the oven off and let it rest inside.

Serves at least 12

1 skin-on, bone-in pork shoulder
   (7 to 10 lb/3.15 to 4.5 kg)
3 fresh bay leaves, stems removed
¼ cup (60 mL) flaky sea salt
2 tbsp (30 mL) fennel seeds
Cracked black pepper
2 yellow onions (unpeeled),
   quartered
5 carrots, peeled and roughly
   chopped
5 stalks celery, peeled and roughly
   chopped
4 heads garlic, cut in half crosswise
3 sprigs fresh rosemary
3 sprigs fresh thyme
2 cups (500 mL) water
3 tbsp (45 mL) chopped Italian
   parsley
1 tbsp (15 mL) unsalted butter

THE NIGHT BEFORE . . .

With a sharp utility knife, score the pork skin ½ inch (1 cm) deep and 1 inch (2.5 cm) apart. You can go the straight-line route or, as I like to, the criss-cross. Using a mortar and pestle, pound the bay leaves with a bit of the salt (try to pound them pretty fine, but you don't need a paste). Add the fennel seeds and give them a little discipline with the pestle. Add the rest of the salt and the pepper and stir together. Massage this into the score marks. In a roasting pan, combine the onions, carrots, celery, garlic, rosemary and thyme. Set the pork on top. Cover it with a dry kitchen towel and leave it in a cool, dry place overnight. Don't worry—it's going to be fine.

THE NEXT DAY . . .

Eight hours before serving, preheat the oven to 450°F (230°C). Place the pork and vegetables in the oven and give them a 30-minute sizzle, during which the skin will start to crackle. After 30 minutes, add the water to the pan and turn the oven down to 325°F (160°C). Roast for another 3½ hours, adding more water if necessary so the pan does not dry out. DO NOT baste the pork, or you will kill all hopes of crackling. Turn the oven down to 300°F (150°C) and roast for another 2½ hours.

Turn the oven off and let that juggernaut of meat rest in the oven for 1 hour. Transfer it to a serving platter and put it back in the warm oven while you prepare the pan sauce.

Strain the roasting liquid into a saucepan and ladle off the fat. Remove the garlic, onions, carrots and herbs from the strainer. Discard the herbs and onion skins. Squeeze the garlic back into the strainer, discarding the skins. Using the back of a ladle, force the celery and garlic through the strainer and into the sauce. Bring the sauce to a boil and cook until it has thickened a little. Remove from the heat and season with salt and pepper. Pull the onions into leaves and add those to the sauce along with your porky carrots. Fold in the parsley and butter.

Carve the pork and serve with the pan sauce, along with salsa verde (see page 235), if desired.

Sweet-and-Sour Sweetbreads

I would be lying if I said this dish wasn't the result of some late-night McNugget eating. I cook my sweetbreads from raw instead of starting with the traditional court bouillon poaching method. To my taste this gives a better result, creamier, more tender, and you get the natural flavour of the sweetbread. You still need to peel them, though, and this is a little more tedious to do with raw ones. But one bite and you'll forgive me.

Serves 8

FOR THE RICE DREDGE
½ cup (125 mL) arborio rice
1 cup (250 mL) all-purpose flour
1 tbsp (15 mL) sea salt
1 tsp (5 mL) black pepper

FOR THE SWEET-AND-SOUR SAUCE
⅓ cup (75 mL) white wine vinegar
3 tbsp (45 mL) sugar
½ cup (125 mL) nonpareil capers, rinsed
¼ cup (60 mL) good-quality olive oil
Kosher salt

FOR THE SWEETBREADS
4 whole veal sweetbreads
Kosher salt and black pepper
1 cup (250 mL) arborio rice dredge (see above)
¼ cup (60 mL) canola oil
3 sprigs fresh rosemary
3 tbsp (45 mL) cold unsalted butter, divided
½ cup (125 mL) chicken jus (see page 237)
Flaky sea salt

FOR THE RICE DREDGE
In a spice grinder, blitz the rice to a fine powder. Sift through a fine-mesh sieve into a bowl. Whisk in the flour, sea salt and pepper. (Rice dredge can be made several days ahead.)

FOR THE SWEET-AND-SOUR SAUCE
In a small saucepan, simmer the vinegar and sugar to make a light syrup. Allow to cool.
In a blender, purée the capers with the vinegar syrup, then slowly drizzle in the olive oil until emulsified. Season with kosher salt. (Sauce may be made a day ahead and refrigerated; bring to room temperature before using.)

FOR THE SWEETBREADS
Soak the sweetbreads under cold running water for 30 minutes. The membrane should pull away easily. Break the sweetbreads apart with your fingers into roughly 2-inch (5 cm) pieces—follow the natural separations. Season the sweetbreads with kosher salt and pepper, then dust them with the rice dredge.

Heat the canola oil in a large sauté pan over medium-high heat until it begins to smoke. Working in batches so you don't crowd the pan, sauté the sweetbreads until they are golden and crispy on all sides but not cooked through. Transfer to a plate.

Turn down the heat to medium. Return all the sweetbreads to the pan and add the rosemary and 2 tbsp (30 mL) of the butter. Constantly baste the sweetbreads until they are firm to the touch but still have a little bit of spring to them, another 8 to 10 minutes depending on their size. (You can check with a skewer to make sure they're cooked through, if you like.) Remove the smaller pieces first so they don't overcook. Transfer to a plate lined with paper towels and allow to rest in a warm place.

Meanwhile, in a small saucepan, bring the jus to a simmer and reduce until it just starts to coat the back of a spoon. Remove from the heat and swirl in the remaining 1 tbsp (15 mL) butter.

Pile the sweetbreads onto eight warmed dinner plates and spoon a bit of the jus around each one. Dollop each sweetbread with the sweet-and-sour sauce and top with a few flakes of sea salt. Serve with buttery braised carrots and greens with garlic.

BBQ Lamb Shoulder

Cooking this lamb at a low temperature in an immersion circulator and finishing it over charcoal yields an amazing result. You get the best of both worlds: pull-apart tender meat that is cooked to a perfect medium right through to the bone, with a barbecue-crusted glaze and that distinct BBQ flavour. This is our standard charcoal BBQ glaze; it's stupidly simple, but there's something about the way it works in combination with the salted meat that picks up the grill flavour so well.

Normally, whole lamb shoulder cooked medium would never be shreddable, but the long cooking breaks down the protein structure, leaving you with succulent meat. Don't rush out and buy an immersion circulator just to make this recipe, though (although it would be worth it). You can easily go the traditional route and either slow roast it or cook it slowly for a few hours over low coals. It will still be delicious.

Serves 6

FOR THE BBQ GLAZE
½ cup (125 mL) maple syrup
½ cup (125 mL) cider vinegar
1 tbsp (15 mL) finely chopped
  fresh rosemary

FOR THE LAMB SHOULDER
1 cup (250 mL) kosher salt
Zest of ½ orange
2 cloves garlic, peeled
6 sprigs fresh thyme
4 star anise
2 tbsp (30 mL) black peppercorns
1 tsp (5 mL) cumin seeds
1 tsp (5 mL) coriander seeds
1 tsp (5 mL) dried lavender flowers
1 bone-in lamb shoulder
  (3 lb/1.35 kg)

TO FINISH THE DISH
1 cup (250 mL) chicken jus
  (see page 237)
12 charred onion petals
  (see page 243)
Flaky sea salt and black pepper
2 tbsp (30 mL) cold unsalted
  butter, cubed
1 tsp (5 mL) torn fresh lavender
  blossoms
1 tsp (5 mL) torn fresh chive
  blossoms
1 tsp (5 mL) torn fresh anise
  hyssop blossoms

FOR THE BBQ GLAZE
Stir all the ingredients together. (Glaze keeps, refrigerated, for up to 6 weeks.)

FOR THE LAMB SHOULDER
In a mortar, combine half of the kosher salt, the orange zest, garlic, thyme, star anise, peppercorns, cumin seeds, coriander seeds and lavender flowers. Pound with a pestle until you have a fragrant spice mixture. Stir in the rest of the salt. Rub the spiced salt liberally all over the lamb shoulder. Place the lamb on a wire rack set over a baking sheet and refrigerate, uncovered, for 4 hours.

Rinse the lamb well to remove the salt mixture and pat dry. Place the lamb in a vacuum bag and vacuum-seal.

Heat a water bath or immersion circulator to 135°F (57°C). Drop in the lamb, tightly cover the cooking vessel with plastic wrap, and cook for 36 hours.

Remove the lamb from the water bath and allow it to rest for 20 minutes. If you are going to finish it later, plunge it into ice water to chill it completely. Reheat it in a water bath at 135°F (57°C) for 1 hour before continuing.

Have your grill ready, with the coals pushed slightly to one side and very casually glowing hot. You don't want full-on animal mode on the grill here; slow and steady will render you the tastiest finished result.

TO FINISH THE DISH
Remove the lamb from the bag, reserving the juices. Place the shoulder on the slowest part of the grill, baste it with the BBQ glaze and close the lid. After a few minutes you will start to see a steady stream of smoke, which signals that everything is working. Every few minutes, turn and baste the meat until only 1 tbsp (15 mL) of the glaze remains and the shoulder is caramelized. Remove the meat from the grill and allow it to rest for 20 minutes.

While the meat rests, in a small saucepan, combine the chicken jus and the reserved juices from the vacuum bag and gently reduce to sauce consistency. Stir in the remaining 1 tbsp (15 mL) BBQ glaze, then strain the sauce through a fine-mesh sieve into a clean saucepan.

Transfer the shoulder to a serving platter and scatter the charred onion petals over and around the meat.

Gently reheat the sauce and season with sea salt and pepper. In a small pan over medium-high heat, cook the butter, swirling the pan frequently, until the butter is browned and smells nutty. Slowly whisk the brown butter into the sauce. Spoon the sauce over and around the meat. Garnish the dish with the lavender, chive and hyssop blossoms.

Well-Done Lamb Chops with Charmoula

In the end this is fairly well done meat, but it's also a beautiful thing. Cooking the chops a bit past medium allows the fat to really melt into the meat and creates a nice, deep crust all around. Make sure you are getting good-quality lamb from a young animal. And don't be a cowboy with the grill. You're giving these just as much love as you would any other piece of food. The lamb is already dead—don't go killing it again.

Frenching your own chops isn't that hard and is considerably cheaper than buying already frenched chops.

Serves 6

FOR THE CHARMOULA
2 tbsp (30 mL) cumin seeds
2 cloves garlic, peeled
Kosher salt and black pepper
2½ cups (625 mL) fresh cilantro
  leaves and tender stems
1 cup (250 mL) Italian
  parsley leaves
1 tbsp (15 mL) sweet
  smoked paprika
½ tsp (2 mL) cayenne pepper
¾ cup (175 mL) extra virgin
  olive oil
2½ tsp (12 mL) rice vinegar

FOR THE LAMB CHOPS
2 racks of lamb
Leaves from 2 sprigs fresh
  rosemary, finely chopped
Leaves from 4 sprigs fresh
  thyme, finely chopped
1 chile de árbol, crumbled
2 cloves garlic, crushed
Zest and juice of ½ lemon
½ cup (125 mL) olive oil
Kosher salt and black pepper
2 tbsp (30 mL) chopped
  Italian parsley
2 tbsp (30 mL) chicken jus
  (see page 237)
Good sea salt to finish
Lemon wedges

FOR THE CHARMOULA
Toast the cumin seeds in a small, dry pan over medium heat until they smell fragrant.

Using a mortar and pestle (or a food processor), pound the cumin seeds to a powder. Add the garlic and pound until you have a paste. Season with kosher salt and pepper, then pound to combine. Add the cilantro and parsley and pound again, scraping down the sides of the mortar until you have a smooth green paste. Stir in the paprika, cayenne, olive oil and vinegar. Adjust the seasoning with kosher salt and pepper.

FOR THE LAMB CHOPS
French the racks halfway down the bone and cut between each bone to form neat chops.

In a large bowl or resealable plastic bag, combine the rosemary, thyme, chile, garlic, lemon zest and juice, and olive oil. Toss with the chops, cover and marinate in the refrigerator for 12 hours.

Prepare a charcoal grill.

Remove the lamb chops from the marinade and wipe off any excess marinade. Wrap each lamb bone in foil so it won't burn. Give each chop a little flatten with the palm of your hand. Season chops with kosher salt and pepper.

Once the coals are glowing, add the lamb chops. (You can cook them in batches if you don't feel comfortable grilling them all at once.) Grill each chop for 2 minutes exactly, then flip them over and grill for 2 minutes on the other side.

Repeat this process, rotating each chop slightly when you turn it so that you get diamond-shaped grill marks, and cooking for another 2 minutes on each side or until medium-well. The grill is going to have hot spots, so move the chops about accordingly. Transfer the chops to a bowl and allow to rest for 5 minutes.

Toss the chops with the parsley and the chicken jus. Transfer them to a serving plate and pour over the juices from the bowl. Season with sea salt, dot the chops with the charmoula and garnish with lemon wedges. Serve the rest of the charmoula in a bowl at the table.

Pork and Tuna

Think of this as a modified vitello tonnato. We used to make this at Zambri's all the time, using veal, and now that I have pigs raised for me, I use those. I go the route of a kind of porchetta, cooking the rolled pork on a rotisserie over charcoal so it develops an amazing flavour. The sodium nitrate, which is available at better grocery stores and online, helps with the curing process, gives the meat a slightly cured texture, locks in the colour and picks up the charcoal taste like nobody's business. But you could always leave it out—just know what you'll be missing.

Serves 10

FOR THE BRINED PORK
24 cups (5.6 L) water
2 cups (500 mL) kosher salt
1 cup (250 mL) sugar
1 tbsp (15 mL) sodium nitrate
2 heads garlic, cloves separated
  and crushed
Leaves from 6 sprigs fresh rosemary
Leaves from 10 sprigs fresh thyme
10 sprigs Italian parsley
3 fresh bay leaves
2 tbsp (30 mL) black peppercorns
1 boneless pork loin (about
  3 lb/1.35 kg)
1 skinless, boneless pork belly
  (about 9 lb/4.1 kg)

FOR THE TUNA MAYONNAISE
3 oz (85 g) good-quality canned
  tuna in olive oil, drained
2 tbsp (30 mL) capers, rinsed
1 tbsp (15 mL) white wine vinegar
1 tbsp (15 mL) lemon juice
2 large egg yolks
½ cup (125 mL) extra virgin
  olive oil
½ cup (125 mL) canola oil
Kosher salt and black pepper

TO FINISH THE DISH
A few handfuls of wild arugula
Lemon vinaigrette (see page 240)
Sea salt and freshly cracked
  black pepper
A nice cheese for shaving
  (I use Avonlea Clothbound
  Cheddar from PEI)
Good-quality olive oil

FOR THE BRINED PORK
Bring 2 cups (500 mL) of the water, the kosher salt, sugar and sodium nitrate to a boil, stirring to dissolve the sugar and salt. Transfer to a blender. Add the garlic, rosemary, thyme, parsley, bay leaves and peppercorns. Purée on high speed until smooth. Pour into a deep nonreactive container and stir in the remaining 22 cups (5.2 L) water.

Cut the pork loin lengthwise into thinner pieces so that it will fit end to end along the length of the pork belly. Add the loin pieces and the belly to the brine, cover and refrigerate for 3 days.

Prepare a charcoal grill with the rotisserie attachment.

Drain the pork, rinse well and dry completely. Lay the belly skin side down on a work surface. Arrange the loin pieces end to end in an even column along the length of the belly. Roll the belly tightly over the loin. Truss the meat log, starting in the middle and working to the ends, so that you have a tight, even roll without any air pockets.

Spit-roast the pork over glowing coals for about 1½ hours, until the internal temperature is 145°F (65°C). Remove the pork from the grill and allow it to rest with the spit attached until completely cool. At this point it can be refrigerated until you are ready to serve.

FOR THE TUNA MAYONNAISE
In a blender, combine the tuna, capers, vinegar, lemon juice and egg yolks. Blend on high speed. Slowly drizzle in the olive and canola oils to form an emulsion. If the mixture becomes too thick, add a splash of water to achieve the correct consistency. Season with kosher salt and pepper.

TO FINISH THE DISH
Using a meat slicer or a very sharp knife, slice the pork as thinly as you can. Arrange the slices on a platter. Spoon the tuna sauce over the pork as artistically as you feel.

Dress the arugula with the lemon vinaigrette, season with sea salt and pepper and scatter it over the pork and the sauce. With a potato peeler, curl off a few shavings of the cheese and finish with a drizzle of the olive oil.

Lovage Maccheroni alla Chitarra
with Cured Goat Liver and Pangritata

The idea for this recipe came from some incredible cured tuna hearts I had in Sardinia. I wanted to do a Canadian version and gave goat livers a try. It turned out a treat, garnished with an egg yolk, dried clay pepper (a type of espelette pepper made in Quebec) and pangritata (aka poor man's Parmesan, at its most basic just bread crumbs toasted in olive oil). The cured liver needs to be made in advance, but it's well worth the wait.

You could do this with veal, pig or lamb liver. Beef would probably be too strong, but if you're super into beef liver, go for it. Chicken livers, however, are just too small. You won't use all the pangritata; keep the rest in an airtight container, refrigerated, and use over salads or gratins.

Serves 6 as a starter

FOR THE GOAT LIVER
1 goat liver (3 lb/1.35 kg)
8 oz (225 g) kosher salt
4 oz (115 g) sugar
1 oz (28 g) pink curing salt
6 fresh bay leaves
Leaves from 2 bunches fresh thyme
Leaves from 2 bunches fresh
  rosemary
¼ cup (60 mL) black peppercorns
1 tbsp (15 mL) juniper berries
1 tbsp (15 mL) allspice berries
1 tbsp (15 mL) red chili flakes

FOR THE PANGRITATA
(MAKES 2 CUPS/500 ML)
1 cup (250 mL) fresh bread crumbs
½ cup (125 mL) + 2 tbsp (30 mL)
  olive oil
⅓ cup (75 mL) dried currants
1 sprig fresh rosemary
1 tsp (5 mL) red chili flakes
¾ cup (175 mL) finely diced
  red onion
Sea salt and black pepper
¼ cup (60 mL) balsamic vinegar
½ cup (125 mL) almonds,
  chopped but not too finely
2 tbsp (30 mL) finely chopped
  Italian parsley

FOR THE GOAT LIVER
Peel the goat liver and set aside.

In a mortar, combine the kosher salt, sugar, pink salt, bay leaves, thyme, rosemary, peppercorns, juniper berries, allspice and chili flakes. Pound with a pestle not to a paste but to marry the flavours and crack the peppercorns and berries.

Spread half the salt mixture in a nonreactive container, place the liver on top and cover with the remaining cure. Cover the container and allow to cure in the refrigerator for 8 days, flipping the liver and redistributing the cure after 4 days.

Remove the liver from the cure, rinse off the salt and pat dry. Wrap in cheesecloth and tie with butcher's string. Hang in a cool, dark place until firm enough to finely grate, 18 to 24 days.

FOR THE PANGRITATA
Preheat the oven to 375°F (190°C).

Toss the bread crumbs with 2 tbsp (30 mL) olive oil. Spread on a baking sheet and toast in the oven, stirring once halfway through, until golden brown and crunchy, about 10 minutes.

Soak the currants in hot water for 10 minutes.

While the currants soak, in a sauté pan over medium heat, combine ½ cup (125 mL) olive oil, the rosemary and the chili flakes. When they start to sizzle, add the onion and season with sea salt. Turn down the heat to low and allow the onions to stew for about 10 minutes, until very tender, stirring occasionally. Transfer to a bowl and discard the rosemary. Do not wipe out the pan.

Drain the currants. Add the balsamic vinegar to the pan that the onions were in and reduce it over medium heat to 1 tbsp (15 mL). Stir the reduced vinegar into the onions, then stir in the currants, bread crumbs, almonds and parsley. Season with sea salt and pepper. (Pangritata keeps, refrigerated in an airtight container, for up to 2 weeks.)

recipe continues . . .

FOR THE LOVAGE PASTA

1 cup (250 mL) lovage leaves, blanched, squeezed dry and coarsely chopped
4 large eggs, plus 1 more if needed
1½ tsp (7 mL) olive oil
3½ cups (875 mL) all-purpose flour

TO FINISH THE DISH

4 tbsp (60 mL) Fromagerie le Détour Ancestral Butter or other artisanal butter
¼ cup (60 mL) extra virgin olive oil
6 cloves garlic, thinly sliced
3 tbsp (45 mL) Société-Orignal dried clay pepper (or 1½ tbsp/20 mL sweet smoked paprika)
1 tbsp (15 mL) chopped fresh thyme
¼ cup (60 mL) chopped Italian parsley
2 tbsp (30 mL) lemon juice
Sea salt and black pepper
6 egg yolks
Parmesan cheese to finish

FOR THE LOVAGE PASTA

In a blender, combine the lovage, eggs and oil; purée until completely smooth and bright green. Pour into a bowl and tap on the counter several times to remove the air from the eggs.

Place the flour in a large bowl. Make a well in the centre and add the lovage mixture. Using a fork, start to incorporate the flour from the sides. The dough will start to come together when about half of the flour has been incorporated. At this point, start kneading with your hands to make a cohesive mass. If the mixture is too dry, add a little more egg. If it is too wet, work in a little more flour.

Remove the ball of dough from the bowl, scrape up and discard any scraps left in the bottom of the bowl, then knead the dough in the bowl for 10 minutes or until it is smooth and soft and just a touch tacky, but no longer sticking to your hands or the bowl. Wrap in plastic wrap and allow it to rest in the refrigerator for at least 2 hours before rolling.

Using a pasta machine and working in batches, roll out the dough, starting with the widest setting and rolling to #2. Cut the dough into 8-inch (20 cm) lengths. Place one dough strip at a time on your chitarra and press the dough through with a rolling pin, using gentle but constant pressure. Toss the noodles in flour and set aside until ready to cook. (You can also cut the noodles by hand; try to achieve fairly square noodles.)

TO FINISH THE DISH

Bring a large pot of salted water to a boil for the pasta.

In a large, heavy saucepan over medium heat, melt the butter with the oil. Add the garlic and sweat it until it starts to melt. Turn down the heat to low, add the clay pepper and thyme and swirl together. The mixture may seem oily, but that's okay, the pangritata will soak it up.

Cook the maccheroni for 6 minutes or until al dente. Drain the pasta, adding a bit of the pasta water to the saucepan. Add the pasta, parsley and lemon juice to the pan and season with sea salt and pepper.

Spread 2 tbsp (30 mL) pangritata on each of six warmed plates, then top with the pasta. Make a small well in the centre of each pile of noodles and carefully place a raw egg yolk in it. Sprinkle each yolk with a little sea salt and pepper. Grate a small amount of Parmesan over each serving, followed by a generous grating of cured goat liver.

Serve immediately, telling your guests that they are to break the yolk and stir it into the hot noodles.

Lamb Brain Profiteroles with Tartar Sauce

This is a great gateway brain recipe. The dough puffs up golden on the outside and leaves a creamy-brainy interior. Like most fried things, these profiteroles benefit immensely from a good homemade tartar sauce.

Makes about 25 small profiteroles, for a light starter

FOR THE TARTAR SAUCE
1 cup (250 mL) mayonnaise
  (see page 236)
2 shallots, finely chopped
½ cup (125 mL) finely chopped dill
  pickles (see page 230)
½ cup (125 mL) capers, finely
  chopped
¼ cup (60 mL) finely chopped
  Italian parsley
¼ cup (60 mL) white wine vinegar
Sea salt and black pepper to taste

FOR THE PROFITEROLES
½ cup (125 mL) water
4 tbsp (60 mL) unsalted butter
⅔ cup (150 mL) all-purpose flour
2 small eggs
½ lb (225 g) fresh lamb brains,
  soaked for 12 hours in several
  changes of cold water
Sea salt
Canola oil for deep-frying

FOR THE TARTAR SAUCE
Stir all the ingredients together. (The sauce is best made a day ahead and refrigerated. If you go this route, add the herbs just before serving.)

FOR THE PROFITEROLES
In a medium, heavy saucepan, bring the water and butter to a boil over medium-high heat. Add the flour all at once and cook, stirring vigorously with a wooden spoon, until the dough forms a ball that pulls away from the sides of the pot. Turn down the heat to low and cook, beating constantly, for 5 minutes. Remove from the heat and allow to rest for 2 minutes.

Add the eggs, beating until smooth. Set aside and allow to cool.

Drain the lamb brains and pat dry with paper towels. Transfer the cooled dough to a food processor. Add the brains and process until smooth. Pass through a fine-mesh sieve and season with salt. Scoop into a pastry bag fitted with a medium plain tip.

Heat the oil in a deep-fryer or deep, heavy pot to 350°F (180°C).

Pipe out about 25 balls slightly smaller than a Ping-Pong ball and carefully lower them into the hot oil. Fry for 2 minutes or until golden on each side. Drain on paper towels and season with salt. Serve hot with the tartar sauce.

✕ Tundra

The food traditions of the Arctic are some of the least understood and least explored on earth. I spent the first ten years of my life living in the Northwest Territories, in places like Norman Wells, Inuvik and Yellowknife. When I met my wife, she was living in the eastern part of the Arctic, in Iqaluit, the capital of Nunavut, and I've spent some time up there as well.

I've eaten muktuk (the fat and skin of bowhead whales) both raw and fermented, and akutaq (berries mixed with whipped walrus fat) and I can tell you that neither is likely to become the next food fad. Yet even those dishes, so foreign to most of us, are tame compared to other traditional delicacies such as fresh seal blood, or the fermented and half-digested contents of caribou and muskox rumen.

Nonetheless, there are still plenty of ingredients and food traditions from that part of the country that we can learn from. Incredibly, there are almost no poisonous plants, mushrooms, roots or berries in the Arctic. Once you get north of the treeline, you're pretty much free to eat any growing thing you come across. The best of them—bright orange cloudberries; black and delicate crowberries, the stems of which can be used to smoke fish; woolly fernweed, like an Arctic carrot; and Labrador tea—are starting to appear on southern menus.

Anyone who's ever foraged for food, put a foraged ingredient on their menu or ingested a foraged food would lose their mind for "mouse food," the roots of various tundra plants that voles store in underground burrows. Inuit collect these caches for themselves but always remember to leave half behind for the "mouse."

Canadian chefs are recognizing how delicious caribou, ptarmigan, muskox and seal are. Derek, through his association with Société-Orignal, is at the forefront of working with these products and introducing them to a wider audience, but when it comes to food from the tundra, there's much more waiting to be discovered.

Smoked Caribou Carpaccio

This is one of my favourite recipes: lightly brined and cold-smoked caribou with pickled blueberries makes for a beautiful early-fall first course. (Purée leftover pickled blueberries into a jam to serve with paté or charcuterie.) Ideally, you'd have a smoker for this dish. If you don't have one, buy one. You'll find yourself using it often.

Serves 8 to 10

FOR THE BALSAM FIR SALT
3 tbsp (45 mL) dried balsam fir tips
½ cup (125 mL) sea salt

FOR THE PICKLED BLUEBERRIES
1 tbsp (15 mL) juniper berries
1 tbsp (15 mL) black peppercorns
1 star anise
1 whole clove
2 allspice berries
½ cinnamon stick
2½ cups (625 mL) red wine
1 cup (250 mL) red wine vinegar
1 cup (250 mL) water
½ cup (125 mL) ruby port
½ cup (125 mL) sugar
3 tbsp (45 mL) Labrador tea leaves
4 cups (1 L) fresh wild blueberries

FOR THE TENDERLOIN
10 cups (2.4 L) water
1 cup (250 mL) kosher salt
3 tbsp (45 mL) juniper berries,
  toasted and coarsely chopped
1 caribou tenderloin (3 lb/1.35 kg),
  cleaned of any silverskin, chain
  and tail removed

TO FINISH THE DISH
½ cup (125 mL) mayonnaise
  (see page 236)
A few button mushrooms, thinly
  shaved with a mandoline
½ cup (125 mL) brown butter
  (see page 242)
4 to 5 cups (1 to 1.25 L) various
  lemony and bitter herbs and
  lettuce hearts
Lemon vinaigrette (see page 240)
Black pepper

FOR THE BALSAM FIR SALT
Using a mortar and pestle, pound the balsam fir tips with half of the sea salt until you have a smooth mixture. Stir in the remaining salt. (Salt mixture keeps well in an airtight container.)

FOR THE PICKLED BLUEBERRIES
In a dry medium pan, toast the juniper berries, peppercorns, star anise, clove, allspice and cinnamon stick until fragrant, then slightly crush them with a mortar and pestle.

In a medium saucepan, combine the spice mix, wine, vinegar, water, port, sugar and tea leaves. Bring to a simmer and reduce by half. Remove from the heat and allow to cool to room temperature.

Place the blueberries in a nonreactive container and pour the pickling liquid through a strainer over the blueberries. Cover and refrigerate overnight.

FOR THE TENDERLOIN
Bring 2 cups (500 mL) of the water to a boil and add the kosher salt and juniper berries. Turn off the heat and allow to infuse for 15 minutes and to dissolve the salt. Add the remaining 8 cups (2 L) water and cool in the fridge. Submerge the tenderloin in the brine and refrigerate for 4 hours.

Drain the tenderloin and pat it dry. Place it on a wire rack set over a baking sheet and refrigerate, uncovered, for 12 hours.

Prepare a smoker. Heat 4 cups (1 L) of maple wood chips in the heating pan until they start to smoke. Place the tenderloin on the upper smoking rack. Place large bowls or trays full of ice on the lower smoking rack. Cold-smoke the caribou for 15 minutes. Turn the meat over. Replenish the ice if necessary and cold-smoke for another 15 minutes. Open the smoker door and allow the smoke to finish its cycle. The key here is for the meat to stay raw.

Remove the caribou from the smoker and cut the meat in half crosswise. Tightly wrap each half in plastic wrap, making sure each piece is perfectly round, and freeze until solid. This will make it easier to slice and give you nice round thin pieces.

TO FINISH THE DISH
Unwrap the caribou. You have two choices here: you can slice it paper thin with a meat slicer or use a sharp knife to cut ¼-inch (5 mm) slices. I prefer the latter, as I find it has a better mouthfeel. Arrange the slices on a cold plate—try for a natural tumbling look—and season with some of the balsam fir salt. Dot the mayo in and around the sliced meat. Arrange the pickled blueberries (you won't use them all) and the shaved mushrooms on the plate.

Stir together the brown butter and ¼ cup (60 mL) of the blueberry pickling liquid and pool this between the slices.

Dress the herbs and lettuces lightly with lemon vinaigrette and season to taste. Arrange the salad neatly on the plate and finish the dish with a couple of turns of a pepper mill.

Seal Mortadella

A lot of controversy surrounds the seal hunt in Canada, but I think a lot of it has to do with misinformation and a lack of education. One of the main issues that I have with the way the hunt is portrayed is that images from past hunts have become iconic symbols for conservation, animal welfare and animal rights advocates, even though practices have changed. It is illegal to hunt newborn seals (whitecoats) in Canada, and Fisheries and Oceans Canada regulates the hunt very carefully. It sets quotas, monitors the hunt, studies the seal population and works directly with the Canadian Sealers Association to train sealers on new regulations. It is important also to remember that in the northern regions of Canada, the hunt was historically for the procurement of seal meat for sustenance and not for financial gain.

I've made this a user-friendly dish. You could always opt out of the seal and replace it with lean pork for a more traditional mortadella; at the very end, fold in some pimento-stuffed Manzanilla olives and macaroni cooked just short of al dente. If you're lucky enough to have on hand some Alkermes, an infused spirit that's difficult to find in North America, use it in place of the apple brandy.

Makes one 2-lb (900 g) sausage

FOR THE BRINE
4¼ cups (1 L + 60 mL) water
¾ cup (175 mL) kosher salt
1 clove garlic, crushed
1 whole clove
1 fresh bay leaf
4 juniper berries

FOR THE MORTADELLA
14 oz (400 g) skinless, boneless
   fresh pork leg, cubed
7 oz (200 g) skinless fatty pork
   belly, cubed
7 oz (200 g) seal meat, cubed
1½ tsp (7 mL) apple brandy
   or Alkermes
1½ tsp (7 mL) kosher salt
½ tsp (2 mL) sodium nitrate
1 cup (250 mL) crushed ice,
   divided
1 cup (250 mL) toasted pistachios
   (optional)
2 tsp (10 mL) sweet smoked
   paprika
1 tsp (5 mL) black pepper
10 feet (3 m) hog casings,
   well rinsed

FOR THE BRINE
Combine all the brine ingredients in a nonreactive pot and bring to a boil, then chill completely.

FOR THE MORTADELLA
Submerge the pork leg cubes in the brine and refrigerate for 12 hours. Refrigerate the bowl and blade of a food processor along with the sausage-stuffer attachments.

Drain the pork, rinse under cold water, pat dry and place in a bowl. Place the pork belly and seal meat in separate bowls; keep the meats refrigerated.

In a food processor, pulse the pork leg meat with the apple brandy until smooth. Place the bowl the pork was in over ice and force the mixture through a fine-mesh sieve into the bowl. Purée the pork belly next and return it to the fridge. (You do not need to sieve the belly.)

Process the seal meat with the salt and sodium nitrate until it is quite pasty. (The salt will pull out the proteins in the meat, which aids in the emulsification.) Add half of the crushed ice and process until smooth. Add the pork belly purée and process for 1 minute. Add the remaining ice and process until the mixture is smooth and shiny, almost like mayonnaise.

Transfer the meat paste to a large bowl set over ice and fold in the leg purée, pistachios (if using), paprika and pepper until the texture is uniform and the spices are evenly mixed through.

Using a sausage stuffer, fill the casings with the meat, making one large sausage and making sure it does not have any air pockets. Seal each end with butcher's string.

Cook the sausage in a water bath set at 155°F (68°C) for 3 hours. Submerge the sausage in ice water to chill completely. Drain and refrigerate, uncovered, for at least 12 hours.

Remove the casing before slicing. The mortadella can be eaten as is with pickles or sliced a bit thicker, lightly sautéed until golden brown and served with a nice apple purée.

Phoque Jésus

Traditionally, a coarsely ground salami seasoned with red wine, spices and garlic is called a Petit Jésus. It gets its name from the fact that it ages for close to nine months and weighs about nine pounds. I discovered that seal meat paired nicely with the robust spicing. The name for my version is therefore a little tongue-in-cheek: phoque is French for seal.

This is one of the easiest fermented sausages to make, and the flavour of the seal really shines through. I do this in hog casings to ensure even and safe drying. You could certainly cure it in a beef bung as a nine-pound specimen, but it will take much longer.

Makes six 1-lb (450 g) salamis

¼ cup (60 mL) black peppercorns
2 lb (900 g) seal shoulder, cubed
2 lb (900 g) boneless pork shoulder, cubed
2 lb (900 g) pork back fat, cubed
1 cup (250 mL) milk powder
¼ cup (60 mL) red wine, plus more for spraying
6 tbsp (90 mL) kosher salt
6 tbsp (90 mL) hot paprika
2 tbsp (30 mL) powdered dextrose
1 tbsp (15 mL) garlic powder
1 tbsp (15 mL) sodium nitrate
10 feet (3 m) hog casings, well rinsed

Soak the peppercorns in plenty of water overnight, then drain. Meanwhile, spread the seal meat on a wire rack set over a baking sheet and allow it to drain overnight, covered and refrigerated. Refrigerate the bowl and paddle attachment of a stand mixer as well as the meat-grinder and sausage-stuffer attachments.

Fit the meat grinder with the large die and grind the seal, pork shoulder and back fat into the bowl of a stand mixer set in a larger bowl of ice. Add the drained peppercorns, the milk powder, wine, salt, paprika, dextrose, garlic powder and sodium nitrate. Fit the bowl onto the stand mixer. Using the paddle attachment, mix on low speed until well combined, about 1 minute.

Using the sausage stuffer, fill the casings with the meat and tie them off into 10- to 12-inch (25 to 30 cm) lengths. Using a sterilized pin, prick the casings to remove any air bubbles and to facilitate drying. Make a note of the weight of the sausages.

Hang the sausages in a dark, humid place—ideally at 60°F (15°C) with 65% humidity—until they are stiff throughout and have decreased in weight by one-third, 6 to 8 weeks. Every couple of days, use a spray bottle to give the salami a spritz of red wine.

Peel off the casings and slice to your desired thickness either by hand or with a meat slicer. Serve with plenty of crusty bread and a nice young Canadian wine made in the Burgundian style.

✕ Charcuterie

I have a picture of Derek standing in a doorway at Jamones de Juviles, a boutique producer of some of the best Spanish charcuterie in the world. In it he's completely surrounded by hams. They line up five deep on all sides, crowding out the frame. It looks like he's caught in some kind of hamvalanche. He looks thrilled.

That was a great trip. Derek, chef Grant van Gameren from Bar Isabel in Toronto and I were invited by the Spanish food importer Michael Tkaczuk to run around the country finding the best preserved products and charcuterie left to be discovered. We ate *berberechos* (cockles) and *morcia* (blood sausage) in Pontevedra, chorizo and baby eels in Bilbao, aged ox and phenomenal *cecina* (smoked and sun-dried beef) in León, sea cucumber in Barcelona and *lomo embuchado* (cured pork tenderloin) in Grenada, among many, many other things.

For me that trip was a chance to taste some of the finest cured meats in the world with some of the most knowledgeable people on the subject. Derek and Grant are already both well known in Canada for making some of the best charcuterie this country has ever seen, but I think it was fun and educational for them to meet some of the people who have been doing it for generations.

Compared to Spain, Italy, France and China, Canada doesn't have a strong charcuterie tradition—peameal bacon and pemmican notwithstanding. Which is understandable. The techniques started as ways to preserve meat before the days of refrigeration, and coldness is not something Canada ever lacked for.

Today, however, chefs like Derek and Grant, Ségué Lepage from Le Comptoir in Montreal, Robert Belcham from Campagnolo in Vancouver, and Connie DeSousa and John Jackson, the team at Charcut Roast House in Calgary, are using local ingredients and putting their own spin on these ancient techniques to create some truly exceptional charcuterie.

Derek first got interested in charcuterie when he was fresh out of cooking school and working for Peter Zambri at Zambri's in Victoria. I was a regular customer in those days and remember that they always had the most incredible sausages and little hams, pancetta and prosciutto. At the time it seemed that nobody—besides hardcore first-generation

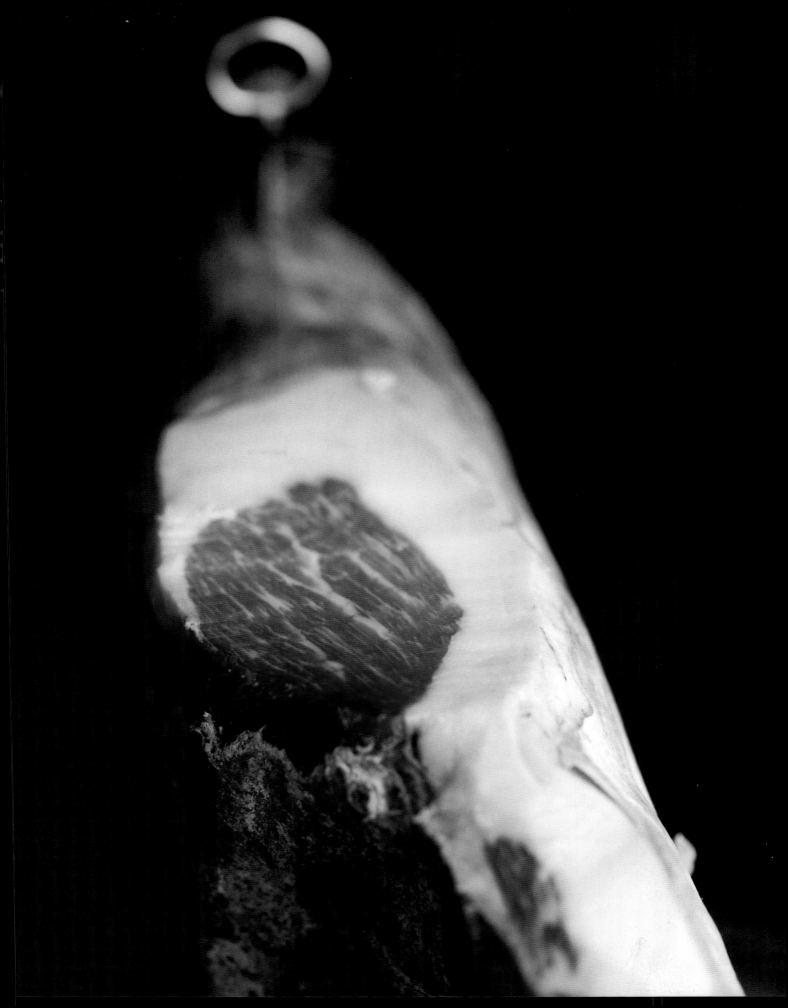

Italian, French and Chinese immigrants—was curing and preserving their own meat in Canada. "Every other restaurant I worked in before that, you'd just call up your supplier, and magically pancetta would arrive," Derek recalls. "Pancetta was made in Italy and that's where ours would come from: salami, pepperoni, ham. You got it by making a phone call."

The idea that you could take a piece of meat and leave it out for weeks or months and not only would it be fine but it would be even better never failed to impress Derek, and so he started experimenting with his own charcuterie.

By the time he got to London and started working for Jamie Oliver at Fifteen, one of his favourite projects was to introduce the students who trained there to little charcuterie projects. "We started out trying to make things like duck prosciutto," Derek says, calling it "the gateway meat of charcuterie." The turning point came when Gennaro Contaldo, Jamie's mentor, gave a class on cotechino, a kind of boiled salami. "He just blew my mind," Derek recalls. "I loved how he was just using all the scraps, the skin and the cartilage. If I could take a pill and have the knowledge of one person, it would be Gennaro. He knows everything." Derek started seriously researching charcuterie, learning the history behind certain cuts of meat, certain cures, the way they'd make lardo in Colonnata, the way they'd make the ham in the ash in Bayonne.

By the time he got back to Canada he'd already started making basic fermented sausages like salami and pepperoni. "There were some hits, some misses, but you can't enjoy a sunny day without a few rainy ones," he says. By the time he was ready to open DNA, his first restaurant in Montreal, charcuterie plates were starting to become trendy in the city, so he had to find a way to make it his own. "Rather than just put everything on the plate, I wanted to focus on things that I wasn't seeing around: porchetta di testa, 'nduja, coppa, just using odd cuts of meat or scraps and putting together homemade charcuterie plates with house-made pickles."

Now, at Maison Publique, Derek is one of the few chefs bringing in whole animals. He'll get a two-year-old pig from Richard Semmelhaack at Gereli Farm, and he and Phill Viens, the restaurant's sous chef, will sit down and decide where they'll dedicate the various cuts. "It's about a ten-day project to break the whole thing down," Derek says. "Basically, the loins get used for service and everything else goes to Phill to work with. The shoulder will go to the speck, the hoof goes for the culatta, the legs we use for mini prosciuttos that are done in six months rather than two years."

A lot of home cooks are intimidated by charcuterie because of the time it takes and the potential for serious problems if things go wrong. But if you work with good products under sanitary conditions, there's nothing to fear. The following recipes, worked on over several years, help to take the guesswork out of the process. And besides, every good Canadian should know how to make their own bacon.

Lardo and Strawberries

Lardo is cured pork back fat. I use the section of fat from just in front of the shoulder, as it's the thickest part. I prefer to make this in the fall, when the sows have naturally fattened themselves up to get ready for winter. This also means the lardo will be ready in late spring, just in time for strawberry season. I would make the effort to source out fat from a well-raised pig—as with any cured meats, you want the best. Factory-raised pigs make awful charcuterie and can be dangerous to work with—the meat's water content is very high because of all the garbage they get fed, affecting pH levels.

You could use belly instead, and end up with nice striations of meat in each slice. The addition of strawberries is in keeping with the Italian tradition of prosciutto with melon, but you could serve this with nothing more than slices of crusty bread and good olive oil.

Makes 3 lb (1.35 kg) lardo

FOR THE DRY CURE
1 lb (450 g) kosher salt
8 oz (225 g) sugar
2 oz (55 g) sodium nitrate

FOR THE LARDO
8 fresh bay leaves, julienned
Leaves from 2 bunches fresh
   rosemary, lightly pounded with
   a mortar and pestle
3½ lb (1.6 kg) skinless pork back
   fat, in one piece, 1½ to 2½
   inches (4 to 6 cm) thick
¼ cup (60 mL) white peppercorns,
   ground

**TO FINISH THE DISH
(FOR 4 SERVINGS)**
16 perfectly ripe in-season
   strawberries (don't even
   bother if it's winter)
2 tsp (10 mL) Balconville vinegar
   or good-quality balsamic vinegar
2 tsp (10 mL) good-quality
   olive oil
A few flakes of sea salt
Freshly cracked black pepper
Lemon thyme tips

FOR THE DRY CURE
Combine all the ingredients.

FOR THE LARDO
In a nonreactive bowl, stir together the dry cure, bay leaves and rosemary. Add the back fat and massage some herby cure all over it.

Spread a layer of the loose cure in a nonreactive pan. Place the back fat on top of it and distribute the remaining cure over the fat. Cover with plastic wrap, then place the pan in a garbage bag to keep the light off it and keep the fat pearl white. Place another pan on top and weight down with some heavy cans or bricks. Refrigerate for 12 days, flipping the fat over every few days and massaging the cure into the meat to redistribute the mix. After 12 days, the fat should feel uniformly dense. It may need a few more days—use your judgment.

Rinse the fat well under cold running water. Pat dry and place it on a wire rack set over a baking sheet. Refrigerate, uncovered, for 24 hours.

Wrap the fat in several layers of cheesecloth and hang it in a cool, dark, humid place—ideally 60°F (15°C) with 65% humidity—for 6 weeks.

Unwrap the fat and massage the top generously with the white pepper. Seal the fat in a bag with a vacuum sealer and refrigerate for at least 1 week before using, so the fat and the pepper become friends.

TO FINISH THE DISH
Chill the lardo in the freezer for 20 minutes to firm it up. Preheat the broiler to high.

Wash and hull the strawberries and cut them into irregular shapes, maintaining a natural look. Dress the berries with the vinegar, oil, sea salt and black pepper and macerate for 5 minutes.

Slice the cold lardo whisper thin along the full length of the fat, preferably with a meat slicer.

Arrange half of the strawberries on four ovenproof plates, drape the lardo slices over the berries and top with the remaining berries, reserving the juices in the bowl.

Slide the plates into the oven and broil for 3 seconds. This will cause the lardo to turn translucent and drape even better. Spoon a little bit of the vinegar mixture onto each plate and scatter the lemon thyme tips over top of the strawberries.

Summer Sausage and Green Sauce

This is a lightly smoked, fermented sausage, but in this case the finished product isn't hung in a dark, humid place. Instead, the ground meat is mixed with the cure and placed in the refrigerator to lightly sour. Then it's ground again and stuffed into the casings before it is cold-smoked first and then hot-smoked. The story goes that it was called summer sausage because it kept well in the summer's heat without refrigeration.

Makes 5 lb (2.25 kg) sausages

FOR THE SUMMER SAUSAGE
3 lb (1.35 kg) boneless beef chuck, fat and sinew removed, cubed

1½ lb (675 g) skinless, boneless pork shoulder, cubed

3 tbsp (45 mL) kosher salt

3 tbsp (45 mL) powdered dextrose

1 tsp (5 mL) sodium nitrate

½ cup (125 mL) milk powder

1½ tbsp (20 mL) Colman's or other hot dry mustard

2 tsp (10 mL) ground coriander

1½ tsp (7 mL) garlic powder

8 oz (225 g) pork back fat, cut into ½-inch (1 cm) cubes

10 feet (3 m) hog casings, well rinsed

FOR THE GREEN SAUCE
12 anchovy fillets

4 cloves garlic

¼ cup (60 mL) capers

Dill pickles (see page 230; eyeball about ¼ cup/60 mL)

Leaves from 1 bunch Italian parsley

Leaves from ½ bunch fresh mint

Leaves from ¼ bunch fresh chervil

¼ bunch fresh dill

1 tbsp (15 mL) fresh tarragon leaves

1 tbsp (15 mL) red wine vinegar

Good-quality olive oil

Kosher salt and black pepper

FOR THE SUMMER SAUSAGE
Combine the beef, pork shoulder, salt, dextrose and sodium nitrate and mix well. Chill thoroughly. Refrigerate the bowl and paddle attachment of a stand mixer as well as the meat-grinder and sausage-stuffer attachments.

Fit the meat grinder with the large die and grind the mixture into the bowl of a stand mixer set in a larger bowl of ice.

In a small bowl, combine the milk powder, mustard, coriander and garlic powder. Stir in just enough cold water to make a slurry and add this to the meat. Fit the bowl onto the stand mixer. Using the paddle attachment, mix on low speed until the sausage mixture is thoroughly combined. Using a rubber spatula, fold in the back fat.

Transfer the mixture to a nonreactive container and cover with plastic wrap, pressing the wrap directly onto the surface of the meat. (Alternatively, vacuum-seal the mixture.) Refrigerate for 4 days.

Fit a meat grinder with the small die and again grind the meat mixture into a bowl set over ice. Quickly sauté a small piece of the sausage to taste for seasoning.

Using the sausage stuffer, fill the casings with the sausage mix and tie them off into 8-inch (20 cm) links. Tie the sausages to a dowel and hang them in an area a little warmer than room temperature for 2 hours.

Prepare a smoker. Heat 4 cups (1 L) of maple wood chips in the heating pan until they start to smoke. Place the sausages on the upper smoking rack. Place large bowls or trays full of ice on the lower smoking rack. Cold-smoke the sausages for 1½ to 2 hours, replenishing the ice as necessary. Remove the bowls of ice and hot-smoke the sausages at 175°F (80°C) until the internal temperature is 153°F (67°C), about 1½ hours.

Return the sausages to the dowel and once again hang them in an area a little warmer than room temperature for 2 hours.

Refrigerate for at least 4 days before serving. The sausages also freeze nicely.

FOR THE GREEN SAUCE
This sauce is much better chopped by hand with a sharp knife—don't use a food processor. Finely chop the anchovies, garlic, capers and pickles and transfer to a bowl. Finely chop the parsley, mint, chervil, dill and tarragon; add to the bowl.

Stir in the vinegar and just enough olive oil to bring everything together in a spoonable consistency, but you don't want an oily mixture. Season with salt and pepper.

TO FINISH THE DISH
You could always use a charcoal grill, but I prefer to skewer the sausages on a branch and slowly cook them over the embers of a campfire. It reminds me of hunting with my dad.

Serve the sausage, sliced with a pocketknife, in a crusty bun smeared with the green sauce.

Grilled Pepperoni and Sweet Pickles

If you don't love pepperoni, then we can't be friends. In this recipe, I stuff them into hog casings, but you could certainly go the Slim Jim route and put them into sheep casings if you wanted. You don't have to grill this sausage at all, but I like the contrast of the hot charred spicy sausage against the cold sweet pickles.

Makes 5 lb (2.25 kg) pepperoni

FOR THE PEPPERONI
3 lb (1.35 kg) skinless, boneless pork shoulder, cubed
2 lb (900 g) beef chuck, fat and sinew removed, cubed
3 tbsp (45 mL) kosher salt
1 tsp (5 mL) sodium nitrate
¾ cup (175 mL) milk powder
¼ cup (60 mL) powdered dextrose
2 tbsp (30 mL) red wine
1 tbsp (15 mL) hot smoked paprika
1 tbsp (15 mL) sweet smoked paprika
1 tbsp (15 mL) cayenne pepper
1 tsp (5 mL) ground fennel seeds
½ tsp (2 mL) ground allspice
10 feet (3 m) hog casings, well rinsed

FOR THE SWEET PICKLES
Use the bread and butter pickles recipe (see page 230), but replace some of the cucumbers with other vegetables from the list below, or freestyle with any vegetable you like:
• pattypan squash
• zucchini
• pearl onions
• baby fennel
• wax beans
• lipstick or mini peppers
• cauliflower
• Romanesco cauliflower

TO FINISH THE DISH (FOR 4 SERVINGS)
2 tbsp (30 mL) coarsely chopped Italian parsley
Good-quality olive oil

FOR THE PEPPERONI
Refrigerate the paddle attachment of a stand mixer as well as the meat-grinder and sausage-stuffer attachments.

Combine the cubed meats, salt and sodium nitrate; mix well.

Fit the meat grinder with the small die and grind the meat into the bowl of a stand mixer set in a larger bowl of ice. Add the milk powder, dextrose, wine, hot and sweet paprikas, cayenne, fennel seeds and allspice. Fit the bowl onto the stand mixer. Using the paddle attachment, mix on low speed for 2 minutes to incorporate everything evenly.

Using the sausage stuffer, fill the casings with the sausage mix, twisting them into 8- to 10-inch (20 to 25 cm) links. With a sterilized pin, poke a few holes around the sausage to remove any air pockets and facilitate drying.

Hang the sausages over a dowel and hang them in an area a little warmer than room temperature for 16 hours to start the fermentation process.

You can now either air-dry or hot-smoke the pepperoni, whichever you feel more comfortable with.

To air-dry: Hang the pepperoni in a dark, humid place—ideally 60°F (15°C) with 65% humidity—for 18 to 24 days.

To hot-smoke: Hot-smoke the pepperoni at 175°F (80°C) until the internal temperature is 145°F (65°C).

Once the sausages are ready, they can be vacuum-sealed and kept in the fridge for up to 6 months or frozen. They can also be pickled in vinegar just as you'd make dill pickles, but without the dill.

FOR THE SWEET PICKLES
Prepare as directed.

TO FINISH THE DISH
Prepare a charcoal grill and allow the coals to break down and start to glow. Meanwhile, cut two of the pepperoni in half lengthwise and score the cut side in a criss-cross manner.

Grill the pepperoni cut side down over a cooler part of the grill so that it takes on as much flavour from the charcoal as possible. Cook until the sausage is hissing and the edges start to caramelize, 10 to 12 minutes. Remove from the grill and allow to rest on a plate for 5 minutes.

Toss some of the pickles with some parsley and place a small mound to the side of four plates. Place a piece of the grilled pepperoni next to the veg. Tip any resting juices accumulated from the sausage into a small bowl and stir in a little olive oil; drizzle over the pickles.

Head Cheese Torchon

Pig heads are delicious and fairly inexpensive. This makes a tasty first course with a little salad dressed with mustard vinaigrette, or a handsome addition to a charcuterie board. The torchon is a great technique for head cheese: instead of pressing it as in a terrine, it is rolled and submerged back into the braising liquid.

Makes 2 torchons

FOR THE HEAD AND BRINE

1 pig's head (about 10 lb/4.5 kg)
—ask the butcher to split it in
two for you
12 quarts (12 L) water
4 cups (1 L) kosher salt

FOR BRAISING THE HEAD

4 pig's trotters (or 2 pig's knuckles)
3 sprigs Italian parsley
6 sprigs fresh thyme
2 fresh bay leaves
12 black peppercorns, lightly cracked
4 juniper berries, cut in half
½ cup (125 mL) chopped celery
½ cup (125 mL) chopped carrot
½ cup (125 mL) chopped onion
¼ cup (60 mL) sodium nitrate
¼ cup (60 mL) kosher salt
12 quarts (12 L) water
1 cup (250 mL) white wine
Cider vinegar

FOR THE HEAD AND BRINE

Remove the brains from the head cavity and reserve for another use. (Try the brain profiteroles on page 91.)

In a large nonreactive saucepan, heat 8 cups (2 L) of the water with the kosher salt just enough to dissolve the salt. Transfer the liquid to a nonreactive container large enough to hold the head and all the brine, and add the remaining water. Place the head in the brine and put a few plates on top to keep it completely submerged. Refrigerate for 12 hours.

Drain the head, return it to the container and rinse under cold water for 5 minutes, then drain and pat dry with paper towels.

FOR BRAISING THE HEAD

Preheat the oven to 325°F (160°C).

In a stockpot, combine the trotters, parsley, thyme, bay leaves, peppercorns, juniper berries, celery, carrot, onion, sodim nitrate, kosher salt, water and wine. Bring to a simmer over medium heat and simmer for 15 minutes. Carefully add the head and cover with a round of parchment paper. Transfer to the oven and slowly cook for 6 hours or until the meat is melting off the skull, checking halfway to make sure it isn't boiling.

Remove the pot from the oven and allow to rest until the head is cool enough to handle.

Transfer the head to a platter or cutting board. Strain the braising liquid into a large nonreactive container, discarding the solids.

Pick all the meat and skin from the head, trying your best to keep it in larger chunks if possible. Slice the ears crosswise and cut the skin into smaller pieces. Combine the head meat, ears and skin in a large bowl. Season to taste with kosher salt and a little cider vinegar. Mix well.

Place half the meat mixture on the far end of a large double layer of cheesecloth, leaving a couple of inches (5 cm) free on each end so you can tie it. Tightly roll the cheesecloth around the meat to form a compact, even log about 2½ inches (6 cm) in diameter. Tie the ends with butcher's string. Repeat with the remaining meat mixture to make a second torchon.

Submerge the torchons in the braising liquid. Cover and refrigerate for 48 hours.

Remove the torchons from the liquid, discarding the liquid. Carefully unwrap the logs, then wrap them in plastic wrap for ease of storage and slicing. (Head cheese keeps, refrigerated, for up to 5 days and also freezes well.)

Pancetta BY PHILL VIENS

It's been said many times, but you really do get out what you put into curing meat. Make sure you use fresh herbs and spices and the best-quality pork you can find. You can make pancetta out of any cut from the belly of a pig, but make sure to get a piece that is free of any deep cuts or flappy bits: these can create little havens for mould and bacteria. Also, don't buy or pick the herbs at the same time you get the pork: they'll lose too much of their lustre by the time you need them.

FOR THE CURE MIX AND PORK BELLY

25 g kosher salt
12 g brown sugar
10 g red chili flakes
3 g nitrite cure mix such as
  Insta Cure #1 or DQ curing salt
  #1 (optional)
8 juniper berries, crushed
20 black peppercorns, cracked
1 whole nutmeg, grated
2 fresh bay leaves, thinly sliced
1 skin-on, boneless pork belly
  (2 lb/900 g), no thicker than
  2 inches (5 cm)

FOR THE HERB RUB

4 sprigs fresh sage
8 sprigs fresh savory
8 sprigs fresh thyme

FOR THE CURE MIX AND PORK BELLY

Thoroughly combine the salt, sugar, chili flakes, cure mix (if using), juniper berries, peppercorns, nutmeg and bay leaves. A couple of pulses in a spice grinder or mini food processor wouldn't hurt.

Working over a nonreactive container large enough to hold the pork belly snugly (and preferably with a lid), sprinkle the cure over the surface of the belly as evenly as you can, taking care that all the excess falls into the container. Lay the belly down in the dish and massage the cure all over it. Pay extra attention to the sides and to any little nooks and crannies. Keep working the cure into the belly until the cure starts becoming wet.

Tuck the belly into the container skin side down and spread the excess cure over the top. Cover and refrigerate for 2 days.

After 2 days, a lot of the cure will have become liquid, saturating the rest. Flip the belly over and redistribute the cure all over it. Cover and refrigerate for another 2 days. Repeat this process until the belly has been curing for 8 days. The belly should be firm all over, just a little giving to the touch, and it shouldn't bounce back when pressed the way raw meat does. If you don't think it's ready, give it another couple of days.

FOR THE HERB RUB

Pick the leaves from the herb sprigs and chop them as finely as you possibly can, making sure to blend them together well.

Rinse off the belly. You don't need to get all the spices off, but make sure you remove all the salt crystals. Pat it dry with a clean kitchen towel. Rub the chopped herbs all over the belly, rubbing them in as best you can. You should just be able to catch little glimpses of the meat through the herb covering. If this isn't the case, chop some more herbs and rub them in. Don't expect all the herbs to stay on the skin—they won't.

Upend four juice glasses or tall shot glasses on a baking sheet and set a wire rack on top of them—you need at least 2 inches (5 cm) of clearance between the rack and the pan. Lay the belly skin side down on the rack.

ON NITRITES

The nitrites in this recipe are optional. I prefer using nitrites for curing because they are safer and maintain the natural colour of the meat. Many say that the only thing nitrites do is lock in the red colour of cured meats. This isn't entirely true. They actually add their own little tang to the flavour, as well as preserve against oxidation—that is, delay the onset of rancidity—which means your cured meat will taste good for longer. Nitrites also help protect against all sorts of little nasties, including *Clostridium botulinum*.

You can buy nitrite cure mixes online, or visit a trusted local butcher, preferably the one you buy your pork from. Tell them what you plan on doing, and they should be able to sell you a small amount of the right product. Make sure that it is equivalent to the cure mixes I specify in the recipes; if it's not, ask your butcher for an appropriate amount to add.

TO AGE THE PANCETTA

Leave the pancetta to age in a cool, humid place—below 65°F (18°C) and above 70% humidity. If you aren't using the nitrite cure mix, keep it below 60°F (15°C). If you use your fridge, it'll take a longer time to dry. Clear an entire shelf (preferably the top one), as air circulation is key for proper drying. Also mind what else is in the fridge: like butter, the pancetta will take up the aromas of other foods, especially expiring ones.

The pancetta will take several weeks to be ready. Flip it over every week or so. When it is ready, it should be quite firm to the touch, with almost no give (depending on fat content and temperature). The skin will have hardened slightly and become almost translucent. Ready weight should be somewhere around 1½ lb (675 g).

Cut back the skin as you use it; wrap any remaining pancetta tightly in plastic wrap and store it in the fridge for up to 2 weeks. If you store it for too long, it will start to bloom mould and taste stale and fridge-y. The pancetta can be stored for longer if it's vacuum-sealed.

✕ FARM

We've been sledding through this maple forest for over an hour and our beans still aren't hot. Seems like the claims for the Muffpot, an ingenious device that allegedly cooks food with the radiant heat of a snowmobile's muffler, are not all they're cracked up to be.

It hasn't been a total waste, though, since we're spending the day with Richard Semmelhaack, one of Canada's coolest farmers. Richard runs Gereli Farm, a former "resort for racehorses," as he calls it, about an hour outside Montreal. The horses are long gone and today the farm produces some of the world's best maple syrup as well as happy, tasty cows, lambs and pigs.

It's well below zero, but the skies are blue and the wind is calm when we arrive, and Richard has plenty to show us. "We had six new lambs last night," he tells us as we pick our way through the cow pen on our way into the barn, where it's warm and bright and noisy with the sounds of lambs and sheep bleating to one

with the herd with this guy around," he says.

"Want to hold one of the new lambs?" Semmelhaack asks. Of course we do. The little black and white creatures, a cross between Dorset (good mothers and milk producers) and Romanov (a prolific breeder), look equal parts adorable and delicious. Their sweetness is matched only by a dozen or so unbelievably cute little piglets a couple of stalls over, who are frantically nursing from their long-suffering mother. Their pen is piled high with fresh hay and looks kind of comfortably domestic.

Richard practises what he calls reverse caging. He's taken one of the metal pens typically used in pig farms, rigged it with warming lights and set it off to one side so the piglets have somewhere to sleep. "It's basically the opposite of what they would do at a factory farm," Derek points out. "Normally all the sows would be in the pen so they can barely move, but Richard's using it as a little place for the piglets to hang out, so they don't have to worry about their mother rolling on them." In the summer they'll all be let out to dig for crabgrass and root around in the fresh air.

This is old-school farming at its finest. Richard calls it multi-farming, to distinguish it from monoculture, in which one crop is grown over a long period of time across a vast area. Multi-farming is what we all grew up imagining what farming was like: some crops, some animals, the one feeding the other. "It works well for me to farm this way," Richard says. "Let's say I've got some low-quality hay, maybe it's been rained on or spoils somehow. We just let it dry out anyway. The protein levels are no good, but I use that for bedding. My smaller bales of second crop I'll give to the sheep, and then if I have some lesser hay, the cows will eat it."

To make this viable, Semmelhaack has to be a bit unconventional. "I used to work with one of the big grocery chains," he says, "but I just couldn't keep up. They kept ordering more and more stuff, especially the low-end cuts, hamburger mainly, so I started working only with stores that would take the whole beast. That's what Derek does, too. That's why I do business with him—because he takes the whole lamb, the whole pig."

Semmelhaack had never raised pigs before meeting Derek. "We used his veal and lamb at DNA," Derek recalls, "and I really liked the way he raised his animals. He didn't feed them any corn, it was all oats and farro and split peas and stuff like that, so one day I asked him if he'd try to raise pigs to our specifications. We'd give him all the organic compost we get, peelings and eggshells, and the leftover whey from our cheese maker. He said, 'I can try, but I've never raised a pig.' I remember he was really antsy about killing it. He really wanted to whack it, but I kept saying let it go, and we kept it for about a year and a half. Normally they kill them at eight months. He kept saying, 'It'll be huge,' but that's what we wanted for charcuterie, it's got better flavour. You go to Italy and they use these massive pigs, so you get this great lardo from the back. We wanted to take it to the fall, so it would eat, eat and eat and put on as much fat as possible to get ready for winter. When we got it, it was phenomenal. That was the best pig I'd ever seen in my life. The carcass was 480 pounds."

Despite the cold outside, it's getting too warm in this barn, and Richard wants to take us into the forest, so we all climb onto snowmobiles (after strapping the Muffpot to one of the engines) and make tracks across the snowy fields. Soon we're carving lines around white pines and red oaks, black cherry, butternut and, most important, sugar maples. At a small clearing we stop to admire the ruins of an ancient sugar shack, now mostly collapsed and long since abandoned.

Semmelhaack only started tapping trees in 1999 and built his sap house the following year, but he now makes one of the most exclusive and delicious maple syrups on earth. Alex Cruz and Cyril Gonzales of Société-Orignal approached him about doing a specialty syrup. "After doing some tastings," Richard says, "we realized that syrup that was taken much farther and reduced to a deeper caramelization and sweetness than is standard just tasted better."

To produce Remonte-Pente ("ski lift"), the team harvests sap only from mature trees that are an average 150 years old and then reduces the liquid over fires built from wood collected from the same forest. The resulting syrup is so intensely flavoured and complex that it's become a favourite not only of Derek's but of chefs all over. Mario Batali uses it at Del Posto, and it's on the menu at Daniel and Betony, as well as at Quince in San Francisco.

It is precious stuff, but we've brought along a little to add to our beans—if we can ever get them hot. Several high-speed runs across an open meadow later and the Muffpot is barely warm to the touch. Defeated but undaunted, we take it into the farmhouse and dump the beans into a pot on the stove. The method's not as romantic as muffler cooking, but the results are delicious. Even without the exhaust flavour.

Potato Croquettes

These make a great addition to your playoff platter and are a hit with the kids. Make either the ketchup or the mayo for dipping.

Makes enough for 2 people snacking

POTATO CROQUETTES

2 tbsp (30 mL) unsalted butter, at room temperature, divided
1 cup (250 mL) finely minced onion
2 tbsp (30 mL) whole milk
½ lb (225 g) mashed potatoes, at room temperature
2 tbsp (30 mL) finely chopped chives
2 tbsp (30 mL) all-purpose flour, plus more for dusting
½ tsp (2 mL) baking powder
Kosher salt to taste
2 eggs, beaten
1½ cups (375 mL) panko
Canola oil for deep-frying

KETCHUP (MAKES 2½ CUPS/625 ML)

3 lb (1.35 kg) ripe tomatoes, coarsely chopped
1 lb (450 g) Cortland or other baking apples, peeled, cored and chopped
3 onions, coarsely chopped
6 black peppercorns
6 allspice berries
6 whole cloves
A pinch of cayenne pepper
2 cups (500 mL) sugar
2 cups (500 mL) malt vinegar
1 tbsp (15 mL) kosher salt

MAYONNAISE (MAKES 3 CUPS/ 750 ML)

1 egg, plus 3 egg yolks
2 tsp (10 mL) Dijon mustard, plus more if desired
½ tsp (2 mL) lemon juice
½ tsp (2 mL) white wine vinegar
2½ cups (625 mL) canola oil
Kosher salt and black pepper
Lemon zest (optional)
chopped fresh herbs (optional)
2 anchovies, finely chopped (optional)

FOR THE POTATO CROQUETTES

Melt half of the butter in a small sauté pan over medium heat. Add the onion and sweat until it is soft and translucent.

Beat the remaining butter and the milk into the mashed potatoes. Mix in the onion, chives, flour, baking powder and salt. Roll the potato mixture into logs 1 inch (2.5 cm) wide and about as long as your index finger.

Dust the potato logs with flour. Coat in the egg wash, letting excess drip off, and roll them in the panko. Transfer to a baking sheet and refrigerate for 1 hour.

Heat the oil in a deep-fryer or deep, heavy pot to 350°F (180°C). Fry the croquettes in batches until they are golden brown and heated through. Drain on paper towels and season with salt. Serve immediately with something to dip them in.

FOR THE KETCHUP

Combine all the ingredients in a large, heavy pot and bring to a simmer over medium heat. Cook gently, stirring occasionally to make sure the mixture doesn't catch on the bottom, for 2 hours or until everything is mush.

Pass the mixture through a food mill fitted with the fine disc into a clean pot. Return to a simmer and cook for 20 minutes, stirring often. Adjust the seasoning. Cool the ketchup and keep refrigerated.

FOR THE MAYONNAISE

In a bowl, whisk together the egg, egg yolks, mustard, lemon juice and vinegar. Whisking constantly, slowly dribble in the oil. Season with salt and pepper. Flavour if you wish with lemon zest, chopped fresh herbs, finely chopped anchovy or more Dijon.

Swiss Chard Gratin

This is an incredibly tasty way to prepare chard. Plus you get to make an onion piqué, using that classic French culinary technique where you use cloves to stick a bay leaf to a whole onion.

Serves 4

FOR THE MORNAY SAUCE
2 tsp (10 mL) unsalted butter
2 tsp (10 mL) all-purpose flour
3 cups (750 mL) whole milk
3 whole cloves
1 fresh bay leaf
½ onion, peeled
½ cup (125 mL) grated Avonlea
   Clothbound or other aged artisanal
   cheddar
Kosher salt and white pepper
A few gratings of nutmeg

FOR THE GRATIN
2 bunches rainbow chard
4 tbsp (60 mL) unsalted butter
1 cup (250 mL) finely diced onion
¾ cup (175 mL) chicken stock
   (see basic stock, page 238)
1 cup (250 mL) diced smoked ham
Kosher salt and white pepper
A few gratings of nutmeg
½ cup (125 mL) grated Avonlea
   Clothbound or other aged artisanal
   cheddar

FOR THE MORNAY SAUCE
In a medium saucepan, melt the butter over medium heat. Stir in the flour and cook, stirring with a wooden spoon, until the roux starts to smell nutty and is on the edge of turning golden brown. Slowly whisk in the milk until there are no lumps. Bring the mixture to a simmer. Using the cloves, stud the bay leaf to the onion and add to the pot. Turn down the heat to medium-low and gently simmer the sauce for 35 minutes, stirring occasionally.

Remove the sauce from the heat and take out the onion. Whisk in the cheddar and season the sauce with the salt, pepper and nutmeg. Strain through a fine-mesh sieve.

FOR THE GRATIN
Preheat the oven to 425°F (220°C).

Thoroughly wash the chard and separate the leaves from the stems. Cut the stems into ¼-inch (5 mm) dice and coarsely chop the leaves.

Melt the butter in a large sauté pan over medium heat. Add the chard stems and the onion and sweat for about 5 minutes, until the onions start to become translucent. Add the chicken stock, bring to a simmer, cover and cook for another 5 minutes.

Add the chard leaves and cook until wilted, stirring constantly. Remove from the heat. Stir in the ham and season with salt, pepper and nutmeg.

Spread 1½ cups (375 mL) of the Mornay sauce in a medium gratin dish. Top with the Swiss chard/ham mixture, spreading it evenly. Cover with the remaining Mornay sauce. Evenly sprinkle the grated cheese over the top. Bake for 20 minutes, until starting to bubble around the edges. Turn the broiler on high and broil the gratin for 45 seconds to 1 minute, until golden brown.

Beer-Battered Beans

This recipe came about when we ended up getting a bounty of wax beans from Jocelyn at Jardins Bio-Santé. I love fish and chips and I love wok-fried beans, so why not have the best of both worlds? So the plate doesn't look like a one-trick pony, I make two different batters from the same base recipe, one with a blonde beer and one with a red. The same two batters reappear in my fish and chips on page 218.

Serves 4 to 6

FOR THE TARTAR SAUCE
See page 91

FOR THE RED AND BLONDE BEER BATTERS
2 tbsp (30 mL) active dry yeast
1¼ cups (300 mL) red beer
   (for the red beer batter) OR
   1¼ cups (300 mL) blonde beer
   (for the blonde beer batter)
1¼ cups (300 mL) cold water
2½ cups (625 mL) all-purpose flour
1 tsp (5 mL) kosher salt

TO FINISH THE DISH
Canola oil for deep-frying
1 lb (450 g) green wax beans,
   trimmed
1 cup (250 mL) all-purpose flour
Kosher salt
1 lb (450 g) yellow wax beans,
   trimmed
1 clove garlic, crushed but
   kept whole
1 tbsp (15 mL) finely chopped
   Italian parsley
2 tsp (10 mL) finely chopped
   fresh summer savory
1 lemon, cut into wedges

FOR THE TARTAR SAUCE
Prepare as directed. (Sauce can be made up to a day ahead.)

FOR THE RED BEER BATTER
Dissolve the yeast in the red beer and water. Allow to sit until foamy, about 5 minutes. Combine the flour and salt in a large bowl. Stir in the beer mixture until the batter is smooth. Transfer to another large bowl to prevent batter on the sides from drying out, cover tightly with plastic wrap and let sit in a place that's slightly warmer than room temperature until doubled in size, 45 minutes to 1 hour.

FOR THE BLONDE BEER BATTER
Do everything the same as above, except use blonde beer instead of red beer.

TO FINISH THE DISH
Heat the oil in a deep-fryer or deep, heavy pot to 375°F (190°C).

Dredge the green beans in the flour. Working in batches, dip them into the red beer batter, letting the excess drip off, and drop them as individuals into the hot oil, agitating them with a slotted spoon so they don't clump into one mass. Fry them for about 4 minutes, until the batter is crispy. Remove them with a slotted spoon and drain on paper towels. Season them immediately and generously with salt. Repeat with the remaining green beans.

Repeat with the yellow beans, except dipping them in the blonde beer batter.

When all the beans are fried and salted, drop little streams of each batter into the hot oil and fry until crispy. Drain on paper towels and season with salt.

If you have a large wooden bowl, now is the time to use it. Rub the garlic around the sides of the bowl, add the yellow and green beans, the parsley, savory and the crispy batter bits. Toss well. Transfer to the serving vessel of your choice and serve with paper ramekins of tartar sauce and the lemon wedges.

Wedge Salad

Here's a timeless salad, elevated with a bit of finessing. Think steak and summer.

Serves 6

**FOR THE BRIOCHE CROUTONS
(MAKES AS MANY AS YOU WANT)**
Red Fife brioche (see page 145),
  crust removed, torn into ¼- to
  ½-inch (5 mm to 1 cm) pieces

**FOR THE BLEU D'ÉLIZABETH
DRESSING (MAKES 2½ CUPS/625 ML
—YOU WILL HAVE LEFTOVERS)**
1½ cups (375 mL) crumbled Bleu
  d'Élizabeth or other delicious raw
  milk blue cheese, divided
1 cup (250 mL) mayonnaise
  (see page 236), divided
¼ cup (60 mL) buttermilk
¼ cup (60 mL) sour cream or
  crème fraîche (see page 241)
1 tsp (5 mL) minced chives
1 tsp (5 mL) minced Italian parsley
1 tsp (5 mL) minced fresh mint
¾ tsp (4 mL) champagne vinegar
½ tsp (2 mL) onion powder
¼ tsp (1 mL) garlic powder
Kosher salt and black pepper

FOR THE SALAD
½ lb (225 g) smoked bacon
  (see page 239), cut into lardons
1 large or 2 small heads iceberg
  lettuce
Extra virgin olive oil
Kosher salt and black pepper
8 oven-dried tomatoes
  (see page 234)
A few Italian parsley leaves,
  coarsely chopped
Flaky sea salt to finish

FOR THE BRIOCHE CROUTONS
Preheat the oven to 350°F (180°C).

Spread the brioche pieces on a parchment-lined baking sheet and toast in the oven for 5 minutes. Rotate the pan, stir and flip the brioche pieces, and toast for an additional 5 minutes or until lightly golden and crispy. Allow to cool. (Croutons can be stored in an airtight container.)

FOR THE BLEU D'ÉLIZABETH DRESSING
In a small bowl, combine half of the cheese and half of the mayo. Cream together using a rubber spatula. You want a semi-smooth mixture.

Add the remaining mayo, the buttermilk, sour cream, chives, parsley, mint, vinegar, onion powder and garlic powder; stir until evenly incorporated. Add the remaining cheese and fold to incorporate. Season with kosher salt and pepper. (Dressing, without the herbs, can be made up to 1 week ahead and refrigerated. Stir in the herbs just before serving.)

FOR THE SALAD
In a medium, heavy saucepan over medium heat, bring ¼ cup (60 mL) of water to a simmer. Add the bacon and cook, stirring often, until the fat renders out and the lardons start to crisp. (Using water allows the fat to render out evenly.) Drain the bacon on paper towels and allow to cool to room temperature.

Trim off a little bit of the root end of the lettuce and cut each head into 6 wedges. Soak the lettuce wedges in ice water for 15 minutes, then gently spin them dry, being careful to keep them intact.

Drizzle the wedges with the olive oil and season with kosher salt and pepper. Arrange them on a large, decorative platter or on six plates. Drizzle some of the dressing neatly over the iceberg wedges, and sprinkle with the lardons and brioche croutons.

Neatly arrange the tomatoes in and around the other ingredients, shower the parsley over the salad and finish with a few crystals of flaky sea salt. Serve extra dressing in a jug on the side.

Bagna Cauda with Winter Vegetables

This is a pretty traditional dish in all aspects, mainly because it's pretty much perfect already. As simple as it is, though, when it hits the table it's a real showstopper. I offer a guideline as to the vegetables you can use, but ultimately, it's up to you. The important thing is to cook each vegetable separately to make sure it's done properly. It's also nice to cut each type of vegetable a bit differently so the finished dish has a mix of textures and shapes. And make sure the cooked vegetables never see the fridge—they should be at room temperature.

Makes enough for 6 people to be very happy

FOR THE DRESSING

40 anchovy fillets in oil
½ lb (225 g) unsalted butter
12 cloves garlic, finely chopped
1 fresh red chili pepper, split in
   half lengthwise, seeds intact
1 generous sprig fresh rosemary
1½ cups (375 mL) white wine
4 cups (1 L) whipping cream
Black pepper
2 tbsp (30 mL) finely chopped
   Italian parsley

FOR THE VEGETABLES

2 fennel bulbs, quartered lengthwise
   and steamed (save the fronds for
   garnish if you like)
8 parsnips, peeled, cut into 3-inch
   (8 cm) lengths and boiled with a
   bit of lemon
1 head cauliflower, cut into florets
   and steamed
4 carrots, peeled, steamed whole,
   then cut into quarters
1 bunch Swiss chard, steamed
   until tender
½ endive, cut into lengths and
   soaked in ice water for 1 hour
4 beets, peeled, boiled with a splash
   of cider vinegar, then sliced

FOR THE DRESSING

Drain the anchovies, reserving the oil. In a large, heavy saucepan over medium heat, melt the butter with the anchovy oil. Add the garlic and allow to sizzle for about 30 seconds without taking on any colour. Add the anchovies, chili and rosemary sprig and stir with a wooden spoon until the anchovies have broken up and completely melted into the butter and oil. Add the wine and turn up the heat to cook off most of the alcohol. Add the cream, turn down the heat to medium-low and simmer the mixture until it is thick enough to coat the back of a spoon. Remove from the heat, discard the rosemary and the chili, and season with a couple of healthy turns of a pepper mill. Stir in the chopped parsley just before serving.

FOR THE VEGETABLES

Arrange the vegetables in separate piles on a platter. You can pour over the warm dressing or pour it into a warmed jug and pass it around at the table.

Asparagus à la Berlinoise

Phill Viens, the chef de cuisine at Maison Publique, came up with this combination of ingredients. It's truly a magical thing to eat when white asparagus is at its peak. Asparagus and hollandaise is a classic combination, and the sauce is very easy to make. Once you have it in your back pocket, you will find that it is a valuable workhorse of a sauce. You could add chopped tarragon for a classic béarnaise, or use dried mint in the reduction for a sauce paloise.

Serves 4

FOR THE POTATO CONFIT
12 German Butter or other new
  potatoes (unpeeled)
3 cloves garlic, lightly crushed
3 sprigs fresh thyme
1 fresh bay leaf
2 tbsp (30 mL) kosher salt
4 cups (1 L) olive oil
8 cups (2 L) chicken stock
  (see basic stock, page 238)
2 tbsp (30 mL) red wine vinegar
1 tbsp (15 mL) grainy mustard
Black pepper

FOR THE ASPARAGUS
24 thick spears white asparagus

FOR THE HOLLANDAISE
2 shallots, finely chopped
1 fresh bay leaf
12 black peppercorns
1 sprig fresh tarragon
1 sprig parsley
⅔ cup (150 mL) white wine vinegar
7 tbsp (100 mL) white wine
4 egg yolks
1 cup (250 mL) unsalted butter,
  melted and cooled to just above
  body temperature
Kosher salt
The lightest showing of cayenne
  pepper

TO FINISH THE DISH
12 slices speck, or jambon blanc
  (see page 113)
Kosher salt and black pepper

FOR THE POTATO CONFIT
Preheat the oven to 300°F (150°C).

Combine the potatoes, garlic, thyme, bay leaf and salt in a casserole dish large enough to hold the potatoes snugly in a single layer. Pour over the oil (it should just come up to the top of the potatoes), cover with foil and bake for 2 hours, or until the potatoes are tender when pierced with a paring knife. Cool the potatoes to room temperature in the oil.

In a medium, heavy saucepan over medium heat, reduce the chicken stock to 1½ cups (375 mL). Stir in the vinegar and mustard and season with salt and pepper.

Remove the potatoes from the oil, discarding the oil and flavourings. Carefully peel the potatoes and add them to the marinade. Cover and refrigerate for 12 hours, gently shaking the container from time to time to redistribute the marinade.

When ready to serve, cover the container with foil and gently reheat the potatoes in a 300°F (150°C) oven for about 20 minutes.

FOR THE ASPARAGUS
Shortly before serving, trim off the woody ends and carefully peel the asparagus from the base to just under the tip.

Blanch the asparagus in boiling, salted water for 6 minutes. Immediately transfer to salted ice water to cool completely. Drain and pat dry.

FOR THE HOLLANDAISE
Shortly before serving, in a small saucepan combine the shallots, bay leaf, peppercorns, tarragon, parsley, vinegar and wine. Cook over medium-high heat until the liquid is reduced to 3 tbsp (45 mL). Strain through a fine-mesh sieve, pressing on the solids to extract all of the liquid. Discard the solids.

Combine the egg yolks with the reduction in a metal bowl set over a pot of gently simmering water. Vigorously whisk the yolk mixture until it is light and fluffy, 6 to 8 minutes, taking care not to start to cook the eggs. (Remove the bowl from the heat if you find it is getting too hot.) Whisking constantly, drizzle in the melted butter in a slow, steady stream. Remove from the heat and season with salt and cayenne.

TO FINISH THE DISH
Reheat the potatoes (see above), and have four warmed plates ready. Place the asparagus in a warm spot for about 20 minutes, until it is just above room temperature (or pop in the oven for 3 minutes).

Season the asparagus with salt and pepper and pile it like a stack of kindling to one side of each plate. Place three potatoes neatly on the plate, next to the asparagus, and nap the hollandaise evenly over the asparagus. Arrange 3 slices of the speck neatly and organically in the empty space on the plate.

Ravioli al Sole with the Best Parts of the Duck

This was one of the greatest hits at DNA. "The best parts" refers to the offcuts of the duck that you don't see every day. This recipe might take a bit of leg work. If you're not feeling up to the challenge, you could make the sauce just with duck livers, without all the bells and whistles. This recipe isn't meant to shock people or be macho. Rather, it is a way to show that you can use everything the animal has to offer, and in a very tasty way.

You'll only use half the duck jus, but it's a tricky recipe to scale down, so freeze half for another use.

Serves 8

DUCK PARTS YOU WILL NEED IN ADDITION TO THOSE IN THE FOLLOWING RECIPE PARTS
8 duck hearts
24 duck testicles
24 duck tongues
Kosher salt

FOR THE DUCK JUS
(MAKES 4 CUPS/1 L)
10 lb (4.5 kg) duck bones, coarsely chopped
2 tbsp (30 mL) duck fat
3 cups (750 mL) sliced onions
1 cup (250 mL) diced carrots
1 cup (250 mL) diced celery
1 cup (250 mL) diced leeks
1 cup (250 mL) diced peeled celery root
3 tbsp (45 mL) tomato paste
1 cup (250 mL) ruby port
1 cup (250 mL) Madeira
2 cups (500 mL) red wine, divided
4 sprigs Italian parsley
6 sprigs fresh thyme
2 fresh bay leaves
12 black peppercorns
3 whole cloves
2 pig's trotters
8½ quarts (8 L) chicken stock (see basic stock, page 238)

FOR THE PASTA DOUGH
4 cups (1 L) all-purpose flour
3 duck eggs
½ tsp (2 mL) olive oil

FOR THE DUCK HEARTS
Split the hearts in half and rinse them under cold water to remove any blood clots. Dry on paper towels and refrigerate until needed.

FOR THE DUCK TESTICLES
Rinse the testicles well under cold water. Remove any excess membrane, dry on paper towels and refrigerate until needed.

FOR THE DUCK TONGUES
Season the tongues liberally with salt and refrigerate for 2 hours. Rinse well under cold water. Pat dry on paper towels and place them in an even layer in a vacuum bag. Seal the bag and cook in a water bath or immersion circulator set at 180°F (82°C) for 8 hours.

Transfer the bag to ice water to cool the tongues. Remove the tongues and pull out and discard the hard piece of cartilage in the centre of each one. Refrigerate until needed.

FOR THE DUCK JUS
Preheat the oven to 350°F (180°C).

Spread the bones in an even layer on a baking sheet and roast, turning once halfway, for about 1½ hours, until the bones are golden brown.

Meanwhile, in a stockpot melt the duck fat over medium-high heat. Add the onions, carrots, celery, leeks and celery root; sauté until they start to caramelize, 15 to 20 minutes. Stir in the tomato paste and cook, stirring frequently, for 3 minutes. Add the port and Madeira and cook until reduced by half, about 10 minutes.

Add the duck bones. Deglaze the baking sheet with half of the wine, making sure to scrape up any caramelized bits. Add this liquid to the pot along with the remaining wine. Cook until reduced by half.

Add the parsley, thyme, bay leaves, peppercorns, cloves, trotters and chicken stock. Bring to a simmer, then turn down the heat to maintain the barest simmer. Simmer, uncovered and without stirring, for 6 hours, skimming frequently.

Strain through a fine-mesh sieve into a clean pot. Reduce the stock over medium heat, skimming frequently, until it is reduced to 4 cups (1 L), about 1½ hours. (Jus can be made a day or two ahead.)

FOR THE PASTA DOUGH
Follow the instructions for basic pasta dough on page 244.

recipe continues . . .

⚔ Foie Gras

We like foie gras, because it's delicious. Yes, it's controversial, and there's no denying it's acquired in a way that is a little harsh. Compared to the life of a battery chicken or pen-raised pig, though, a well-raised foie gras duck probably has it better. Most Canadian producers, like Élevages Périgord and Rougié, are located in Quebec, and they take great effort to ensure the well-being of their ducks. Anyway, it's not an everyday staple—it's a special-occasion splurge, and having a piece every once in a while is a real treat.

We prefer a cold preparation to a hot one. The flavour and texture of the foie come through a little more with a terrine or mousse. If you really want it hot, try this: Put a baking sheet in the fridge for a couple of hours. Turn the oven to 375°F (190°C). Score the foie gras—don't season it—and get a frying pan super hot. Sear the slices fast-fast on both sides just to give it the colour you want without rendering out too much fat. Put the seared foie on the cold baking sheet and pop it into the oven to warm through and set. After about 5 minutes it should be ready, depending on the size. Season it with some good-quality fleur de sel.

Foie Gras and Maple Syrup

This recipe captures autumn in Quebec. All of the flavours are there: pain d'épices, maple, apples and ice cider. Once you've made the foie gras terrine, this is an easy dish to assemble.

Serves 8

FOR THE PAIN D'ÉPICES
2½ cups (625 mL) all-purpose flour
1½ tsp (7 mL) ground ginger
1 tsp (5 mL) cinnamon
1 tsp (5 mL) ground cloves
1 tsp (5 mL) baking soda
½ tsp (2 mL) kosher salt
1 cup (250 mL) unsalted butter,
   at room temperature
1 cup (250 mL) white sugar
½ cup (125 mL) brown sugar

FOR THE STREUSEL
3½ tbsp (52 mL) all-purpose flour
3 tbsp (45 mL) almond flour
3 tbsp (45 mL) sugar
3 tbsp (45 mL) cold unsalted
   butter, cubed

FOR THE APPLE PURÉE
4 tbsp (60 mL) canola oil, divided
6 Gravenstein apples, peeled, cored
   and cut into ½-inch (1 cm) cubes
½ cup (125 mL) white wine
1 tsp (5 mL) apple vinegar (see
   page 163)
Kosher salt

FOR THE PAIN D'ÉPICES
Preheat the oven to 350°F (180°C).

In a bowl, whisk together the flour, ginger, cinnamon, cloves, baking soda and kosher salt. In a stand mixer fitted with the paddle attachment, cream the butter with the white and brown sugars until fluffy. Add the dry ingredients and stir to incorporate thoroughly.

Scrape the batter onto a sheet of parchment paper. Top with a second sheet and roll out to ¼-inch (5 mm) thickness. Slide onto a baking sheet, remove the top sheet of parchment and bake until golden brown, 14 to 16 minutes. Cool the bread in the pan to room temperature.

Break the bread into large pieces and grind in a food processor until the mixture resembles coarse sand. (Crumbs will stay crisp for up to 1 week in an airtight container. You will not use all the crumbs. Use the extra crumbs as cheesecake crust or topping for ice cream.)

FOR THE STREUSEL
Preheat the oven to 350°F (180°C).

Combine the all-purpose flour, almond flour and sugar in a bowl. Using your fingertips, rub in the butter until the mixture resembles coarse sand. Tip the mixture into a measuring cup, note how much there is, and return it to the bowl. Add an equal amount of pain d'épices crumbs, stirring to fully incorporate.

Spread the mixture evenly onto a parchment-lined baking sheet and bake, stirring once halfway through, for 16 to 18 minutes, until the mixture is toasted and fragrant. Allow to cool to room temperature in the pan.

In a food processor, pulse the mixture until it is the texture of sand. (Streusel keeps for up to 1 week in an airtight container.)

FOR THE APPLE PURÉE
Heat 2 tbsp (30 mL) of the oil in a large sauté pan over medium heat. Add the apples and cook gently until just soft, but do not let them colour. Add the wine and vinegar. Bring to a simmer. Turn down the heat to low and cover the apples with a round of parchment paper. Slowly stew the apples until they are tender and the liquid has reduced by half.

Transfer the mixture to a blender and purée until smooth. With the motor running, add the remaining 2 tbsp (30 mL) oil. Strain the purée through a fine-mesh sieve into a bowl set over ice. Season with kosher salt. (Apple purée can be made ahead and refrigerated, covered.)

FOR THE APPLE BALLS

1 cup (250 mL) ice cider
1 cup (250 mL) white wine
½ cup (125 mL) sugar
½ cup (125 mL) apple vinegar
  (see page 163)
5 whole cloves
1 cinnamon stick
1 tsp (5 mL) kosher salt
3 Gravenstein apples

TO FINISH THE DISH

8 slices foie gras terrine (see page
  141) the size of your index finger
Flaky sea salt
Société-Orignal Remonte-Pente or
  other top-quality maple syrup

FOR THE APPLE BALLS

In a small saucepan, combine the ice cider, wine, sugar, vinegar, cloves, cinnamon stick and kosher salt. Simmer until reduced to ½ cup (125 mL).

Meanwhile, peel the apples. Using a ½-inch (1 cm) melon baller, scoop 24 nice clean balls out of the apples. Add the apple balls to the syrup and simmer for 2 minutes. Remove the pan from the heat and allow the balls to cool in the liquid.

TO FINISH THE DISH

Preheat the broiler to high.

Place a finger of the foie gras just off the centre of each of eight ovenproof dinner plates. Arrange 3 apple balls on each plate. Spoon 1½ tsp (7 mL) of the streusel mixture to the side of each slice of foie gras, making sure to get a bit on the apple balls. Place the plates under the broiler for 10 seconds to warm the streusel.

Spoon a pool of the apple purée around the foie gras. Sprinkle the terrine with a few flakes of sea salt and generously drizzle the maple syrup over everything.

Prairies

For six thousand years the broad plains and big skies of the Canadian prairies provided rich hunting grounds for the Plains people: Cree, Ojibwa, Blackfoot. Buffalo was the main food source, along with deer, moose, elk, berries and tubers. With the arrival of European settlers—primarily Ukrainian, German, French and Scandinavian—in the late nineteenth century, open-range ranching and widespread agriculture began to shape the region.

Today the Canadian Prairies are not only this country's bread basket but much of the world's. So abundant are they that much of what's produced there gets shipped out of the country and sent back to us in the form of products we think of as international. That fancy French mustard? The seeds probably came from a Saskatchewan field. Your favourite Italian pasta? The durum wheat was probably grown in Alberta. That clean, smooth IPA or thick, rich imported stout almost certainly has some Canadian hops or barley in it.

Although good food was abundant in the prairies for as long as people have lived there, by the time I arrived in Alberta in the early 1980s, with a few notable exceptions, good food was mostly a home-cooked affair. Despite being surrounded by some of the best farmland in the country, the restaurant scene was limited to a few dusty old hotel dining rooms, some crepuscular steakhouses specializing in well-done beef and the occasional "fusion" restaurant offering "Chinese and Canadian cuisines." It was a big deal when one place started cutting their pizzas into squares, and the arrival of ginger beef was a momentous event. That was a long time ago, though, and the restaurant scene in the Prairies in the past few years has taken a dramatic turn for the better.

Much like its best agricultural products, for a long time, the Prairies' best chefs had to leave the region to develop and to be fully appreciated. Dale MacKay worked in Japan, Hong Kong and New York before returning to Saskatoon to open Ayden Kitchen and Bar. John Jackson and Connie DeSousa honed their skills in New York, London and San Francisco before opening Charcut Roast House in Calgary. Justin Leboe staged in Napa, New York and Virginia before opening Model Milk in Calgary.

Now that young cooks are seeking out these places and coming from around the world to learn in those kitchens, the future of dining in the Canadian Prairies seems as big and bright as a prairie sky.

Steak for Two

There is nothing better than steak. Cooked properly and served with just about anything, it is delicious. When I think of the Prairies, I think of hauling huge bales of hay, playing hockey outdoors in minus 40 degrees Celsius weather, and eating meat. My cut of choice is rib steak, cut at least 2 inches (5 cm) thick from the best end of a piece of very aged and well-marbled beef. In this recipe, the steak is rubbed with a spice and dried mushroom blend, which puts a light cure on the meat and develops into an amazing crust. The dried mushrooms pick up the flavour of the charcoal very well and really bring out the qualities of the beef. In the summer I serve this along-side a tomato salad (see page 150) with a beautiful blue cheese from Quebec and lots of raw onion.

FOR THE STEAK RUB
5 cloves garlic, peeled and crushed
¼ cup (60 mL) dried wild
   mushrooms, preferably porcini,
   ground
2 tbsp (30 mL) sugar
1 tbsp (15 mL) kosher salt
1 tbsp (15 mL) red chili flakes
1 tbsp (15 mL) black pepper
¼ cup (60 mL) canola oil

FOR THE MAÎTRE D'HÔTEL BUTTER
1 lb (450 g) unsalted butter, at room
   temperature
1 tbsp (15 mL) finely chopped chives
1 tbsp (15 mL) finely chopped curly
   parsley
1 tbsp (15 mL) finely chopped fresh
   chervil
1 tbsp (15 mL) finely chopped fresh
   tarragon
1 tbsp (15 mL) flaky sea salt
Finely grated zest of 1 lemon

FOR THE STEAK
1 bone-in rib steak (about 36 oz/
   1 kg), 2 inches (5 cm) thick
Flaky sea salt
Very good olive oil

FOR THE STEAK RUB
In a mortar, combine the garlic, ground mushrooms, sugar, kosher salt, chili flakes and pepper. Pound with a pestle, making sure to pound the garlic to a paste. Stir in the oil. (Rub keeps, refrigerated, for up to 1 week.)

FOR THE MAÎTRE D'HÔTEL BUTTER
Place all the ingredients in a bowl and combine well with a wooden spoon or a rubber spatula. You can roll this up into a log in plastic wrap, refrigerate it until firm and then slice it, or pipe it into rosettes or simply spoon it on top of the meat. (Any leftover butter can be frozen.)

FOR THE STEAK
Massage all the steak rub into both sides of the steak. Cover and allow to cure in the refrigerator for 24 hours.

Remove the steak from the fridge at least 2 hours before grilling it. Wipe off the excess rub.

Prepare a charcoal grill. When the coals are good and glowing, place the steak on the hottest part of the grill and sear on both sides until you achieve a nice char. Move the steak to the cooler part of the grill and continue cooking until the internal temperature is 120°F (48°C) for perfect medium-rare, about 40 minutes total. (The temperature will rise to 125°F/50°C during the resting.) While the steak cooks, you can make a tomato salad (see page 150). Remove the steak from the grill and allow it to rest for at least 15 minutes before serving or slicing.

Serve the steak with maître d'hôtel butter and pots of flaky sea salt. Stir a little bit of very good olive oil into the resting juices and spoon over the meat. Serve with a tomato salad—that's my preferred pairing, but it's also delicious with grilled zucchini.

WHY A THICK CUT?

Get your steak from a good butcher shop that ages its meat well, and ask the butcher to custom cut your steak from the best end. It's called "best" for a reason. You want a thick cut because when cooking over fire or charcoal, the longer your steak stays on the grill, the better it's going to taste. I prefer to slow cook these cuts for maximum charcoal flavour. Use any charcoal you like, but in my opinion Kingsford is superior for that childhood taste and nostalgia. Plus, it burns long, making it an economical choice.

Tomato Salad

A fantastic summer salad, perfect with grilled steak.

Serves 2

FOR THE DRESSING

1½ tsp (7 mL) fresh marjoram leaves
½ clove garlic, peeled
Flaky sea salt and freshly cracked
  black pepper
2 tsp (10 mL) red wine vinegar
1½ tsp (7 mL) Balconville vinegar
  or good-quality balsamic vinegar
¼ cup + 1½ tsp (67 mL) olive oil

FOR THE TOMATO SALAD

½ red onion
1 lb (450 g) very ripe in-season
  tomatoes
Sea salt
Lemon juice
1½ tsp (7 mL) finely chopped
  Italian parsley
Leaves from 1½ sprigs purple basil
Leaves from 1½ sprigs green basil
2 oz (55 g) Bleu d'Élizabeth or
  other blue cheese

FOR THE DRESSING

Place the marjoram, garlic and a pinch of salt in a mortar and pound to a paste. Stir in the red wine and Balconville vinegars and the olive oil. Season with salt and pepper. (Dressing can be made several hours ahead.)

FOR THE TOMATO SALAD

Slice the onion ¼ inch (5 mm) thick and soak in ice water for 10 minutes. Drain.

Cut the tomatoes into natural-looking chunks. Spread them on a plate and season with the salt and lemon juice. Allow to stand for 5 minutes.

Transfer the tomatoes (without their juices) to a large bowl. Add the drained onion, parsley and dressing; toss to combine. Add the basils and mix in gently with your hands. Adjust the seasoning. Mound the salad into a decorative bowl and crumble the blue cheese over the top.

Chanterelle Pasties

Saskatchewan is known for some of the best chanterelles in Canada. Out West you can get hit with some pretty big storms, so the wild mushrooms tend to get waterlogged. But the weather in this part of the country is very consistent during midsummer, when the mushrooms are in season, resulting in perfect chanterelles with aromas of apricots and the forest floor.

Makes 4 pasties

FOR THE PASTRY
2½ cups (625 mL) all-purpose flour
½ tsp (2 mL) kosher salt
½ cup + 1 tbsp (140 mL) cold
   unsalted butter, cut into ½-inch
   (1 cm) cubes
1 egg, beaten
A few drops of milk

FOR THE CHANTERELLE FILLING
2 tbsp (30 mL) canola oil
¾ lb (340 g) chanterelle mushrooms,
   cleaned, small ones kept whole,
   big ones torn
Kosher salt and black pepper
1 clove garlic, sliced
2 tbsp (30 mL) finely chopped
   shallot
2 tsp (10 mL) chopped fresh thyme
1 tbsp (15 mL) red wine vinegar
1 tbsp (15 mL) unsalted butter
¼ cup (60 mL) whipping cream
2 tbsp (30 mL) sour cream
1 tbsp (15 mL) finely chopped
   Italian parsley

TO FINISH THE PASTIES
1 egg yolk, lightly beaten, for
   egg wash

FOR THE PASTRY
In a large bowl, stir together the flour and salt. With your fingertips, rub in the butter until the mixture looks like fine bread crumbs. Quickly stir in the egg and just enough milk to form a stiff dough, taking care not to overmix the dough. Shape the dough into a disc, wrap it in plastic wrap and refrigerate for at least 1 hour.

FOR THE CHANTERELLE FILLING
Heat the oil in a large, heavy sauté pan over medium-high heat. Add the mushrooms with a pinch of salt and sauté until they start to turn golden. Add the garlic, shallots and thyme and sauté until the shallots start to turn translucent. Drain the mushroom mixture in a colander set over a bowl (you don't want the mushrooms absorbing liquid).

Add the vinegar to the pan and bring to a boil. Swirl in the butter, then add the mushrooms with any liquid collected in the bowl. Add the cream and cook until reduced by half.

Transfer half of the mushroom mixture to a food processor and blend until smooth. Return the purée to the pan and fold in the sour cream. Season with salt and pepper. Cover and refrigerate until cold and set. Stir in the parsley.

TO FINISH THE PASTIES
Divide the pastry into 4 equal pieces. Roll out each piece on a lightly floured work surface to a 10-inch (25 cm) circle.

Spread a quarter of the mushroom mixture over half of each circle, leaving a 1-inch (2.5 cm) border. Brush the edges with some of the egg wash and fold the dough over the filling. Crimp the edges to form a decorative seal. Place the pasties on a parchment-lined baking sheet and refrigerate for 30 minutes.

Preheat the oven to 350°F (180°C).

Brush the pasties with egg wash. Bake for 18 to 20 minutes, until they are golden brown. Allow to rest for 10 minutes before serving.

Bone Marrow and Anchovies

St. John, Fergus Henderson's massively influential restaurant in London, and one of my favourite places to eat in the world, basically put bone marrow on the map. This is an interesting way to prepare the marrow, using a classic panade, or bread crumb thickener. Don't be put off by the anchovies; they are simply there as a seasoning element.

Serves 6

FOR THE MARROW

6 centre-cut veal marrow bones
  (ask your butcher to cut these
  "canoe style"), chilled
1½ cups (375 mL) sourdough rye
  bread, crusts removed and torn
  into small pieces
2 cups (500 mL) chicken stock
  (see basic stock, page 238), at
  room temperature
½ cup (125 mL) unsalted butter
½ cup (125 mL) finely diced shallots
1 fresh bay leaf
1 cup (250 mL) white wine
6 salt-packed anchovy fillets, rinsed,
  dried and finely chopped
2 tbsp (30 mL) finely chopped
  Italian parsley
2 tsp (10 mL) finely chopped
  fresh thyme
Zest of ½ lemon
Kosher salt and white pepper

FOR THE SALAD

1 banana shallot, peeled
2 cups (500 mL) Italian parsley,
  disciplined a few times with a
  sharp knife
¼ cup (60 mL) nonpareil
  capers, rinsed
2 tsp (10 mL) apple vinaigrette
  (see page 240)
Sea salt and black pepper

TO FINISH THE DISH

Flaky sea salt
½ cup (125 mL) pangritata (see
  page 88)

FOR THE MARROW

Preheat the oven to 350°F (180°C).

Remove the marrow from the cold bones, reserving the bones, and cut it into ½-inch (1 cm) cubes.

Spread 1½ cups (375 mL) of the bread pieces on a baking sheet and toast in the oven, stirring halfway through, until golden brown and completely dry, 12 to 15 minutes. Allow to cool to room temperature.

Place the toasted bread in a medium bowl and pour over the stock. Allow to soak until the bread has absorbed as much stock as it can. Squeeze out as much moisture as you can. Wipe out the bowl, return the bread to it, and add the marrow.

In a medium saucepan, melt the butter over medium heat. Add the shallots and bay leaf and sweat until the shallots are soft and translucent, stirring occasionally. Add the wine and reduce until the liquid is almost all evaporated, 12 to 15 minutes. Allow to cool to room temperature, then remove the bay leaf.

Add the anchovies, parsley, thyme and lemon zest to the marrow/bread mixture and stir until thoroughly incorporated. Season with kosher salt and white pepper.

FOR THE SALAD

Slice the shallot into thin rings with a mandoline and soak in ice water for 5 minutes; drain. In a large bowl, toss the shallot with the parsley, capers and vinaigrette. Season with sea salt and black pepper.

TO FINISH THE DISH

Preheat the oven to 425°F (220°C). Divide the marrow/bread mixture among the 12 bone halves, arrange on a baking sheet and roast for 10 minutes.

Turn on the broiler. Carefully broil just until the filling is golden brown. Sprinkle the filling with a few flakes of sea salt and garnish the bones with the parsley salad and a shower of pangritata.

ORCHARD
& VINEYARD

When you drive in from Vancouver, there's that moment when the car crests the final hill and the first glimpse of Okanagan Lake explodes into view. "That never gets old," Derek says as we start the descent into the valley. "That's one of my favourite sights in the world."

The scene is no less impressive late in the day when we arrive at JoieFarm at the very southern end of the lake just as the golden-hour light is settling in the valley, basting the whole scene in buttery hues. Boats carve white wakes in the water's black surface, steep cliffs rise slowly from the shore and tidy rows of vineyards line their edges. Farther up, sagebrush and massive pine trees dig deep into the soil.

Derek and I both have roots here as well. A set of grandparents and an annual hockey camp brought Derek to the region every summer when he was growing up, while I lived here for several years off and on as a kid and still have family in the area's main city, Kelowna.

Back in the day, the Okanagan Valley was known mainly for its orchards, and dozens of brightly painted farm stands still line both sides of the highway. Throughout the summer and fall, produce spills out into the parking lots, piled high in big pallets. Cherries are first: pale, delicate Rainiers with their creamy yellow flesh, and extra-large, hardy Bings, Lapins for jam and Lamberts for baking. Then come the apricots: sweet-fleshed orange Tomcots; blushing, glossy Goldbars; giant sweet Tiltons; and sharp Sundrops for canning.

By the time the lakes are warm enough for swimming in July, the Early Sweetheart peaches are ready, followed by juicy Red Havens and Glohavens through August, when it's time for the pears to take over: Bartlett, Flemish Beauty, Anjou and super-sweet Red Clapp. Fall brings plums: black-skinned damsons for jam, greengage and Bluefres for eating right off the tree. Apples, king of the Okanagan orchard industry, are last on the trees. Dozens of varieties are grown here, including some, like the Spartan with its sweet, snow-white flesh and the pale yellow Sinta, that were developed at the nearby Summerland Research Station.

While orchards remain an important part of what makes the Okanagan special, these days it's the wineries that are bringing the region global recognition. The northern end of the valley is dominated by crisp whites: primarily pinot gris, Gewürztraminer and riesling from such wineries as Gray Monk, CedarCreek and Mission Hill, while the far south is home to the big reds from Road 13 Vineyards, Cassini Cellars and Orofino, among others.

One of our favourite winemakers in the valley is Heidi Noble of JoieFarm. Since starting her winery in 2004, she and co-founder Michael Dinn have won just about every wine award there is for their crisp, clean Alsatian and Burgundian-style wines. Her celebrated rosé is on nearly every restaurant menu in Western Canada and is one of the country's great wines. On the day we show up, Michael is just getting off the phone after learning that Joie just won, for the second year in a row, a prestigious Decanter World Wine Award. Unlabelled bottles of sparkling wine—"A little experiment we've been working on," Michael says—are uncorked and toasts are raised.

Heidi, a chef before she was a winemaker, is already well into dinner preparations. Great spears of the season's first asparagus and bunches of sorrel are laid out on the counter waiting to be combined into a soup. The brick oven out on the patio is warming up, and Theo, the former couple's towheaded young son, is regaling everyone with tales of his day, the highlight of which seems to be the stash of quail eggs he found out beside the chicken coop.

There's quail on the menu tonight, too, albeit from a store. Our feeble and, frankly, half-assed attempts at catching them with an old wine box, a handful of seeds and very little patience have gone unrewarded. We have better luck finding piles of morels that are growing all around the property. "When we landscaped the house we used what's called interior mulch. It's from forest fires and land clearings around here, and it was full of morel spores," Heidi explains. Those morels—which we toss into a duxelles to stuff the quail with before wrapping the birds in pancetta—are a testament to the almost absurd fertility of this region.

Much of the produce Heidi has laid out—including whole bunches of grapes that we'll roast and toss with tarragon, chive blossoms and goat cheese before mixing them with torn shards of toasted bread for a vibrant panzanella—comes from the renowned Penticton organic farmer's market. "It's one of the best things about living here," Michael says. "The food that you get at that market stands alongside anything I've had anywhere: Italy, France, Spain. It's phenomenal."

Dinner's ready just as the sun slips below the horizon. The patio table overlooking the vineyard and beyond to the lake is set with fresh linens. Toasts are raised (again), wine is popped, jokes are cracked and, exactly as promised, it's a meal that stands alongside anything anywhere. We're just glad it's here.

A-pear-itif

This is a boozy pear cocktail, and the only one in the book as I don't want to be classified as a mixologist of any sort. I don't have a moustache ironic enough or a wardrobe full of my great-grandfather's clothes . . . I'm talking about you, Chris Morgan.

Serves 1 or 2

FOR THE ELDERFLOWER CORDIAL
(MAKES 8 CUPS/2 L)
6 cups (1.5 L) water
25 elderflower clusters
Finely grated zest and juice of
  3 lemons
Finely grated zest and juice of
  1 orange
2 lb (900 g) sugar
1 tsp (5 mL) citric acid

FOR THE APERITIF
2 tbsp (30 mL) chopped Lebanese
  cucumber
3 tbsp (45 mL) pear vodka
3 tbsp (45 mL) elderflower cordial
3 tbsp (45 mL) London No. 1 or
  other good gin
3 tbsp (45 mL) fresh lime juice

FOR THE ELDERFLOWER CORDIAL
Bring the water to a boil. Place the elderflowers in a large container and add the lemon and orange zests. Pour the boiling water over the elderflowers and zests, cover and refrigerate overnight.

Strain the mixture into a large saucepan and add the sugar, citric acid and lemon and orange juices. Bring to a simmer to dissolve the sugar. Cool to room temperature, transfer to a jug or bottle and keep refrigerated. Use to make boozy or virgin cocktails or sorbet.

FOR THE APERITIF
Muddle the cucumber with the vodka. In a shaker two-thirds full of crushed ice, combine the muddled cucumber, cordial, gin and lime juice. Shake well. Strain into one or two chilled cocktail glasses and add a large square ice cube.

Apple Vinegar

If you can get hold of Gravenstein apples, a tart cooking apple that's still found in a lot of small orchards and backyards, they work beautifully here. Otherwise, just use your favourite apple.

Makes about 6 cups (1.5 L)

6 Gravenstein apples
5 cups (1.25 L) cider vinegar
1 cup (250 mL) maple syrup
1 tbsp (15 mL) kosher salt

Cut the apples into quarters and place them in a nonreactive container.

Combine the vinegar, syrup and salt in a saucepan and bring to a boil. Pour the hot liquid over the apples, then place a plate over the apples to keep them submerged. Cool to room temperature. Cover and refrigerate for at least 6 weeks. Remove the apples before using. (Vinegar keeps, refrigerated, for up to 6 months.)

Schiacciata

Popular in the wine-growing regions of Italy, this focaccia-like bread is always baked at harvest time when there's an abundance of grapes available. The word schiacciata *means "flattened out," and although you don't really flatten the dough, the fingerprints you leave in it make great little indentations for the toppings to gather. In a perfect world you'd use freshly harvested vinifera grapes from local vineyards, but any kind of red or blue grape works well. This bread is traditionally served with some cured meats and marinated vegetables, but makes an excellent companion to the foie gras parfait on page 140.*

You can make this dough a day in advance and keep it in the fridge, but it will take almost twice as long to prove.

Serves 8 to 12

1½ tsp (7 mL) active dry yeast
2 cups (500 mL) warm water
4 cups (1 L) all-purpose flour
1½ cups (375 mL) Red Fife flour
½ tsp (2 mL) sea salt
2 lb (900 g) Concord or your
   favourite red or blue grapes,
   seedless if preferred
⅓ cup (75 mL) olive oil
4 sprigs fresh rosemary
⅓ cup (75 mL) good honey
1 tbsp (15 mL) fennel seeds
Flaky sea salt

In the bowl of a stand mixer, stir the yeast into the water until it dissolves; let sit for 10 minutes, until foamy. Mix the flours and the salt together. Using a dough hook and, with the mixer on the lowest speed, slowly add the flour to the dissolved yeast. Knead on low speed for 15 minutes, or until the dough is soft and moist, just forming a loose ball that comes away from the sides of the bowl. Add a little more all-purpose flour if it seems too wet, or a little more water if it is too dry. Cover and allow to rise until doubled in size, about 2 hours.

While the dough is rising, stem, wash and dry the grapes. Heat the olive oil over medium heat and fry the rosemary sprigs until just crisp—do not let them burn. Set aside to cool in the oil.

Place a pizza stone, if you have one, in the lower third of the oven and preheat the oven to 450°F (230°C). Oil a 20- × 12-inch (50 × 30 cm)—or as close as you have—rimmed baking sheet.

Turn the risen dough into the baking sheet and stretch and press it with your hands until it fills the pan. Let the dough rest for 15 minutes.

Dimple the surface with your fingers. Spread the grapes over the top and drizzle with the honey. Remove the rosemary from the oil, strip off the leaves and scatter them over the top. Pour over the oil, then sprinkle with the fennel seeds and some flaky sea salt.

Bake for 15 to 20 minutes. Remove from the oven and use a pastry brush to spread the syrupy liquid collecting in the centre from the grapes and honey all over the bread. Bake for another 15 to 20 minutes, until the bottom and sides are golden, the dimples are filled with jammy liquid and the peaks between them are crisp and golden. Use a spatula to loosen the sides and bottom, then slide the schiacciata onto a wire rack to cool completely.

Grapes and Tarragon

I made this salad (pictured on pages 166 and 167) when we were in the Okanagan at JoieFarm winery, and the flavours really worked. The licorice and slightly medicinal quality of the tarragon play so well with the different textures and levels of sweetness in the grapes.

Serves 4

FOR THE ROASTED GRAPES
2 bunches seedless red grapes
1 tsp (5 mL) olive oil
Kosher salt and black pepper

FOR THE DEHYDRATED GRAPES
2 cups (500 mL) seedless
  green grapes
2 cups (500 mL) sugar
2 cups (500 mL) water

FOR THE CROUTONS
1 loaf sourdough rye, sliced, crusts
  removed
½ cup (125 mL) olive oil
Kosher salt and black pepper
3 sprigs fresh thyme

TO FINISH THE DISH
2 banana shallots, peeled
Leaves from 6 bunches
  fresh tarragon
2 bunches seedless Concord
  grapes, picked
2 tbsp (30 mL) apple vinaigrette
  (see page 240)
Kosher salt and black pepper
½ cup (125 mL) fromage blanc
3 tbsp (45 mL) torn fresh chive
  blossoms
3 sprigs fresh dill
Flaky sea salt

FOR THE ROASTED GRAPES
Preheat the oven to 450°F (230°C).

Using scissors, snip the grapes into small clusters. Toss the grapes with the oil, kosher salt and pepper, then spread them on a parchment-lined baking sheet. Roast for 12 to 15 minutes, until the skins start to blister. Allow to cool to room temperature.

FOR THE DEHYDRATED GRAPES
Preheat the oven to 200°F (100°C).

Pierce each grape with the tip of a paring knife. Combine the sugar and the water in a medium saucepan and bring to a boil over medium heat. When the sugar has dissolved, turn down the heat to low and add the grapes. Gently poach the grapes for 5 minutes. Drain well.

Spread the grapes on a parchment-lined baking sheet and dehydrate in the oven until they have shrivelled and are about two-thirds their original size, 1¾ to 2 hours.

FOR THE CROUTONS
Preheat the oven to 350°F (180°C).

Tear the bread into natural-looking crouton-sized pieces and toss with the olive oil, massaging the bread with your hands so that the oil is evenly absorbed. Season with kosher salt and pepper.

Spread the croutons on a parchment-lined baking sheet. Tuck the thyme sprigs among the bread pieces. Bake, rotating the pan and stirring the bread halfway through, until the croutons are golden but still a bit chewy inside, 20 to 25 minutes. Allow to cool to room temperature.

TO FINISH THE DISH
Make the salad at the very last minute. Very thinly slice the shallots and soak in ice water for 10 minutes; drain.

In a large bowl, combine the shallots, croutons, tarragon, fresh grapes, roasted grapes and dehydrated grapes. Lightly dress with the apple vinaigrette, season with kosher salt and pepper and combine gently.

Spread the salad in an even layer on a serving platter—you don't want to stack this one. Dot with small spoonfuls of the fromage blanc, scatter over the chive blossoms and tear the dill sprigs over the top. Season the salad with a few flakes of sea salt.

Heidi's Spring Asparagus and Sorrel Soup

This soup can be served with some sautéed morels, a bit of fresh Dungeness crab meat or a piece of seared salmon in the bowl for a treat. For a vegetarian soup, use vegetable stock instead.

Serves 6

8 cups (2 L) chicken stock (see basic stock, page 238)
1 tbsp (15 mL) unsalted butter
1 onion, diced
3 stalks celery, diced
1 carrot, peeled and diced
1 fresh bay leaf
1 cup (250 mL) white wine
Kosher salt and black pepper
1 lb (450 g) asparagus, trimmed
1 bunch fresh sorrel leaves
A handful of fresh tender herbs such as parsley, chervil or tarragon
2 tbsp (30 mL) rice vinegar
Zest of 1 lemon
Finely chopped chives and torn fresh chive blossoms or borage flowers or other edible petals to garnish

Timing is everything in this recipe, so set up a blender and have ready a bowl of ice water. In a large pot, bring the stock to a boil.

Meanwhile, melt the butter in a large sauté pan over medium-high heat and sauté the onion, celery, carrot and bay leaf until the vegetables are soft. Remove the bay leaf and deglaze the pan with the wine. Let the alcohol simmer off. Season with salt and pepper. Remove the mirepoix from the heat.

Plunge half the asparagus into the boiling stock and cook, uncovered, until it is tender and bright green, just 1 or 2 minutes. Using a slotted spoon or spider, skim the asparagus out of the boiling stock and plunge it into the ice bath to cool. Bring the stock back to a full boil and blanch the remaining asparagus; cool it in the ice bath. Drain the asparagus and pat dry.

Add the mirepoix to the stock. Bring back up to a boil, then turn down the heat and simmer for 2 minutes.

In the blender, and working in batches, blend some of the asparagus, sorrel and herbs with 2 cups (500 mL) of the stock mixture until very smooth. Strain the soup through a sieve into a bowl set in a larger bowl of ice water to stop the cooking and maintain the bright green colour. Repeat until all the vegetables have been blended.

Stir in the vinegar and lemon zest, then season with salt and pepper. The soup should have a fresh, bright flavour.

To serve, gently reheat the soup and serve in warmed bowls. Garnish with the chives and chive blossoms.

⚔

Canadian Plateau
de Fruits de Mer

Have you ever seen a fifteen-pound lobster? It's kind of terrifying. They could make a horror movie out of it: *Claws*.

John Bil, former world oyster shucking champion, has acquired just such a monstrosity for us, along with about two dozen normal-sized lobsters and just about every other kind of good thing to eat from the Atlantic Ocean, including several types of clams, oysters galore and a plethora of periwinkles. Derek has called on his suppliers from the west coast: there's geoduck the size of dinner plates, spiny urchin that look like medieval weapons, roe in a rainbow of colours and much, much more.

For months we've been planning this meal, waiting for the perfect moment when the maximum amount of fresh ingredients is available to us to build a shellfish platter of epic proportions. For the past two days Derek and John have been camped out at Norman Hardie's winery scaling, gutting and shucking the finest selection of Canadian seafood ever assembled.

While those two are prepping, I've been running around Prince Edward County with our host, winemaker Norman Hardie. We stop at Vicki's Veggies to pick up several pounds of just-picked salad greens and bottles of homemade hot sauce, toast sparkling rosé with winemaker Jonas Newman at Hinterland Wine Company and devour chef Elliot Reynolds's corn bread with molasses butter at Angeline's Inn. Everyone we meet gets invited back to the winery for dinner.

By the time Norm and I get back, a small crowd has already started to gather. The usual motley crew of winemakers, vineyard workers, cooks, servers, beekeepers and gardeners who populate the winery in the summer is setting tables and stoking fires. Derek is coating poached arctic char in a court bouillon he's reduced down to gelatin and mixed with ham and chervil. The brick oven is heated up: whole skate scattered with thyme flowers and basted with brown butter go in along with trays of bug-eyed redfish.

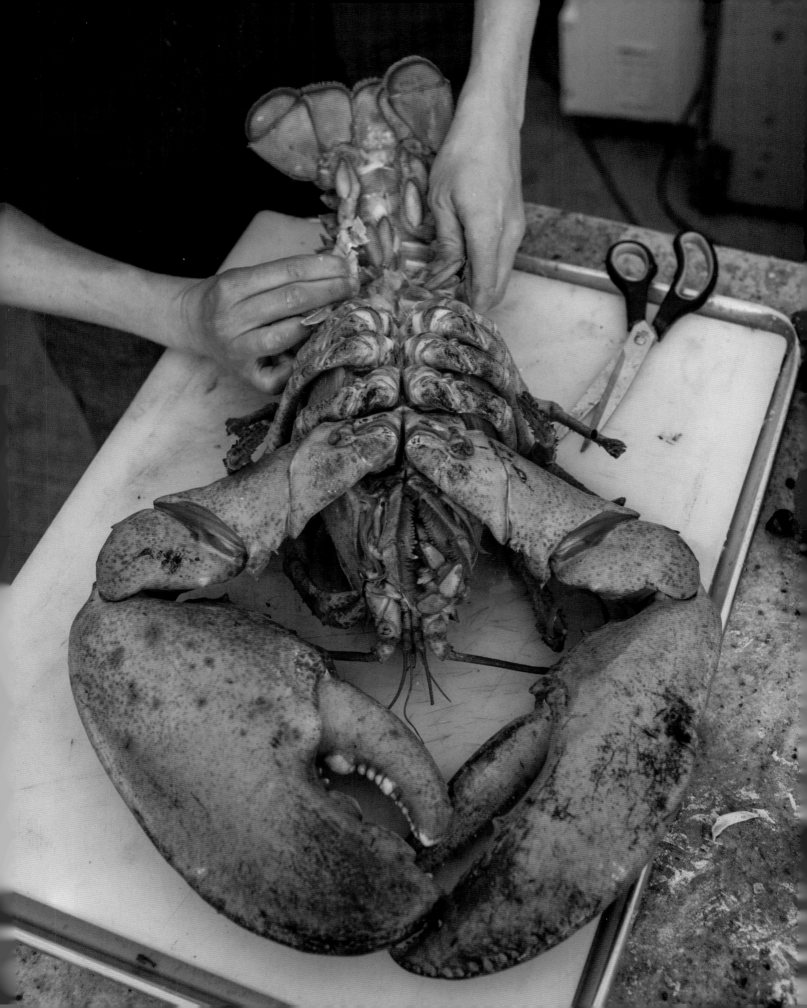

There's an entire clam station, and in keeping with the desire to keep everything in as close to its natural state as possible, steamer and littleneck clams are simply steamed, cleaned and returned to their shells. Surf clams are blanched and then cooked over hardwood in the Big Green Egg. Lobster are boiled in salt water, and Gaspé mussels are steamed with some of Norman Hardie's wine, shallots and herbs from the garden.

Oysters by the dozen, representing the best of both coasts: Fanny Bay, Kusshi, Black Pearl, Royal Miyagi and Ships Point from the Pacific, and Beausoleil, Malpeque, Bras d'Or, Caraquet and Tatamagouche from the Maritimes are shucked and ready. Princess scallops from Gaspésie, along with their roe, sit open to be sliced into three so that each bite contains a bit of scallop and a bit of roe.

It takes a good half-hour of intense focus to get everything laid out on the fifteen-foot table. Derek arranges a whole octopus between a phalanx of spiky snow crab legs and a small school of poached spot prawns. Jars of freshly made mayonnaise, bowls of melted butter and grilled lemon slices are there for dressing. Gooseneck barnacles poke out between whole fish; super-thin slices of geoduck topped with Acadian caviar beckon from icy shoals. Whole fish ranging from bite-size to trophy winners are arrayed in groups, some dressed simply with chilies and mint, others bedecked in glistening roe. Everywhere, shells: clams and mussels, oysters and whelks give the display an orgiastic quality.

It's gloriously too much. At first people are civilized, approaching the table with plates, returning to their seats to sip Calcaire and using cutlery. But as the double magnums are cracked, all propriety is abandoned. We start to attack the melting table with our bare hands, pulling limbs from lobsters, double-fisting molluscs.

Norm gets someone to turn the music off and manages to make a toast: "Thank you all for coming and taking part in this unbelievable feast. Seriously, I've never seen anything like it. I'm honoured that you picked the winery as the place you wanted to bring all of this phenomenal seafood together. It's appropriate, too. The Hillier limestone soil we're standing on, the soil that made me want to come here and grow grapes, was once at the bottom of a sea. So go ahead and toss your oyster shells. They'll help make great wine in a few thousand years. Cheers."

⚔

PACIFIC

Much too early in the morning we're sailing out of False Creek Harbour, on the edge of downtown Vancouver. The sun is just beginning to rise as we pass under the Burrard St. Bridge. As we move out into English Bay, the luxury apartment towers along Beach Avenue give way to the dense forest of Stanley Park, the whole scene framed by the blue peaks of the North Shore Mountains. Even fishermen Frank and Steve, who have made this trip thousands of times, can't help but admire the beauty of the city on this perfect late-May morning.

There's only so much time to enjoy the view, though, as we're on the hunt for spot prawns, and there are traps out there, full from their overnight soak, just waiting to be hauled up. Picking up speed, we move farther into the bay and thread our way between the massive tankers that wait to unload their cargo.

"You need to be careful around these big ships," Steve Johansen tells us over the roar of the engine. "They're big, but you'd be surprised how fast they can move." Johansen, along with his partner, Frank Keitsch, who is currently pulling on a pair of bright yellow rain pants and matching jacket, run Organic Ocean, the country's leading supplier of sustainably harvested Pacific seafood. In addition to catching some of the most sought after salmon, halibut, ling and albacore from the pristine waters off Canada's west coast, the duo also practically invented the local market for spot prawns, a seasonal product that inspires a veritable mania these days among the seafood savvy.

"It used to be that 90 percent of the spot prawns were exported out of the country," Johansen says. "In 2006 chef Robert Clark"—owner of The Fish Counter and a renowned champion of sustainable seafood—"came out fishing with us. He loved the shrimp and wanted to get it for his restaurant, but I explained that wasn't as easy as it should be." Together, the duo, in collaboration with the Chefs' Table Society of British Columbia, launched the first ever Spot Prawn Festival. "Now every prawn we catch stays right here in Canada," Johansen says with some pride.

We pull alongside our first string of traps not far from Keats Island (even giving this much information might get me in trouble with the fishermen who guard their secret spots jealously). Frank passes the hook to Derek. "When we get up beside the buoy, grab the line with this," he tells him. Derek snags it, and Frank guides the rope into a pull wheel and feeds the line into a tall bucket where it unspools its entire kilometre length. Everyone goes quiet as we wait for the first trap to surface.

A full minute passes before it does. It's empty except for a lethargic octopus. If it's possible for an octopus to look self-satisfied, this one does. "They're so smart," Steve says, "they get into the traps and devour every last prawn." The next trap is much better, with about a dozen wriggling, fleshy shrimp piled up, and the next one better still. "We've hit the honey hole with this one," Frank announces, handing the trap to Steve, who pulls a string and releases the prawns onto a sorting table. He flicks the small ones back into the water and puts the rest in plastic tubs. As soon as each tub is full, it's dropped into the ship's saltwater hold. "They need to be kept alive," Steve says. "Once they die they start to decompose and get mushy. Every minute they're out of the water they're getting less delicious."

He hands me one fresh from the trap, and it wriggles and flaps until I pop its head off. The tail throbs as I peel it open, revealing the sweet, translucent flesh. For the next few hours we get into a rhythm: traps are pulled and stacked while the prawns are sorted. Then the traps are baited and dropped back into the water.

Derek has offered to make everyone lunch, so we grab a bucket of wriggling prawns and start peeling. I feel a little bad tearing into the live creatures, but they get their revenge by cutting my hands to shreds with their sharp legs. Once we have a healthy pile of the freshest shrimp imaginable, Derek slices up a pint of cherry tomatoes, dices some shallots and chilies and juices a few limes. He mixes in a handful of capers, along with some chives, and finishes the dish with torn leaves of mint, basil and dill.

The ceviche looks so good that even the deckhand, Jason, who despite growing up in a fishing family has never eaten a prawn in his life—never mind a raw one—is persuaded to have a taste. "Not bad," he says after an epic struggle to get it down.

With the engine idling and everyone tired after a successful, busy morning, we float off the edge of the city and enjoy the feast. "You guys have the most beautiful office in the world," Derek says.

Baked Oysters with Marmite

As everyone except the Brits seems to know, Marmite is gross, but its depth of flavour makes this dish. It's a total umami bomb, offset by the cucumber-metallic finish of the oyster and the rich mushroom duxelles made with the great unsung mushroom: the button.

I get amazing beach oysters from Out Landish Shellfish Guild in Heriot Bay on Quadra Island. They raise their oysters for around nine years, and when they're harvested they are about the size of your hand. If you can't find Beach Angels, use another large oyster. If you don't have access to bull kelp, use kombu. Plain water will also work, but at the expense of a bit of umami flavour. To keep the shells balanced on the plate, mix some kosher salt with a bit of water and make a salt nest to hold them upright. Some decorative seaweed is a nice touch too.

Makes 6 oysters

FOR THE DUXELLES
9 oz (250 g) white button
  mushrooms
2 tbsp (30 mL) olive oil
1 tbsp (15 mL) unsalted butter
Leaves from 2 sprigs fresh thyme,
  finely chopped
Kosher salt and white pepper
½ cup (125 mL) white wine
¼ cup (60 mL) very thinly
  sliced green onion

FOR THE MARMITE MAYONNAISE
2 cups (500 mL) mayonnaise
  (see page 236)
2 tbsp (30 mL) Marmite
2 tbsp (30 mL) reserved oyster
  liquor, strained through a
  fine-mesh sieve
1 tbsp (15 mL) lemon juice
A pinch of cayenne pepper
Kosher salt to taste

FOR THE OYSTERS
6 extra-large Beach Angel oysters
½ cup (125 mL) water
2 pieces (6 inches/15 cm each)
  bull kelp

FOR THE DUXELLES
In a food processor, pulse the mushrooms until they have the texture of coarse bread crumbs, taking care not to overmix them—you do not want a paste.

Heat the olive oil and the butter in a medium, heavy saucepan over medium heat and cook the mushrooms with the thyme, stirring frequently, until they are softened, about 12 minutes.

Season with the salt and pepper, then deglaze with the wine. Cook the mixture until the wine has completely evaporated and the duxelles holds its shape when stirred.

Remove from the heat, adjust the seasoning and allow to cool completely. Carefully fold in the green onions. (Duxelles can be made up to 2 days ahead. Keep refrigerated.)

FOR THE MARMITE MAYONNAISE
Whisk everything together until smooth.

FOR THE OYSTERS
Under cold running water, thoroughly scrub the oysters to remove any algae and debris.

In a large, heavy saucepan, bring the water and bull kelp to a simmer over medium heat. Add the oysters curved side down, cover with the lid and cook just until the shells pop open slightly and the oyster flesh is just slightly set, 4 to 5 minutes.

Remove the oysters from the pot and immediately shuck them and remove the meat to stop the cooking. Reserve the bottom shells for serving. Allow the oysters to cool to room temperature, then carefully slice each one into three even pieces.

TO FINISH THE DISH
Preheat the oven to 375°F (190°C).

Make six little nests for the oysters by bunching up some foil. On a baking sheet, rest a reserved oyster shell on each nest. Place 1 tbsp (15 mL) of the mushroom duxelles in each shell and spread it out from the lip to the hinge of the shell.

Place 1 sliced oyster on top of the duxelles in each shell and spoon some of the Marmite mayonnaise over top, spreading it out until it is flush with the edges of the shell. (I can't tell you exactly how much, because that depends on the shell size.)

Bake for 12 minutes or until you see slight bubbling around the edges of the shell. Remove from the oven and heat the broiler to high.

Carefully broil the oysters on the middle rack to glaze the tops, about 10 seconds. Remove from the oven again and allow to rest for 3 minutes before serving.

Dungeness Crab and Its Possibilities

Crab is my absolute favourite thing on earth. I grew up on Vancouver Island eating them, and crab is still the dish I request first when I am visiting my folks. A big Dungeness crab with some grilled oysters, spot prawns and mayo, corn with salted butter and a big rib steak is pretty much my favourite feast ever. Dipping buttered sourdough bread into the head meat of a big Dungeness crab that's been simply boiled over a beach fire at low tide and throwing the shells on the ground is one of life's great pleasures.

HOW TO PREPARE DUNGENESS CRAB

When choosing a Dungeness crab, pick one that feels heavy for its size. Drop the crab into a pot of heavily salted boiling water, allow the water to come back to a boil and cook for 10 to 12 minutes depending on the size. Remove from the water, drain and let the crab cool naturally.

Turn the crab upside down with its head facing away from you and pull away the tail flap from the underside of the body. Twist off the claws and legs. Break the legs at the joints with the back of a large knife or a hammer and extract the meat with a crab pick or a skewer. Crack the claws and remove the meat in chunks, taking care not to remove bits of shell and the fine flat bone in the centre.

Push your thumbs against the hard shell close to the crab's tail and push the body section out and away from the shell. Remove and discard the greyish stomach sac behind the eyes and the "dead man's fingers," the soft, yellow, feathery gills attached to the body.

Cut the body in half and poke out any white meat in the crevices with a crab pick or a skewer. Set the white meat aside. Scoop the brown meat out of the shell and chop or mash it up.

Crab with Garlic Mayonnaise

Easy to make, messy and time consuming to eat. Perfect for a first date.

Serves 4

2 large Dungeness crabs, cooked,
  meat chilled (see above)

FOR THE MAYONNAISE
¾ cup + 2 tbsp (200 mL) canola oil
½ cup (125 mL) olive oil
2 cloves garlic, peeled and crushed
  to a paste with a little salt
2 small anchovy fillets
2 large egg yolks
1 tbsp (15 mL) cider vinegar
1 heaping tsp (6 mL) Colman's
  or other hot dry mustard
A small pinch of sugar
Sea salt and black pepper to taste

Combine the two oils in a small bowl. Using a mortar and pestle, mash the garlic with the anchovies. Mix in the yolks, vinegar, mustard, sugar, and salt and black pepper. Whisking constantly, add the oils a few drops at a time until the mayonnaise starts to emulsify. At that point you can add the rest in a steady stream, whisking constantly.

Adjust the seasoning. If the mayo seems too think, whisk in a touch of warm water. Chill until needed. Serve alongside the crab with bowls of lemon, brown bread and butter.

Potted Crab

Like pickling, sousing and curing, potting was originally a way to extend the shelf life of meat and seafood. This recipe makes for an easy starter or light lunch that can be made in advance. Just take it out of the fridge well before serving to let it come to room temperature.

Serves 6

1 cup (250 mL) unsalted butter,
  at room temperature, divided
1 clove garlic
Flaky sea salt and freshly cracked
  black pepper
Zest and juice of 1 lemon
A pinch of mace
3 tbsp (45 mL) water
A few drops of hot sauce
7 oz (200 g) brown crab meat
7 oz (200 g) white crab meat

Melt 3 tbsp (45 mL) of the butter in a small saucepan over low heat. When no more foam rises to the surface, remove from the heat and skim off the foam. Pour the butter through a sieve lined with cheesecloth, being careful to leave behind any solids in the pan. Set aside the clarified butter.

Chop the garlic and crush to a paste with a bit of the salt. In a medium bowl, combine the remaining butter with the garlic paste, lemon juice, mace, water and hot sauce. Using an electric mixer, whip until light and fluffy.

Force the brown crab meat through a sieve and pick through the white meat for any bits of shell. Fold the crab meats and the lemon zest into the butter. Season generously with pepper. Divide the mixture among six 4-oz (125 mL) ramekins or Mason jars and pour the clarified butter over the top. Cover and refrigerate for up to 3 days.

Serve at room temperature with toast and a light salad.

Dungeness Crab Tart

This recipe breaks the no-cheese-with-fish rule, but the Parmesan really brings it all together. I am partial to Dungeness, but you could use any type of crab. You could also make individual tarts if you wanted, though I find one large one less finicky, and it avoids that drastic pitfall of too much crust and not enough filling.

Serves 8

Pâte brisée (see page 132)
1 egg white, lightly beaten
3 tbsp (45 mL) canola oil
1 onion, thinly sliced
3 cloves garlic, finely minced
1 fresh red chili or jalapeño pepper, seeded and finely chopped
1 lb (450 g) cooked Dungeness crab meat (see page 190), picked over for shells
¼ cup (60 mL) finely chopped fresh cilantro
3 tbsp (45 mL) freshly grated Parmesan cheese
1 tbsp (15 mL) lemon juice
Kosher salt and black pepper
2 eggs
2 egg yolks
⅔ cup (150 mL) whipping cream
⅔ cup (150 mL) whole milk

On a floured work surface, roll out the pastry until it is the thickness of a nickel and line a 10-inch (25 cm) fluted tart pan with a removable bottom with it. Transfer the tart pan to a baking sheet and refrigerate for 1 hour.

Meanwhile, preheat the oven to 350°F (180°C).

Prick the tart shell several times with a fork, line with parchment paper and fill with beans to weigh the pastry down. Bake for 25 minutes, rotating the baking sheet halfway through. Remove the parchment and the beans and continue to bake the tart shell for another 10 to 12 minutes, until the pastry is light golden. Remove from the oven and brush the base of the tart shell with the egg white to prevent any filling from leaking.

In a large frying pan over medium-high heat, heat the oil until almost smoking. Add the onions and sauté until they are soft and starting to turn golden brown. Add the garlic and the chili and quickly sauté to take the edge off the garlic. Remove from the heat, add the crab meat and toss to combine.

Transfer the mixture to a bowl and fold in the cilantro, Parmesan and lemon juice. Season with salt and pepper. Spoon the crab filling into the warm tart shell and gently even it out without pressing down on it.

Whisk together the eggs, egg yolks, cream and milk. Carefully pour most of the custard over the crab meat, making sure it fills in all the cracks and crevices. Bake the tart for 7 minutes, then top up with the remaining custard so the filling is flush with the top of the crust. Cook, rotating halfway to ensure even cooking, until the custard is set, 40 to 45 minutes. Allow the tart to rest for at least 1 hour before slicing. I think it's best at room temperature, served with lemon slices. It really doesn't need anything else.

Crab and Carrageen Mousse

It is really satisfying to bring together two ingredients found in the same spot on the same day in the wild. This recipe uses Pacific Dungeness, but carrageen grows out East too, so you could use snow crab, lobster or spot prawns.

Serves 6

1 oz (28 g) dried carrageen
  (or 3 oz/85 g fresh, well rinsed)
5 oz (140 g) crab meat
Zest and juice of 1 lemon
1 tbsp (15 mL) chopped Italian
  parsley
1 tsp (5 mL) chopped fresh dill
Sea salt and freshly cracked
  black pepper
2 cups (500 mL) water
⅔ cup (150 mL) whipping cream
⅔ cup (150 mL) skim milk
1 tsp (5 mL) chopped fresh red
  chili pepper
A few drops of hot sauce

If you are using dried carrageen, soak it in cold water for 20 minutes; drain.

In a small bowl, mix together the crab, lemon zest and juice, parsley and dill. Season with salt and pepper, being generous with the salt.

In a small saucepan, over medium heat, combine the water and carrageen. Bring to a boil, then turn down the heat and simmer for 20 minutes, stirring occasionally.

Meanwhile, in a medium saucepan, heat the cream, milk, chili and hot sauce.

Line a sieve with a double layer of cheesecloth. Whisking constantly, strain the hot carrageen into the warm cream mixture. Put on some rubber gloves, gather up the cheesecloth and squeeze out as much liquid as possible.

Quickly stir in the crab meat and spoon into six 5-oz (150 mL) ramekins or one serving dish. Cover and refrigerate until set.

If using ramekins, turn the mousses out onto individual plates and serve with a green salad and buttered sourdough bread.

Shore Crab Bisque

As kids, we got hours of entertainment from shore crabs. Flipping rocks at low tide looking for the biggest ones, then playing baseball with them and a piece of driftwood. As an adult (albeit a childish one), I'm astonished at how a humble bucket of them can be transformed into something so sophisticated.

Serves 8

2 lb (900 g) shore crabs
2 tbsp (30 mL) unsalted butter
1 tbsp (15 mL) olive oil
1 large onion, finely chopped
1 large fennel bulb, finely chopped
3 stalks celery, finely chopped
2 cloves garlic, peeled and crushed
1 fresh bay leaf
1 tsp (5 mL) paprika (not smoked)
A pinch of cayenne pepper
1 cup (250 mL) white wine
½ lb (225 g) ripe tomatoes, peeled,
   seeded and finely chopped
⅔ cup (150 mL) apple brandy
7 cups (1.75 L) fish stock
2 large sprigs fresh tarragon
¼ cup (60 mL) whipping cream
1 tbsp (15 mL) lemon juice
Sea salt and freshly cracked
   black pepper

Bring a large pot of heavily salted water to a boil. Drop in the crabs, bring back to a boil and cook for 2 minutes. Remove the crabs, allow to cool a little and chop them coarsely with a knife of little value to you.

Heat the butter and olive oil together in a large, heavy pot over medium-low heat. Add the onion, fennel, celery, garlic and bay leaf. Cook gently, stirring occasionally, until the vegetables are soft but not browning, 5 to 7 minutes. Stir in the paprika and cayenne and cook for another minute or two.

Add the wine, tomatoes and crabs and cook for about 6 minutes. Pour in the brandy and bring to a simmer, then flame the brandy. When the flames die down, add the stock and tarragon. Simmer gently until reduced by one-quarter, 30 to 45 minutes. Remove from the heat.

Strain a ladleful of the soup at a time through a fine-mesh sieve, pushing as much liquid through as you can. Pass the soup through a fine strainer into a clean pot. Bring to a simmer, stir in the cream and simmer until reduced to a napping consistency. Add the lemon juice and season with salt and pepper. Serve in warmed bowls with buttered brown bread.

Greenling with Seaweed Butter

Greenling are found in the subarctic waters of the North Pacific. Because of the depth, they're difficult to catch, so you don't see them much (ling cod would be a good substitute in this dish). So when fisherman Frank calls to say he has one or two that he isn't going to eat himself, I jump on them right away.

Greenling live in kelp beds, which gave me the idea to grill them in a butter made with sea lettuce, a type of seaweed that gives off the most amazing aroma of truffles when cooked. (Think of it as free truffles!) If you can't get your hands on any, kombu or dulse, which are both readily available in health food stores and Asian markets, would be good substitutes.

Serves 6, with leftover butter

FOR THE SEAWEED BUTTER
2 cups (500 mL) sea lettuce, washed well
1 lb (450 g) unsalted butter, at room temperature

FOR THE CRISPY SEA LETTUCE
A couple of good-sized handfuls of sea lettuce, cleaned
Canola oil for deep-frying
3 tbsp (45 mL) black sesame seeds, toasted
1 tbsp (15 mL) sugar
Sea salt

FOR THE GREENLING
6 centre-cut greenling fillets (6 oz/170 g each)
Canola oil
Good-quality cider vinegar
Flaky sea salt

FOR THE SEAWEED BUTTER
If you have an electric oven, set it to its lowest setting. Place the sea lettuce on a wire rack set over a baking sheet. Put it in the oven, with the door slightly ajar, and leave until dried. If you have a gas oven, leave the lettuce in the oven overnight with the door closed; the heat from the pilot light should dry it out by morning.

In a spice grinder, blitz the lettuce to a fine powder.

In a stand mixer fitted with the paddle attachment, mix the butter and the powdered seaweed on low speed just until the seaweed is completely incorporated. Don't overmix the butter.

Turn out the butter onto a sheet of plastic wrap and roll it into a neat and even log. Wrap tightly and prick with a skewer to remove any air bubbles. Transfer to the fridge to chill completely.

FOR THE CRISPY SEA LETTUCE
Thoroughly wash and dry the sea lettuce. Drying is important, or else the sea lettuce will spit like crazy when it's fried. (Think about frying bacon without a shirt on, then multiply that by ten.)

Heat the oil in a deep-fryer or deep, heavy pot to 350°F (180°C). Working in batches if necessary, fry the sea lettuce until crispy, about 45 seconds. Drain on paper towels. Toss the seaweed with the sesame seeds and the sugar, and lightly season with sea salt. Set aside (lettuce will stay crisp for up to 2 hours).

FOR THE GREENLING
Position a rack in the middle of the oven and heat the broiler to high.

Cut six pieces of parchment paper into squares a bit larger than the fillets; lightly grease them with canola oil. Place a fillet on each piece of paper and transfer to a baking sheet, leaving plenty of room between each piece to baste the fish easily. Top each fillet with 2 generous slices of seaweed butter.

Broil until the butter has melted, then remove the baking sheet from the oven and generously baste the fish with the melted butter. Continue to baste every 2 minutes until the fish has cooked to medium, 10 to 12 minutes total depending on the thickness of the fillets—trust your gut. Remove the baking sheet from the oven and allow the fish to rest for 5 minutes, constantly basting with the melted butter.

Transfer the fish to six warmed plates, spoon a little bit of the butter over the fish and sprinkle with a couple of drops of the cider vinegar. Finish with a few flakes of sea salt and serve with a bowl of the crispy sea lettuce in the middle of the table.

Salmon Candy

This is as classic West Coast as it gets. Originally called Indian candy (and for obvious reasons no longer called that), it is strips of salmon smoked for so long that they are basically jerky. Originally it was a means of preserving the fish so it could be held without refrigeration and was convenient to carry on long trips. Nowadays the fish is usually lacquered with something sweet such as brown sugar, honey, molasses or, as I do it, with maple syrup.

Any type of salmon (except farmed garbage) can be used, but I prefer keta, because the long, uniform shape makes the curing time the same for all the pieces. The bellies and collars are the best bits, and should be considered the "cook's treat" and eaten hot right out of the smoker.

Makes 5 lb (2.25 kg)

1 cup (250 mL) kosher salt
6 cups (1.5 L) water
2 skinless keta (chum) salmon fillets
  (about 5 lb/2.25 kg each),
  pin bones removed
5 cups (1.25 L) maple syrup

In a large bowl, dissolve the salt in the water. Slice the salmon across the fillet into ½-inch (1 cm) slices and place them in the brine. Refrigerate for 8 hours.

Drain the salmon, pat dry and return it to the dried bowl. Add the maple syrup and refrigerate for another 8 hours.

Strain the salmon and set aside the syrup. Place the salmon on a wire rack set over a baking sheet and refrigerate, uncovered and near the fan, for 12 hours to develop the pellicle.

Prepare a smoker. Heat 4 cups (1 L) of maple wood chips on the heating element until they start to smoke. Place the salmon pieces on the smoking racks and put them in the smoker. Hot-smoke the salmon until the maple chips run out. Discard the chips, replenish the chip tray, and repeat this process so that the fish has done two full cycles of hot smoke. This will take about 1½ hours.

The salmon is best eaten straight away while still warm. If you are going to hold it, place the salmon slices in an even layer in vacuum bags with a few spoonfuls of the reserved syrup. Vacuum-sealed, they will hold for up to 3 months in the fridge.

Raw Sockeye Salmon and Tomatoes

Of the five species of salmon indigenous to the Pacific, sockeye is the one that gets people the most excited. The high fat content and deep red flesh give this fish great flavour and visual appeal. August and the first half of September are sockeye season, and I'd go out fishing for them just about every year when I lived out West. These days I trust the boys at Organic Ocean to send me their best sockeye. At the peak of the season, when the fish is pristinely fresh, I like to treat it simply and serve it raw, dressed only with a few tomatoes and basil. This dish looks great and tastes extremely red, if that makes sense. Plan this for a group of friends on a nice summer day.

Serves 6 or more

FOR THE TOMATO WATER
5 lb (2.25 kg) ripe, heavy tomatoes
Leaves from 1 bunch fresh basil
2 cloves garlic
1 tbsp (15 mL) kosher salt

FOR THE TOMATO VINAIGRETTE
1 cup (250 mL) reduced tomato
   water, divided
1½ sheets gelatin
1 tbsp (15 mL) lemon juice
A pinch of cayenne pepper
Kosher salt

FOR THE SOCKEYE SALMON
1 skinless sockeye salmon fillet
   (1½ lb/675 g), pin bones
   removed

TO FINISH THE DISH
Basil seeds
Cherry and currant tomatoes of
   mixed colours and shapes
Sea salt and black pepper
½ cup (125 mL) good-quality
   olive oil
Different varieties of basil
   leaves and basil flowers

FOR THE TOMATO WATER
The day before you plan to serve this dish, remove the core and stem from the tomatoes. In a blender, purée the tomatoes with the basil, garlic and kosher salt until smooth.

Line a large glass bowl with a quadruple layer of cheesecloth. Carefully pour in the tomato purée without spilling any over the sides of the cheesecloth. Bunch up the corners of the cheesecloth to create a pouch and securely tie it closed with butcher's string, creating something that resembles Santa's sack. Do not squeeze the sack.

Transfer the bowl to the refrigerator and tie the sack to a shelf with the string so that it is suspended a few inches above the bowl. (Alternatively, you can hang the bag from the handle of a kitchen cupboard.) Allow to drain overnight; you will be left with crystal-clear, intensely flavoured tomato liquid. Discard the sack or save the tomatoes to make sauce.

Gently simmer the tomato water until it is reduced by one-third. Cool over an ice bath.

FOR THE TOMATO VINAIGRETTE
Bring ¼ cup (60 mL) of the reduced tomato water to a low simmer. Meanwhile, soften the gelatin in cold water. Squeeze the excess water from the gelatin and add it to the warm tomato water, stirring to dissolve. In a bowl, whisk together the gelatinized tomato water, the remaining ¾ cup (175 mL) tomato water, the lemon juice and cayenne. Season with kosher salt. Transfer to the refrigerator to set.

FOR THE SOCKEYE SALMON
Starting at the head end, and using a sharp knife, cut a ⅝-inch (1.5 cm) slice from the fillet in one smooth motion. Continue slicing the rest of the fillet in the same manner until you get close to the tail. (Save the tail piece for tartare or a sandwich for your lunch tomorrow.)

Lay the slices evenly and neatly on your cutting board and gently score the surface of the flesh. This will tenderize the slices and create a nice mouthfeel.

TO FINISH THE DISH
Plump the basil seeds in warm water for 5 minutes, then drain.

Cut the tomatoes into irregular pieces, leaving some of the very small ones whole; season with sea salt and pepper. Season the salmon with sea salt and pepper and arrange how you like on chilled serving plates. Stir the olive oil into the remaining tomato water. Arrange the tomatoes around the salmon and spoon some of the tomato vinaigrette on and around the salmon. Place small mounds of the basil seeds near a few of the tomatoes and garnish with the basil leaves and flowers.

Devilled Spot Prawns

This is essentially a ceviche of spot prawns—just the little bit of acid from the lemon and the tomatoes "cook" them. I made this dish right on Frank and Steve's boat. The prawns were out of the water only as long as it took us to clean them, and their fresh, sweet flavour was phenomenal. You could substitute lobster or wild salmon, but please don't use those crappy tiger shrimp. Serve this on a beautiful platter outside in the summer and let everyone dig in. The spot prawn garum takes a good six weeks to mature. Substitute Thai fish sauce if you prefer.

Serves 6

1 shallot
Zest and juice of 1 lemon
1 jalapeño pepper, seeded and
  finely chopped
Flaky sea salt and black pepper
  to taste
4 lb (1.8 kg) fresh spot prawns,
  peeled and heads removed
1 serrano chili, sliced paper thin
1 Thai bird chili, sliced paper thin
2 cloves garlic, very finely chopped
2½ cups (625 mL) seeded and
  chopped really ripe good tomatoes
  of different varieties, shapes and
  colours
3 tbsp (45 mL) really good olive oil
3 tbsp (45 mL) torn fresh mint leaves
2 tbsp (30 mL) thinly sliced Italian
  parsley
2 tbsp (30 mL) finely minced chives
2 tbsp (30 mL) nonpareil capers,
  rinsed
1 tbsp (15 mL) spot prawn garum
  (see sidebar)
2 tsp (10 mL) Société-Orignal dried
  clay pepper (or 1 tsp/5 mL sweet
  smoked paprika)
Torn fresh chive blossoms and fennel
  fronds to garnish

Slice the shallot into thin rings and soak in ice water for 10 minutes.

In a bowl, whisk together the lemon zest and juice, jalapeño, salt and pepper to make the dressing.

In a large bowl, combine the prawns, serrano and Thai bird chilies, garlic, tomatoes, oil, mint, parsley, chives, capers, spot prawn garum and clay pepper. Toss with some of the dressing. Adjust the seasoning.

Transfer the salad to a large serving plate in a nice organic layer. Drizzle over the remaining dressing and shower the top with the chive blossoms and fennel fronds. Sprinkle with some flakes of salt and a few twists of pepper.

SPOT PRAWN GARUM

This is a Canadian version of the classic Roman fish sauce. Make sure to use the freshest prawn heads to yield the best results. It is especially good in marinades that will eventually see a charcoal grill.

To make this recipe, you'll need as many fresh spot prawn heads as you can get your hands on and 11% salt by weight of the heads.

In a nonreactive container, mix the spot prawn heads with the salt. Cover the container with a quadruple layer of cheesecloth and secure it with butcher's string. Store in a cool, dark place until the mixture smells a little bit worse than death, about 6 weeks.

Carefully decant the mixture through a coffee filter, discarding the solids. (Garum keeps in a sealed container in the fridge for up to 6 months.)

Mussels with Peas and Brown Scones

The mussels that come from Out Landish Shellfish Guild in Heriot Bay on the backside of Quadra Island are the best I've ever tasted. The water is so cold and nutrient rich that they are huge. The meat is the same size as the shell. Briny and sweet, these are the polar opposite of those sad specimens we've all been served at one point or another. The sweetness made me think of peas and, since we were there in the spring, wild garlic bulbs.

Serves 4, with extra scones

FOR THE SCONES
2¼ cups (550 mL) all-purpose flour
¾ cup (175 mL) Red Fife flour
3 tbsp (45 mL) sugar
3 tbsp (45 mL) baking powder
1 tsp (5 mL) kosher salt
½ lb (225 g) cold unsalted butter, cubed
1¼ cups (300 mL) buttermilk, divided

FOR THE MASHED POTATOES
2 lb (900 g) russet potatoes, peeled and cut into quarters
4 tbsp (60 mL) unsalted butter
2 cups (500 mL) chopped wild garlic bulbs and leaves
Kosher salt and black pepper
¼ cup (60 mL) milk
2 tbsp (30 mL) whipping cream
A pinch of nutmeg

FOR THE MUSSELS
⅓ cup (75 mL) olive oil
1 cup (250 mL) finely minced shallots
1 tbsp (15 mL) finely chopped fresh thyme
4 lb (1.8 kg) Pacific mussels, cleaned and debearded
½ cup (125 mL) white wine
½ cup (125 mL) chicken and pork stock (see basic stock, page 238)
1½ cups (375 mL) frozen peas
½ cup (125 mL) unsalted butter, cubed
Kosher salt and black pepper
Lemon juice
¼ cup (60 mL) thinly sliced Italian parsley
¼ lb (115 g) pea shoots

FOR THE SCONES
Preheat the oven to 375°F (190°C).

In a food processor, combine the flours, sugar, baking powder and salt; pulse to mix. Add the butter and pulse just until the mixture resembles coarse sand. Add 1 cup (250 mL) of the buttermilk and process again, stopping the moment the mixture comes together. Do not overwork the dough.

Turn the dough out onto a lightly floured counter and roll it out until it is 1 inch (2.5 cm) thick. Using a round cookie cutter, cut the dough into 12 pieces, or cut into 12 triangles with a knife.

Transfer the scones to a parchment-lined baking sheet and brush the tops with the remaining ¼ cup (60 mL) buttermilk. Bake for 20 to 25 minutes, until they are golden brown. Transfer to a wire rack to cool.

FOR THE MASHED POTATOES
Boil the potatoes in a large pot of salted water until tender. Drain them and allow them to steam in the colander while you cook the garlic.

Rinse and dry the pot, and in it melt the butter over medium heat until it starts to foam. Add the wild garlic, season with salt and pepper, and cook, stirring frequently, until the garlic has softened, about 4 minutes. Remove from the heat.

Add the potatoes and mash them with a wooden spoon. Stir in the milk and cream, taking care not to overwork the mixture. Season with salt, pepper and nutmeg. Keep warm.

FOR THE MUSSELS
Heat a large, heavy pot over medium-high heat and add the olive oil. Once hot, add the shallots and thyme; sauté until the shallots are translucent. Add the mussels and stir to coat them with the oil. Add the wine and bring to a simmer. Add the stock, cover and cook for 3 minutes.

Remove the mussels as they start to open, transferring them to a tray. Discard any mussels that don't open. Once all the mussels have been removed, turn up the heat and reduce the liquid by one-third.

Add the peas and the butter, stirring to incorporate all the butter. Remove from the heat and season with the salt, pepper and lemon juice.

Return the mussels to the pot and add the parsley and pea shoots. Stir to coat the mussels with the sauce and wilt the shoots.

TO FINISH THE DISH
Place a scoop of potato in each of four warmed large bowls. Divide the mussels and the sauce between the bowls. Serve with a plate of scones in the middle of the table.

Pickled Sardines and 'Nduja

A piece of grilled bread smeared with 'nduja, topped with these sardines and some dressed pickled vegetables is a true pleasure.

Makes 10 sardines

FOR THE PICKLED SARDINES
1½ cups (375 mL) water
1 cup (250 mL) white wine vinegar
1¼ cups (300 mL) kosher salt
2 tbsp (30 mL) sugar
1 tsp (5 mL) red chili flakes
1 fresh bay leaf, lightly bruised
10 black peppercorns
1 red onion, thinly sliced
4 cloves garlic, thinly sliced
2 stalks celery, very thinly sliced
2 smaller carrots, peeled and
  finely julienned
2 tbsp (30 mL) finely chopped
  Italian parsley
A drizzle of extra virgin olive oil
10 sardines, filleted and belly
  bones removed

TO FINISH THE DISH
Good extra virgin olive oil
Sea salt and black pepper
2 tbsp (30 mL) chopped
  Italian parsley
'Nduja
Grilled bread
4 sprigs fresh dill
Flaky sea salt

FOR THE PICKLED SARDINES

In a medium bowl, combine the water, vinegar, kosher salt, sugar, chili flakes, bay leaf and peppercorns; stir to dissolve the salt and sugar. Add the onion, garlic, celery, carrots and parsley; fold together and allow the vegetables to soften for 5 minutes.

Using a slotted spoon, spread half of the vegetable mixture in a shallow nonreactive dish large enough to hold the sardines in one layer. Lay the sardine fillets on top, skin side facing the sun. Evenly distribute the remaining vegetables over the fillets, then pour over the pickling liquid. Cover tightly and refrigerate for 8 to 12 hours, depending on the size of your fillets.

TO FINISH THE DISH

When it comes time to serve the fish, remove the sardines from the pickling liquid and set aside. Turn the vegetables and half of the pickling liquid into a bowl, drizzle in some quality extra virgin olive oil and season with sea salt and pepper. Return the fillets to the bowl, add the parsley and gently toss.

Smear some 'nduja on grilled bread and top with some sardine fillets and some of the vegetables. Tear the fresh dill sprigs over everything and sprinkle with flaky sea salt.

Albacore Mojama

On a recent trip to Spain with Grant van Gameren from Toronto's Bar Isabel and Chris, I fell in love with the simple dish of thinly sliced mojama, garnished with only a few almonds and some good olive oil. The tuna loins are salted and hung to dry in the ocean air until they are the texture of stale fudge. I immediately thought of the amazing albacore that I get from Frank and Steve out of Haida Gwaii in northern BC. The water is frigid, resulting in beautiful loins of "fatty luv" as they call it. Why couldn't we take this inspiration and create something Canadian? This makes 500 grams of finished product—more than you'll need to serve four—but it keeps well, vacuum-sealed in the refrigerator, for a couple of months. Like most charcuterie, the quality of the end result depends solely on the quality of the product you start with.

Serves 4

FOR THE TUNA
14 oz (400 g) kosher salt
5 oz (140 g) sugar
2 lb (900 g) centre-cut albacore
  tuna loins

FOR THE LEMON JAM
(MAKES 1 CUP/250 ML)
8 lemons
½ cup (125 mL) sugar
1 cup (250 mL) + 2 tbsp (30 mL)
  water
2 tsp (10 mL) unsalted butter
Kosher salt

TO FINISH THE DISH
32 toasted whole almonds
24 Italian parsley leaves
Very good olive oil

FOR THE TUNA

Combine the kosher salt and sugar. Spread a ½-inch (1 cm) layer of the cure in a non-reactive baking dish. Place the tuna pieces on top and cover with the remaining cure. Cover with plastic wrap, place some weights on top of the tuna (soup cans, for example) and refrigerate for 18 hours.

Rinse the fish thoroughly under cold running water and pat dry with paper towels. Place the tuna on a wire rack set over a small baking sheet and refrigerate, uncovered, for 48 hours to distribute the cure flavours evenly.

Wrap each piece of tuna in cheesecloth and tie with butcher's string. Hang the tuna in a cool, dark place—ideally at 60°F (15°C) with 75% humidity—for 18 to 24 days. The tuna will lose about 40% of its volume and the colour will intensify.

FOR THE LEMON JAM

Using a vegetable peeler, remove the peel from the lemons. Juice the lemons; strain and reserve the juice.

Place the lemon peel in a small pot and cover with water. Bring to a simmer. Drain, return the peel to the pot, and repeat two more times.

Return the peel to the pot and add the sugar and 1 cup (250 mL) water. Bring to a gentle simmer and cook for 30 minutes, until the peels are very tender. Strain, reserving the syrup.

In a blender, combine the peels with 2 tbsp (30 mL) syrup, 2 tbsp (30 mL) reserved lemon juice and 2 tbsp (30 mL) water. Blend on high speed until very smooth. Blend in the butter and season with kosher salt.

Force the jam through a fine-mesh sieve and transfer to a squeeze bottle. (Jam keeps, refrigerated, for up to 2 weeks.)

TO FINISH THE DISH

Thinly slice the albacore mojama into 32 even pieces. Place 8 slices of tuna neatly on four plates. Dot the lemon jam around the slices. Arrange 8 almonds and 6 parsley leaves on each plate. Generously drizzle the olive oil over the mojama.

Halibut with Sauce Messine

Halibut caught in the frigid waters of the Pacific by the hands of Frank and Steve from Ocean Organic is tough to beat. These fish live in deep waters, are caught by hand and are huge, making the centre cut of the loin a perfect canvas for this French sauce from Lorraine. Here I slowly bake the fillets, so as not to colour them, letting the rich halibut flavour be the star.

Serves 4

FOR THE SAUCE

2 tbsp (30 mL) unsalted butter
1 tsp (5 mL) all-purpose flour
1 tsp (5 mL) Dijon mustard
2 egg yolks
⅔ cup (150 mL) whipping cream
2 shallots, finely minced
1 tbsp (15 mL) finely chopped
  fresh tarragon
1 tbsp (15 mL) finely chopped
  fresh chervil
1 tbsp (15 mL) finely chopped
  Italian parsley
1 tbsp (15 mL) finely minced chives
Juice of ½ lemon
Kosher salt and white pepper

FOR THE HALIBUT

4 centre-cut boneless halibut loins
  (8 oz/225 g each)
Kosher salt and white pepper
2 tbsp (30 mL) unsalted butter,
  at room temperature, divided, for
  buttering the parchment

FOR THE SAUCE

In a medium saucepan, bring an inch or so of water to a simmer.

In a small bowl, work together the butter, flour and mustard to make a paste.

In a heatproof bowl, combine the egg yolks, cream, shallots and butter mixture. Place the bowl over the simmering water and whisk until the sauce starts to thicken and become glossy. You're aiming for the texture of a light hollandaise that holds some shape.

Remove from the heat and stir in the tarragon, chervil, parsley and chives. Season with the lemon juice, kosher salt and pepper. Keep in a warm place.

FOR THE HALIBUT

Preheat the oven to 350°F (180°C).

Season the halibut with the kosher salt and pepper and place it on a piece of buttered parchment paper in a casserole dish large enough to hold all the fish without crowding. Cover with another piece of buttered parchment, buttered side down, and bake until a metal skewer or the tip of a sharp paring knife pierces the flesh without resistance, 12 to 15 minutes. Remove from the oven and allow the fish to rest for 5 minutes, basting it a couple of times with any juices that have accumulated in the pan.

Transfer the fish to four warmed plates and nap the sauce over the middle of the fish. Serve the extra sauce on the side with lots of crusty bread.

Pop's Smoked Oysters

These are a staple at my parents' house, and always come out when there is company, part of a spread of smoked salmon, chopped onion, Mom's pickles and Triscuits. My pop has been making these for as long as I can remember, and they are so incredible. My only complaint is that he is super stingy with them. He cans hundreds of oysters each year, and whenever he comes to visit, he asks, "You want me to bring some oysters?" The answer is always yes, and he brings one little jar. Yet my sister seems to have a constant supply in her cupboard.

I suggest buying larger oysters for this so you don't end up with sad specimens after they have been cooked. Pop uses soup oysters for this, which are large oysters that have been damaged while being shucked. You can easily reduce the recipe to make less.

**Makes 16 to 20 cups
(4 to 5 L)**

FOR THE BRINE
4 cups (1 L) water
½ cup (125 mL) kosher salt
½ cup (125 mL) sugar

FOR THE OYSTERS
20 cups (5 L) shucked extra-large
   soup oysters
Olive oil

FOR THE BRINE
In a large pot, bring 2 cups (500 mL) of the water, the salt and sugar to a boil to dissolve the salt and sugar. Remove from the heat and add the remaining water. Allow to cool completely.

FOR THE OYSTERS
Thoroughly wash the oysters under cold water.

Bring a large pot of water to a boil. Working in batches, put some oysters in a large strainer, lower them into the water and blanch for 90 seconds. Rinse under cold water to cool, then spill the oysters into the brine. Repeat with the remaining oysters and allow to marinate for 1 hour.

Drain the oysters, transfer to a wire rack set over a tray and allow to air-dry for 1 hour.

Prepare a smoker. Heat 4 cups (1 L) of alder wood chips in the heating pan until they start to smoke. Place the oysters on the smoking racks and hot-smoke for 1 hour.

Pack the oysters into ½-pint (250 mL) canning jars, leaving ¼-inch (5 mm) headspace at the top. Drizzle 1 tsp (5 mL) olive oil into each jar. Seal the jars. Place the jars in a pressure cooker and cook until the gauge reads 10 psi. Maintain this pressure for 75 minutes. Turn off the heat and allow the gauge to return to zero.

Make sure all the lids have fully sealed and let the jars stand at room temperature for 24 hours before using. (Oysters keep for up to 1 year.)

HOME

Sunday nights were always a big deal when I was growing up. My mom would pull out all the stops: roast beef, Yorkshire pudding, some variation on potatoes that inevitably featured unhealthy amounts of cheese and cream, always carrots. Lemon meringue pie was a favourite dessert, and After Eight wafers if it was a special occasion. Dinnertime was important every night of the week, though, and those fresh, homemade meals, which always made the house smell so good, instilled in me a love of cooking and sharing meals with family and friends. Derek's house was the same. I know this because one day towards the end of our cross-Canada journey we visited his folks in Campbell River, the salmon capital of the world, on the east coast of Vancouver Island, and his mom put on a feast for us that was among the best we ate on our whole trip.

"You've got to try these," Derek says as soon as we arrive, handing me a smoked oyster on a toothpick. "My dad makes them every year. They're the best." They are great, but are even better when topping a Stoned Wheat Thin, that greatest of Canadian crackers. Well, except for the Triscuit, maybe. There are Triscuits, too, of course, and sharp, homemade pickles and No Name cream cheese to go with Derek's dad's smoked salmon.

The table is set with the family's best china, and everyone gets their own little salt and pepper shaker and butter container for the fresh buns that are swaddled in a bowl. We all sit down, and Derek's mom brings out the dishes: vibrant carrots scattered with fresh dill; boiled baby potatoes with butter, salt and pepper; a simple salad dressed with white vinegar and oil. The centrepiece, though, is an enormous pork shoulder topped with a crisp, blistered crackling.

"Derek taught me this recipe," Mrs. Dammann says, admitting that it took some convincing for her to leave the shoulder out on the counter overnight, with salt and fennel seeds rubbed into the scored fat to help draw out the moisture and make the best crackling. "It's a big piece of meat," Derek points out, "and if you put fridge-cold pork into a blistering-hot oven, you just get steam and not that great crackly puff."

You can't argue with results. The pork (see recipe on page 77) is tender, moist and deeply flavourful. Covered in a rich gravy, it's as good a piece of meat as you'll find anywhere. We eat so much of it that by the time the pizzelle—traditional Italian waffle cookies—show up, rolled into coronets and stuffed with aniseed-and-chocolate-flavoured whipped cream, it is a struggle to eat more than two.

Afterwards, as if on cue, we all settle in the living room and wait for digestion to kick in. Now that Derek and I both have kids of our own, it's these kinds of traditions that we want to pass on to them. Big roasts on special occasions, of course, but also the day-to-day dishes that we loved growing up and still love today. These are the recipes we think of when we think of home.

Sausage and Peppers

A toss-up for my favourite meal of all time. Nona and Mom always used green peppers, for which I have a soft spot in my heart, and in my opinion, they really make this dish sing. Here's my version of their classic recipe.

Serves 6

FOR THE SAUSAGE
4 lb (1.8 kg) skinless, boneless
  pork shoulder
2 lb (900 g) pancetta
3 tbsp (45 mL) dried oregano
3 tbsp (45 mL) kosher salt
2 tbsp (30 mL) black pepper
2 tbsp (30 mL) red chili flakes
2 tbsp (30 mL) fennel seeds
½ cup (125 mL) white wine
6 feet (1.8 m) hog casings,
  well rinsed

FOR THE SOFRITO
3½ cups (875 mL) finely diced onion
1 cup (250 mL) olive oil
Kosher salt and black pepper to taste
1½ lb (675 g) Roma tomatoes,
  peeled, seeded and finely diced
1 tsp (5 mL) minced garlic

FOR THE PEPPERS
6 sweet yellow peppers
6 sweet red peppers
Canola oil
Kosher salt and black pepper
1½ cups (375 mL) chicken and pork
  stock (see basic stock, page 238)
¾ cup (175 mL) sofrito
1 tsp (5 mL) Société-Orignal dried
  clay pepper or ½ tsp (2 mL) sweet
  smoked paprika
2 tbsp (30 mL) finely chopped
  Italian parsley
6 leaves fresh basil, torn
A drizzle of good-quality olive oil

FOR THE SAUSAGE
Chill a large bowl along with the meat-grinder and sausage-stuffer attachments.

Fit the meat grinder with the largest die and grind the pork and pancetta, catching them in the chilled bowl. Add the oregano, salt, pepper, chili flakes, fennel seeds and wine. Using your hands, combine thoroughly. (Do this quickly, or the warmth of your hands will start to melt the fat.)

Using the sausage stuffer, fill the casings with the meat and tie them into 8-inch (20 cm) links. Prick the sausages with a sterilized pin, arrange on a wire rack set over a baking sheet, and refrigerate, uncovered, overnight to allow the casings to relax.

FOR THE SOFRITO
In a large, heavy saucepan over medium heat, combine the onions, oil, salt and pepper. Slowly start to sauté. Turn down the heat to the lowest setting and cook, stirring occasionally, until the onions are an even, rich golden brown, about 2 hours.

Add the tomatoes, cover with a round of parchment paper, and cook until the tomato liquid has evaporated and the mixture is starting to fry in the oil, 15 to 20 minutes.

Remove from the heat and season with salt and pepper. Stir in the garlic and allow the sofrito to cool in the pan. Strain the sofrito in a colander, reserving the oil for a nice vinaigrette.

FOR THE PEPPERS
Place the oven racks in the middle and lower third of the oven and preheat the oven to 400°F (200°C).

In a large bowl, toss the peppers with just enough canola oil to coat them. Season with salt and pepper. Transfer the peppers to two parchment-lined baking sheets and roast the peppers, switching and rotating the baking sheets halfway, until the skin is blistering, about 40 minutes. Return the peppers to the bowl, cover tightly with plastic wrap and allow to steam.

When the peppers are cool enough to touch, peel and seed them, reserving the resting juices. Tear them by hand into rough strips about ¾ inch (2 cm) wide.

In a medium, heavy saucepan, combine the peppers, their resting juices, the stock, sofrito, and clay pepper. Season with salt and pepper and bring to a simmer over medium heat. Cook, uncovered and stirring occasionally, for 40 minutes to soften the peppers and reduce the stock. Remove from the heat and stir in the parsley and basil. Allow to sit for a few hours before serving. Anoint with some olive oil.

TO FINISH THE DISH
Grill the sausages over charcoal for 8 minutes per side. Transfer them to a plate.

Spoon the peppers onto a large platter and top with the grilled sausages. Drizzle over any resting juices that have come off the sausages. Serve with lots of crusty bread and aïoli (see page 243).

Cold Roast Chicken

Of my favourite things to eat, this could be No. 2. It's not exactly cold, but just left on the counter for a couple of hours after roasting—call it Counter-Temp Roast Chicken. I adore food after it has sat out for a while.

Serves 4 to 6

FOR THE CHICKEN
1 good-quality chicken (3 lb/1.35 kg)
Leaves from 4 sprigs fresh thyme
Leaves from 2 sprigs fresh rosemary
Leaves from 1 sprig fresh sage
4 cloves garlic, peeled and lightly
   crushed
3 tbsp (45 mL) kosher salt
Freshly ground black pepper

FOR THE COLESLAW
¼ cup (60 mL) red wine vinegar
¼ cup (60 mL) cider vinegar
1 tbsp (15 mL) honey
½ head red cabbage, thinly sliced
½ head green cabbage, thinly sliced
½ red onion, thinly sliced
1 carrot, peeled and grated
Kosher salt and black pepper
½ cup (125 mL) mayonnaise
   (see page 236)
¼ cup (60 mL) finely chopped
   Italian parsley
2 tbsp (30 mL) finely chopped chives
A pinch of cayenne pepper

FOR THE BLACK PEPPER GRAVY
¼ cup (60 mL) reserved chicken fat
3 tbsp (45 mL) all-purpose flour
1½ tbsp (20 mL) freshly cracked
   black pepper
2 cups (500 mL) whole milk
1 tbsp (15 mL) crème fraîche
   (see page 241)
A few drops of apple vinegar
   (see page 163)
Kosher salt

FOR THE CHICKEN
Using your fingers, gently loosen the skin of the chicken around the breasts and thighs.

Finely chop the thyme, rosemary and sage and stir together with the garlic. Stuff the herbs evenly under the loosened skin. Season the chicken all over with the salt. Place the chicken on a wire rack set over a tray and refrigerate for 4 hours.

Rinse off the salt, taking care not to get any water under the skin, and return the chicken to the rack. Refrigerate, uncovered and near the fan, overnight to dry the skin.

Preheat the oven to 475°F (240°C). Truss the chicken to ensure even cooking.

Heat a large cast-iron frying pan in the oven for 10 minutes. When the pan is smoking hot, place the chicken breast side up in the pan and roast in the oven for 40 minutes. Turn the chicken over and roast for an additional 15 to 20 minutes, until the juices run clear when the thigh joint is pierced. Transfer the chicken to a platter to rest. Reserve the fat and juices in the pan and any that gather from the chicken while it rests. You can rest the chicken for 30 minutes before carving and serving, but I like to let it sit for 2 hours on the counter first.

The fats and resting juices will eventually separate. Skim the fat from the juices and reserve the fat and the juices for the gravy.

FOR THE COLESLAW
Combine the vinegars in a small saucepan and reduce by half over medium heat. Remove from the heat and stir in the honey. Allow to cool to room temperature.

In a large bowl, combine the red and green cabbage, onion and carrot. Pour in the vinegar mixture, season with salt and pepper, and mix well. Allow the mixture to sit for 10 minutes, mixing again after 5 minutes.

Stir in the mayonnaise, parsley, chives and cayenne. Adjust the seasoning if necessary.

FOR THE BLACK PEPPER GRAVY
Heat the reserved chicken fat in a medium saucepan over medium heat. Using a wooden spoon, stir in the flour and the pepper until it forms a paste. Continue to cook the roux, stirring constantly, until it starts to smell nutty and is just on the edge of turning golden. Switch the spoon out for a whisk and gradually add the milk, whisking constantly until it comes to a boil, taking care that there are no lumps.

Add the reserved chicken juices. Turn down the heat to low and simmer, stirring frequently, until the gravy is thick and smooth, 7 to 10 minutes.

Remove from the heat and stir in the crème fraîche and vinegar. Season with salt. Strain through a sieve into a clean pot.

TO FINISH THE DISH
Reheat the gravy and pour it into a warmed gravy boat. Cut the chicken in half and place it on a serving plate. Mound the coleslaw in a chilled bowl.

Breakfast of Champions

I find that people are very ritualistic about their breakfast. At home, I really like the smorgasbord approach, with lots of platters of things to pick at and snack on. Not too eggy and not too sweet, with a good mix of land and sea. Plenty of coffee, stout and Caesars.

This is my spread for what I think is a winning brunch. It may look daunting, but you don't have to do everything—these are just the dishes I like to put out. You can do a lot ahead, and you can keep things warm in the oven until serving.

Makes a lot of each

FOR THE BLOOD CAKE
(SERVES 8 TO 10)
¼ cup (60 mL) + 2 tbsp (30 mL)
  rendered smoked pork fat
  (see page 154)
1 onion, finely chopped
6 cloves garlic, finely chopped
Leaves from 10 sprigs fresh
  marjoram, finely chopped
½ tsp (2 mL) mace
½ tsp (2 mL) ground allspice
4 cups (1 L) fresh pig's blood
¾ cup (175 mL) cornmeal (I use
  Société-Orignal sagamité flour)
Kosher salt and black pepper
½ lb (225 g) lardo (see page 105),
  cut into ¼-inch (5 mm) cubes
½ lb (225 g) tongue smoked meat
  (see page 55), cut into ¼-inch
  (5 mm) cubes

FOR THE WELSH RAREBIT
(FOR 4 SERVINGS)
2 tbsp (30 mL) unsalted butter
1 tbsp (15 mL) all-purpose flour
1 tsp (5 mL) Colman's or other
  hot dry mustard
A pinch of cayenne pepper
1 cup (250 mL) stout (I use one
  from Troue du diable in Quebec)
2 tbsp (30 mL) Worcestershire
  sauce, plus more to finish
1 lb (450 g) Avonlea Clothbound or
  other aged artisanal cheddar, grated
Kosher salt and black pepper
4 slices Pullman loaf (each ¾ inch/
  2 cm thick), toasted

FOR THE BLOOD CAKE
Preheat the oven to 350°F (180°C). Cut a piece of cardboard to fit just inside the top of a terrine mould or loaf pan; wrap it in plastic wrap. Line the mould with plastic wrap, leaving some overhang on both sides.

In a large, heavy saucepan over medium heat, heat ¼ cup (60 mL) smoked pork fat. Add the onion and garlic and sweat, stirring occasionally, until they are soft and translucent, but do not brown. Stir in the marjoram, mace and allspice. Slowly whisk in the blood. Whisking constantly, add the cornmeal in a slow, steady stream. Cook, stirring constantly, until the mixture is thick like porridge. (The mixture has to be on the thick side or else the lardo and the tongue will sink to the bottom as the cake cooks.) Season with salt and pepper. Transfer the mixture to a large bowl and fold in the lardo and the tongue.

Scrape the blood mixture into the terrine mould, spreading it evenly. Fold over the plastic wrap and cover the mould with the lid or foil. Place the mould in a deep baking pan and add enough hot water to come halfway up the side of the mould. Place the pan in the oven and cook for 1½ hours or until a wooden skewer comes out clean.

Remove the pan from the oven and allow the mould to cool in the water until you are able to handle it with bare hands. Place the mould on a baking sheet, fit the cardboard in position and put something heavy on top to press it down. Refrigerate overnight.

The next day, carefully unmould the blood cake and, with a sharp knife, cut a 1-inch (2.5 cm) slab for each serving. (Any leftovers keep well, wrapped in plastic wrap in the fridge for up to 5 days, or vacuum-sealed and frozen for up to 6 months.)

Heat a nonstick frying pan over medium-high heat for 2 minutes. Add 2 tbsp (30 mL) smoked pork fat and sauté the blood cake, turning once, until it is lightly crispy and warmed through. Transfer to warmed plates.

FOR THE WELSH RAREBIT
In a medium saucepan over medium heat, melt the butter and the flour together. Cook for 5 to 7 minutes, stirring with a wooden spoon, until the roux starts to smell nutty. Stir in the mustard and cayenne. Switch to a whisk and stir in the stout, whisking constantly to avoid lumps. Turn down the heat to low and gently simmer, stirring occasionally, for about 5 minutes. Stir in the Worcestershire sauce and remove from the heat.

Stir in the cheese until completely incorporated. Season with salt and pepper. Pour the rarebit mixture into a shallow nonreactive container and allow to set completely, about 3 hours.

FOR THE CURRY FRIES

4 lb (1.8 kg) russet potatoes, peeled and cut into chips 2½ × ¾ × ¾ inches (6 × 2 × 2 cm)

Canola oil for deep-frying

Kosher salt and black pepper

½ head cauliflower

4 tbsp (60 mL) canola oil, divided

2 inches (5 cm) fresh ginger, peeled

2 cloves garlic

6 green onions

1 fresh red chili pepper

1 bunch fresh cilantro

1 tsp (5 mL) black mustard seeds

1 tsp (5 mL) fenugreek seeds

1 tsp (5 mL) ground turmeric

1 whole clove, ground

¼ cup (60 mL) dried curry leaves

2 tomatoes, coarsely chopped

1 can (14 oz/400 mL) coconut milk

1 cup (250 mL) frozen peas

Leaves from ½ bunch fresh mint

½ cup (125 mL) plain yogurt

Juice of 1 lemon

2 tbsp (30 mL) fresh cilantro leaves

Put a rack in the middle of the oven and preheat the broiler.

Spread the rarebit mixture about ½ inch (1 cm) thick on each slice of toast. Transfer to a baking sheet and broil until the rarebit has melted smooth and is slightly golden in places, 6 to 8 minutes.

Remove from the oven and allow to rest for 5 minutes on the baking sheet. Any rarebit that has melted over the edges of the bread and onto the sheet will get nice and crispy.

Transfer the toasts to warmed plates. Using a knife, gently press down on the cheese in a criss-cross fashion to score the rarebit. Give each toast a splash of Worcestershire and serve immediately.

FOR THE CURRY FRIES

Place the potatoes in a bowl and rinse under warm running water for 10 minutes to remove any excess starch. Drain the potatoes and place them in a large pot of cold water. Bring to a simmer over medium heat and cook the potatoes until they are nearly falling apart, 18 to 22 minutes. Carefully remove the potatoes and spread them on a wire rack set over a baking sheet. Freeze for at least 1 hour to dry them out.

Heat the deep-frying oil in a deep, heavy pot or a deep-fryer to 300°F (150°C). Fry the potatoes in batches until a light crust forms, 5 to 7 minutes. Carefully transfer the potatoes to the wire rack again and leave them in the fridge near the fan, uncovered, for 24 hours. Reserve the oil in the pot.

Cut the cauliflower into medium florets, then cut each floret in half. Heat a large nonstick frying pan until almost smoking. Add 2 tbsp (30 mL) of the canola oil and the cauliflower florets, cut side down. Cook, without stirring, until the cauliflower is nicely charred on one side. Remove the florets from the pan and set aside.

In a food processor, pulse the ginger, garlic, green onions, chili and cilantro until smooth.

In a large, heavy saucepan, heat the remaining 2 tbsp (30 mL) canola oil until it is almost smoking. Add the mustard seeds; when they start to pop, add the fenugreek, turmeric, ground clove and curry leaves. Sauté until fragrant, then add the ginger-garlic mixture and sauté until everything is fragrant. Add the tomatoes and turn down the heat to medium.

When the tomatoes start to break down, pour in the coconut milk and bring to a simmer. Cook for 5 minutes, then turn the heat down to low. Add the charred cauliflower and the frozen peas and simmer gently for 30 minutes, until the mixture has thickened and the vegetables are quite cooked. Keep warm.

In the meantime, reserve 2 tbsp (30 mL) of the mint leaves for the garnish. Using a mortar and pestle, grind the remaining mint with a pinch of salt until you have a smooth green purée. Stir in the yogurt and season with salt and pepper.

Add the lemon juice to the curry and season to taste.

Just before serving, heat the reserved deep-frying oil to 365°F (185°C) and fry the potatoes until golden brown, 5 to 7 minutes. Drain well and season with salt. Place the fried potatoes on a serving plate and spoon the curry mixture over them. Drizzle the mint yogurt over the curry and tear the cilantro and reserved mint over top.

recipe continues . . .

**FOR THE PANCAKES AND BACON
(MAKES TWELVE 4-INCH/10 CM
PANCAKES)**

3 large eggs, separated
¾ cup + 1 tbsp (190 mL)
  all-purpose flour
1 tsp (5 mL) baking powder
⅔ cup (150 mL) whole milk
1 cup (250 mL) fresh or frozen
  wild blueberries
A pinch of kosher salt
About 3 tbsp (45 mL) unsalted butter
12 slices bacon (see page 239)
1 tbsp (15 mL) finely chopped
  Fresno chili, seeds intact (optional)
Really good maple syrup

FOR THE PANCAKES AND BACON

In a medium bowl, combine the egg yolks, flour, baking powder and milk; whisk to a smooth batter. Fold in the blueberries.

In a separate bowl, whisk the egg whites with the salt until they form stiff peaks. Gently fold the whites into the blueberry mixture.

Use a griddle or however many nonstick pans you feel comfortable handling at once. Heat your pan over medium heat. Add 1 tbsp (15 mL) of the butter to each pan, and when it starts to foam, ladle in some of the batter to make 4-inch (10 cm) pancakes. Gently cook the pancakes until the bottom looks golden and firm, about 2 minutes. Flip them over and do the same on the other side. Transfer the pancakes to a baking sheet (don't stack them) and keep warm in the oven. Repeat with the remaining batter.

In the meantime, cook your bacon how you like it.

Arrange a nice stack of the pancakes on a warmed plate. Mound the bacon on top and sprinkle over the chili, if using. Serve with copious amounts of maple syrup.

TO FINISH THE BREAKFAST

I usually plan on 2 eggs per person. I prefer "facing the sun," so if you have a large, nonstick pan, cook them all at once and slide one big sunny-side-up factory onto a platter. Set it in the middle of the table and let your friends help themselves.

Things that round out the breakfast and bring everything together:

Jars of Pop's smoked oysters (see page 210)
Salmon candy (see page 197)
Big plates of smoked salmon (see page 208)
Pickled sardines and 'nduja toasts (see page 205)
Dungeness crab tart (see page 193)
Swordfish bresaola (see page 19)
Clam chowder (see page 14)
Beer-battered beans (see page 123)

Have bottles of your favourite hot sauce on the table. My favourite, and in my opinion the absolute best, is Diablo's Fuego, made by our friend Rossy Earle in Ontario.

A Few Recipes for Pickles

Everything is better with pickles. My mom was big on canning, so we always had a variety to choose from, and there were always jars of pickles on the table to go with every meal. I don't really go the canning route—I'm more of a bucket-in-the-fridge kind of guy. I also process pickles on a large scale into vacuum bags. Kept refrigerated, they last up to a year. These are based on Mom's recipes. You can play with the amounts based on how many you want to make.

Makes 20 of each kind

DILL PICKLES
20 small pickling cucumbers
4 cups (1 L) white vinegar
4 cups (1 L) water
2 cups (500 mL) fresh dill
½ cup (125 mL) kosher salt
2 tbsp (30 mL) dill seeds
2 tsp (10 mL) red chili flakes
2 tsp (10 mL) coriander seeds
6 cloves garlic, peeled

BREAD AND BUTTER PICKLES
20 small pickling cucumbers
4 cups (1 L) cider vinegar
3 cups (750 mL) sugar
2 cups (500 mL) water
1 cup (250 mL) kosher salt
2 tbsp (30 mL) coriander seeds
2 tbsp (30 mL) celery seeds
2 tsp (10 mL) dry mustard
2 tsp (10 mL) ground turmeric

SPICY PICKLES
20 small pickling cucumbers
4 cups (1 L) white vinegar
4 cups (1 L) water
2 cups (500 mL) fresh dill
½ cup (125 mL) kosher salt
2 tbsp (30 mL) red chili flakes
2 tbsp (30 mL) dill seeds
1 tbsp (15 mL) sugar
1 tbsp (15 mL) black peppercorns
2 tsp (10 mL) coriander seeds
4 jalapeño peppers, sliced into
   ½-inch (1 cm) rings
6 cloves garlic, peeled

Wash the cucumbers well and place in a nonreactive container.

In a saucepan, bring the remaining ingredients to a rolling boil. Pour over the cucumbers. Allow to cool to room temperature.

Transfer the pickles and brine to an appropriately sized bucket and place a plate directly on top of the cucumbers to keep them submerged. Cover the pail and refrigerate for 2 weeks before using.

FUNDAMENTALS

Don't be fooled by their simplicity—the following recipes are some of the most important and versatile in the whole book. Having a great, herbaceous salsa verde, some smoky bacon and sticky, savoury oven-dried tomatoes in your repertoire gives you the chops to make something special out of even the simplest meal. The deliciousness of homemade chicken and pork stock, fresh pasta and a proper aïoli—a few of the most important basics in any cook's kitchen—are equalled only by the deep satisfaction that comes from making them.

Oven-Dried Tomatoes

These can be used in pastas or salads. They also make a nice addition to a charcuterie plate.

Makes 24 pieces

12 ripe Roma tomatoes
½ cup (125 mL) extra virgin olive oil
Leaves from 3 sprigs fresh thyme,
  branches reserved
1 tsp (5 mL) sugar
Kosher salt and black pepper

Preheat the oven to 200°F (100°C).

Bring a large pot of salted water to a boil, and have a large bowl of salted ice water at the ready. Core the tomatoes and score a small X in the bottom. Drop the tomatoes into the salted water, blanch for 15 seconds, then immediately transfer them to the ice water to cool completely. Peel the tomatoes, cut them in half lengthwise and put them in a large bowl.

Toss the tomatoes with the olive oil, thyme leaves and sugar and arrange them cut side up on a baking sheet lined with a nonstick liner. Tuck in the thyme branches, pour over any oil left in the bowl and season with kosher salt and pepper.

Roast for 5 to 6 hours, rotating the tray occasionally to ensure even cooking, until the tomatoes are dehydrated a bit—you don't want them completely dried. Allow to cool to room temperature on the baking sheet.

Store in an airtight container with all the oil from the pan. (Tomatoes keep for up to 1 week. The oil can be used to make a vinaigrette, if you so desire.)

Salsa Verde

I use this salsa verde for the slow-roasted shoulder of pork (see page 77), but it also works well with fish, meat and vegetable dishes. It's a good workhorse sauce—a great recipe to have in your back pocket.

Makes 2 cups (500 mL)

Leaves from 1 bunch Italian parsley
Leaves from 1 bunch fresh mint
Leaves from 1 bunch fresh basil
4 anchovy fillets
1 clove garlic
½ cup (125 mL) capers
½ cup (125 mL) cornichons
1 cup (250 mL) extra virgin olive oil
2 tbsp (30 mL) black pepper
2 tbsp (30 mL) red wine vinegar
1 tbsp (15 mL) Dijon mustard
1 tsp (5 mL) sea salt
1 tsp (5 mL) sugar

Finely chop the parsley, mint and basil and transfer to a bowl. Finely chop the anchovies, garlic, capers and cornichons; add to the herb mixture. Add the oil, pepper, vinegar, mustard, salt and sugar; mix well. Taste for seasoning and balance.

Mayonnaise

Mayo . . . plain and simple.

Makes just over 2 cups (500 mL)

3 egg yolks
1 tbsp (15 mL) Dijon mustard
2½ cups (625 mL) canola oil
1 tsp (5 mL) lemon juice
1 tsp (5 mL) white wine vinegar
Kosher salt and black pepper

Place the egg yolks and mustard in a food processor. With the motor running, very slowly drizzle in the oil. Continue to process until all the oil is used and the mixture is emulsified. If you feel the mayonnaise is getting too thick, add a splash of water to thin it. Add the lemon juice and the vinegar and season with salt and pepper.

NOTE:

If the mayonnaise looks like it is separating—you see little flecks in the mixture—it has "broken." But you don't have to start over. Break an egg yolk into a clean stainless steel bowl. Whisk in the broken mayo drop by drop and continue whisking until you have a new emulsified mayonnaise.

Chicken Jus

I prefer the taste of chicken jus over other meat jus, but this here is really just a guide to basic sauce making. The key to a good sauce is in the feet of the animal: the feet contain lots of collagen that will naturally thicken the sauce, so you won't have to reduce it down as much. This gives you a cleaner flavour because the sauce will not be as cloying, and it will also give you a better yield in the end. The best feet to use are chicken, duck, pork or veal. The other key is starting off with a good stock and taking proper care of it. Skim, skim, skim ... It's really a labour of love, with a big payoff in the end.

Makes 4 cups (1 L)

10 lb (4.5 kg) chicken wings
¼ cup (60 mL) canola oil
4 cups (1 L) thinly sliced onions
2 cups (500 mL) diced carrots
2 cups (500 mL) diced celery
2 cups (500 mL) diced peeled
　celery root
2 cups (500 mL) thinly sliced leeks
⅓ cup (75 mL) tomato paste
¼ cup (60 mL) honey
¼ cup (60 mL) apple brandy
4 cups (1 L) red wine
1 cup (250 mL) Madeira
½ bunch fresh thyme
4 fresh bay leaves
2 tbsp (30 mL) black peppercorns
5 lb (2.25 kg) chicken feet

Preheat the oven to 350°F (180°C).

Spread the wings in a single layer on a baking sheet and roast until golden brown, about 1½ hours, flipping them over from time to time to ensure browning on both sides. Drain the wings on paper towels, reserving the fat for another use.

Meanwhile, heat a stockpot over medium-high heat and add the oil. When the oil is smoking, add the onions, carrots, celery, celery root and leeks; sauté until nicely caramelized all over. Add the tomato paste and cook for 5 minutes, stirring constantly. Stir in the honey and allow this to caramelize slightly, another 5 minutes. Add the apple brandy and flame to burn off most of the alcohol. Add the wine and Madeira and cook until it reaches a syrupy consistency.

Add the thyme, bay leaves, peppercorns, chicken feet and chicken wings. Cover with cold water. Bring to a simmer, turn down the heat to medium-low and cook, uncovered and without stirring, for 6 hours, skimming off any impurities that come to the surface.

Strain through a fine-mesh sieve into a clean stockpot, discarding the solids. Simmer the stock until reduced to 4 cups (1 L), about 1½ hours, again skimming off any impurities that come to the surface.

Strain the jus into a clean container and chill over ice. (Jus keeps in the fridge for up to a week or in the freezer for up to 6 months.)

Basic Stock

I use both chicken and pork bones in my stock. The chicken gives me the flavour of a good roasted-chicken stock, and the pork trotters add texture and richness. This is a basic recipe, so feel free to sub out the chicken for duck, lamb or veal bones. You will just have to add 2 hours onto the cooking time for veal. If you aren't pork friendly, you could replace the trotters with chicken feet for similar results.

Makes 25 cups (6 L)

6 lb (2.7 kg) chicken bones
3 lb (1.35 kg) pig's trotters
2 onions, diced
2 carrots, peeled and diced
3 stalks celery, diced
½ celery root, peeled and diced
1 leek, diced
2 heads garlic, cut in half
  crosswise
20 black peppercorns
3 whole cloves
1 bunch fresh thyme
6 sprigs parsley
2 fresh bay leaves

Preheat the oven to 350°F (180°C).

Spread the chicken bones on a baking sheet and roast them until they are a deep golden brown, 1 to 1½ hours, turning them over from time to time to make sure they are evenly roasted.

Transfer the bones to a stockpot along with the trotters. Add enough cold water to cover the bones by a few inches. Bring to a simmer over medium heat and simmer for 15 minutes, skimming off any scum that rises to the surface.

In the meantime, place the baking sheet over high heat. Deglaze with 1 cup (250 mL) water, scraping up any caramelized bits with a wooden spoon. Add this liquid to the stockpot.

Once the stock has simmered for 15 minutes and no more impurities are rising to the surface, add the onions, carrots, celery, celery root, leek, garlic, peppercorns, cloves, thyme, parsley and bay leaves. Turn down the heat to low and very gently simmer for 6 hours, uncovered and without stirring. Allow to cool.

Strain the stock through a fine-mesh sieve into a clean stockpot. Bring to a simmer and slowly reduce the stock by one-third.

Strain again into a clean container and cool completely. (Stock keeps in the fridge for up to 1 week or in the freezer for up to 6 months.)

Bacon BY PHILL VIENS

Bacon is definitely a funadmental where I come from. Like Phill's pancetta (see page 110), this recipe is easy and delicious. Using a dry cure and smoking gives this bacon a rich, intense flavour, and the slices don't shrink by half when you cook them like supermarket bacon does.

Makes about 2lb (900 g)

25 g kosher salt
25 g brown sugar
10 g red chili flakes
3 g nitrite cure mix such as
   Insta Cure #1 or DQ curing salt
   #1 (optional)
20 black peppercorns, cracked
1 skinless, boneless pork belly
   (2 lb/900 g)

Thoroughly combine the salt, sugar, chili flakes, cure mix (if using) and peppercorns. Working over a nonreactive container large enough to hold the pork belly snugly (and preferably with a lid), rub the cure all over the belly. Attach the lid or cover with plastic wrap. Refrigerate for 2 days.

After the 2 days, check to make sure that the cure is melting away and the belly is giving off liquid. Redistribute the cure all over the belly, flip it over, cover and refrigerate for another 2 days. Repeat this process every 2 days for a total of 8 days. The belly should be firm all over, just a little giving to the touch, and it shouldn't bounce back when pressed the way raw meat does. If you don't think it's ready, give it another couple of days.

Rinse the belly well and pat dry with a clean kitchen towel. Set it on a wire rack set over a baking sheet and refrigerate, uncovered, overnight. This will dry the surface of the bacon to form what is called a pellicle. The surface of the belly should feel slightly tacky. This ensures a good bond with the smoke.

Prepare a smoker. Heat 4 cups (1 L) apple, oak or beech wood chips in the heating pan until they start to smoke. Place the belly on the upper smoking rack and hot-smoke it at 180 to 200°F (82 to 100°C) until the internal temperature is 155°F (68°C). (Alternatively, smoke the bacon in a BBQ or bake it in a 200°F/100°C oven, on a wire rack set over a baking sheet, again until it reaches an internal temperature of 155°F/68°C.) Let the bacon cool a bit, then peel off the skin with a sharp knife.

This bacon won't last more than 1 month. If you don't think you'll get through it in that time, cut it in half and wrap one half well in plastic wrap or freezer paper and freeze for up to 6 months. Once you pull a frozen piece out, you'll need to use it up, as it cannot be refrozen.

UNSMOKED BACON

You don't really need to smoke bacon to have nice cured, cooked pork belly to fry up. Simply skip the smoking if you don't like the delicious, sweet smoky flavour of traditional bacon, aren't allowed to play with matches or have poor culinary judgment. Obviously never smoke anything indoors and always follow the safety instructions that come with your equipment.

Basic Pasta Dough

This is your workhorse dough for making hand-cut noodles and stuffed pastas. You could certainly flavour this dough with herbs, if you wish (see wild garlic pasta, page 39).

Makes 2 lb (900 g)

4 cups (1 L) all-purpose flour
4 large eggs

Mound the flour on a work surface and make a well in the centre. Crack the eggs into the well, add oil if the recipe calls for it, and beat together with a fork. Stirring with the fork, start incorporating the flour from the sides. Keep pushing the outside edge of the flour to maintain the well shape (don't worry if it looks messy).

When about half of the flour is incorporated, the dough will start to come together. Start kneading with your hands to incorporate the rest of the flour. As soon as the dough comes together in a cohesive mass, scrape up and discard any leftover flour and any dried pieces of dough left on the counter.

Lightly flour the counter and knead the dough for about 10 minutes, dusting the counter lightly with flour if the dough sticks. The dough should be smooth and soft and just a touch tacky, but it should no longer be sticking to your hands or the counter. Wrap it in plastic wrap and refrigerate for 1 hour before rolling.

XO Sauce BY BEICHUAN

Beichuan is one of our cooks at Maison Publique. He made this sauce to use up some scallops and served it with simple steamed greens. Everyone who tasted it lost their mind. David (Beichuan's round-eye name) cooks some of the best Chinese food I have ever eaten.

Makes about 6 cups (1.5 L)

12 big scallops
1 cup (250 mL) salt
6 cups (1.5 L) water
⅓ cup (75 mL) + 1 tbsp (15 mL) dry sherry
½ tsp (2 mL) brown sugar
3 oz (85 g) chunk of ham (no fat!)
4 cups (1 L) canola oil
1 cup (250 mL) chopped garlic
1 cup (250 mL) chopped shallots
½ cup (125 mL) seeded and chopped red chilies

Pat the scallops dry and toss with the salt. Refrigerate overnight.

Rinse the scallops and pat dry. Prepare a smoker. Heat 4 cups (1 L) of maple wood chips in the heating pan until they start to smoke. Place large bowls or trays full of ice on the lower smoking rack. Place the scallops on the upper rack. Cold-smoke the scallops for 20 minutes, replenishing the ice halfway if necessary.

Place the scallops on a wire rack set over a plate and allow to dry in a cool, dark place for 2 to 3 weeks.

Combine the water, ⅓ cup (75 mL) sherry and the brown sugar in a bowl. Add the dried scallops and refrigerate for 12 hours.

Drain the scallops, squeeze out any excess liquid and place them in a bowl. Place the bowl in a steamer over boiling water; cover and steam for 15 minutes. Remove the scallops from the bowl, reserving the liquid, and shred the scallops while they are still warm.

Place the ham in a bowl in the steamer over boiling water. Steam, covered, for 15 minutes. Reserve the liquid in the bowl and finely chop the ham.

In a deep, heavy pot, heat the oil to 300°F (150°C). Add the chopped garlic and fry until crispy; remove and drain on paper towels. Working with one ingredient at a time, repeat with the chopped shallots, chopped chilies, chopped ham and shredded scallops.

Turn off the heat. Return all the fried ingredients to the oil along with the reserved scallop and ham liquids and 1 tbsp (15 mL) sherry. Allow to sit at room temperature for 24 hours. (Sauce keeps, refrigerated, for up 1 month.)

ACKNOWLEDGEMENTS FROM DEREK

I would like to thank . . .

My parents, Dwight and Donna, and my sister, Dara.

My main man, Felix, and his mom, Julia.

Nona and Grams, for giving me a love for food and always hosting the family meal.

My extended family, past and present.

Alex Cruz, my brother from another mother.

The Flying Panther Pack: Lee Cooper, Brock Bowes, Josh Clark, Nin Rai.

All my friends back on the island and in the Riv.

My Maison Publique family: Phill Viens, Felix-Leonard Gagne, JF, Harrison, North River David, Darcy, Kylie, Lliana,

J-Boogie Johnson, Lancia, Guillaume, Renée, Soula, Emilie, Jordan Wells.

Chris Johns, Farah Khan, Alison Slattery and HarperCollins.

Peter and Jo Zambri.

Jamie Oliver, Steve Pooley and the 15 team.

Chris Cosentino.

Peter Kiriakos.

Welcome Bienvenue (www.mynameiswelcome.com).

Frank and Steve at Organic Ocean.

Max Climan and the NDG Bruins.

Anthony "Brenda" Benda, Paolo Macchi and the Mojave Desert.

The Northern Chefs Alliance: Matt Jennings, Jamie Bissonnette, Rob Gentile, Jeremy Charles and Matty Matheson.

Melanie Kaye and Erik Doole.

Kim Yorio.

Anita Stewart.

Alicia Vocke.

Medium Rare Chef Apparel.

Richard Semmelhaack at Gereli Farm.

Michael Allemeier.

Cam Neely and the Boston Bruins.

Dave McMillan, Fred Morin and Marc-Olivier Frappier.

Nick Hodge and Nathalie Doucet.

Normand Laprise and Charles-Antoine Crete.

Restaurants and friends: L'Abattoir, Model Milk, Joe Beef/Liverpool House/Le Vin Papillon, Toqué!, Icehouse, Zambri's, Au Pied de Cochon, Gia Ba, Le St-Urbain, EVOO, Garde Manger, Société-Orignal, Le Bremner, Buca, Bar Isabel and Bar Raval, Macchi Inc, Parts and Labour, Canoe, Porzia, Beast, Mallard Cottage, Saint John Ale House, Townsman, Raymonds, Café Myriade, Lawrence, Blackstrap BBQ, Dinette Triple Crown, Ayden, CHARCUT, Waterfront Wines, Park, Hof Kelsten, Appetite for Books, Brasserie Kensington, Cockscomb, Toro, Dagwoods, La Belle Province, L'Emouleur, JAPADOG, 7-Eleven, Impasto and Uniburger.

And all of the farming families we have worked with along the way.

Hopefully, I didn't forget anyone.

ACKNOWLEDGEMENTS FROM CHRIS

Many thanks to . . .

My family, for always making the act of sharing meals such an important part of every day.

Jillian and Harper, for everything.

Rachelle Maynard, for her great eye.

Charlene Rooke, for the break that led to this book.

Derek, Farah and Alison, for being the best road-trip crew a writer could hope for.

David and Antonella, for taking care of business.

Everyone at HarperCollins who believed so strongly in this project and supported us throughout.

All the talented farmers, chefs, winemakers and restaurateurs whose hard work and

dedication made this book possible.

⚔

INDEX

A

Aïoli, 22, 243
Albacore Mojama, 206
Alberta, 100, 146
almond flour
  Sour Cherry Crumble, 171
  Streusel topping, 142
almonds
  Albacore Mojama, 206
  Caponata, 129
  Pangritata, 88
  Trout Amandine, 67
Almost-Raw and Cooked Lobster with Butter and
    Mayonnaise, 9
anchovies
  Bagna Cauda with Winter Vegetables, 127
  Bone Marrow and Anchovies, 153
  Garlic Mayonnaise, 190
  Green Sauce, 106
  Mayonnaise, 120
  Ravioli al Sole with the Best Parts of the Duck, 135–36
  Salsa Verde, 235
Angeline's Inn (Bloomfield, Ontario), 176
A-pear-itif, 162
apricots, 159
  Apricot Mustard, 144
  Flan "Cake Party," 132
  Summer Fruit Tart, 172–73
Arctic char
  Smoked Salmon, 208
asparagus
  Asparagus à la Berlinoise, 131
  Heidi's Spring Asparagus and Sorrel Soup, 169

Atlantica Restaurant (Portugal Cove, Newfoundland),
    4
avocados
  Guacamole, 217
Ayden Kitchen and Bar (Saskatoon), 146

B

bacon
  peameal, 100
  unsmoked, 239
  Bacon (Phill Viens), 239
  Clam Chowder, 14–15
  Pancakes and Bacon, 229
  Roast Grouse, 44–45
  Wedge Salad, 125
  See also pork
Bagna Cauda with Winter Vegetables, 127
Baked Oysters with Marmite, 189
balsam fir tips, dried
  Balsam Fir Salt, 95
  Fried Smoked Rabbit, 43
Bar Isabel (Toronto), 100, 206
barnacles, 179
Basic Pasta Dough, 244
Basic Stock, 238
basil, fresh
  Pistou (pesto), 128
  Raw Sockeye Salmon and Tomatoes, 198
  Tomato Salad, 150
Batali, Mario, 118
BBQ Glaze, 83
BBQ Lamb Shoulder, 83

beans: dried
  Soupe au Pistou, 128
beans: green and yellow wax
  Beer-Battered Beans, 123
  Soupe au Pistou, 128
  Sweet Pickles, 108
  Trout Amandine, 67
beans: haricots verts
  Trout Amandine, 67
Béarnaise, 131
Béchamel, 14, 24
beef
  Grilled Pepperoni and Sweet Pickles, 108
  Steak for Two, 149
  Summer Sausage and Green Sauce, 106
  Swordfish Bresaola and Celery Root Salad, 19
  Taco Kit, 216–17
  Wild Boar and Rosemary Ragù, 41
beef liver
  Lovage Maccheroni alla Chitarra with Cured Goat Liver
    and Pangritata, 88–90
beef tongue
  Moose Tongue Smoked Meat, 55
Beer-Battered Beans, 123
beets
  Bagna Cauda with Winter Vegetables, 127
Beichuan, 245
Belcham, Robert, 100
berries. See fruit and berries
beverages
  A-pear-itif, 162
  Elderflower Cordial, 162
Bil, John, 176
biscuits and cookies
  Oyster Crackers, 15
  Sablé Breton, 172
  Whippets, 155
Black Pepper Gravy, 224
Blonde Beer Batter, 123
Blood Cake, 226
blossom garnishes (chive, lavender, hyssop)
  BBQ Lamb Shoulder, 83
  Devilled Spot Prawns, 200
  Grapes and Tarragon, 165
  Heidi's Spring Asparagus and Sorrel Soup, 169
blueberries
  Pancakes and Bacon, 229

Pickled Blueberries, 95
  Smoked Caribou Carpaccio, 95
  Summer Fruit Tart, 172–73
blue cheese
  Bleu d'Élizabeth Dressing, 125
  Tomato Salad, 150
Bone Marrow and Anchovies, 153
"Boquerónes" and "Anchovies" on Toast, 18
Boudin Blanc with Sauerkraut and Ham Hock, 80–81
Bouillabaisse, 28–29
Braised Hare, 49
Brandade, 24
Bread and Butter Pickles, 230
breads, yeast
  Red Fife Brioche, 145
  Schiacciata, 164
  See also toasts
breads and biscuits, quick
  Brown Scones, 203
  Oyster Crackers, 15
Bread Sauce, 45
Breakfast of Champions, 226–29
Brined Pork, 86
Brioche, Red Fife, 145
Brioche Croutons, 125
British Columbia
  freshwater fishing, 62
  Okanagan Valley, 157–60
  Pacific fish and seafood, 179, 183–210
Brown Butter, 242
Brown Scones, 203
Buttercream, Italian, 172
butter(s)
  artisanal varieties, 90
  to clarify, 191
  Brown Butter, 242
  Maître d'hôtel Butter, 149
  Seaweed Butter, 196
  Smoked Butter, 242
  Smoked Ham Beurre Blanc, 209

C

cabbage
  Boudin Blanc with Sauerkraut and Ham Hock, 80–81
  Coleslaw, 224
  Sauerkraut, 80

Campagnolo (Vancouver), 100
Canadian produce, ingredients and cuisine
    from the Atlantic region, 1–29
    charcuterie, 100, 103
    farmers and farming, 74, 115–18
    field crops, 74–75
    from forests, 35–71
    foraged foods, 36, 43, 50–51, 92
    freshwater fish, 62
    orchards and vineyards, 157–73
    Pacific fish and seafood, 179, 183–210
    plateau de fruits de mer, 176–79
    from the prairies, 146
    from the tundra, 92–99
    using the whole animal, 103, 117–18, 135–36
    wild game, 35–36, 49
Canadian specialty producers
    Élevages Périgord, 138
    Gaspésie Sauvage, 50
    Gereli Farm, 103, 115
    Hinterland Wine Company, 176
    Jardins Bio-Santé, 74, 123
    JoieFarm, 157, 159, 165
    Organic Ocean, 185, 198, 207
    Out Landish Shellfish Guild, 189, 203
    Rougié, 138
    Société-Orignal, 7, 36, 92, 118, 133
capelin, 7
    "Boquerónes" and "Anchovies" on Toast, 18
capers
    Beer-Battered Beans, 123
    Bone Marrow and Anchovies, 153
    Caponata, 129
    Devilled Spot Prawns, 200
    Green Sauce, 106
    Salsa Verde, 235
    Sweet and Sour Sweetbreads, 79
    Tartar Sauce, 91
    Tuna Mayonnaise, 86
Caponata, 129
Caramelized Garlic, 129
caribou, 4, 49, 92
    Smoked Caribou Carpaccio, 95
carrageen. See seaweed
carrots
    Bagna Cauda with Winter Vegetables, 127

cauliflower
    Bagna Cauda with Winter Vegetables, 127
    Curry Fries, 227
    Sweet Pickles, 108
caviar, Acadian, 3, 179
Celery Root Salad, 19
Chanterelle Pasties, 151
charcuterie, 100, 103
    nitrites for, 111
    Albacore Mojama, 206
    Duck and Foie Gras Salami, 112
    Head Cheese Torchon, 109
    Jambon Blanc, 113
    Lardo and Strawberries, 105
    Pancetta (Phill Viens), 110–11
    Seal Mortadella, 96
    Summer Sausage and Green Sauce, 106
Charcut Roast House (Calgary), 100, 146
Charles, Jeremy, 4
Charmoula, 85
Charred Onion Petals, 243
cheeses
– artisanal cheddar
    to smoke, 137
    Lake Fish Quenelles, 69–70
    Mornay Sauce, 121
    Salt Cod Gratin, 24–25
    Smoked Leek Crumble, 137
    Swiss Chard Gratin, 121
    Taco Kit, 216–17
    Welsh Rarebit, 226–27
– blue
    Bleu d'Élizabeth Dressing, 125
    Tomato Salad, 150
– fromage blanc
    Grapes and Tarragon, 165
– mascarpone
    Mascarpone Cheese, 241
– Parmesan
    Dungeness Crab Tart, 193
    Pistou (pesto), 128
cheddar cheese
    to smoke, 137
    Lake Fish Quenelles, 69–70
    Mornay Sauce, 121
    Salt Cod Gratin, 24–25

G

game and hunting, 3–4, 35–36, 44, 46, 49
Gameren, Grant van, 100, 206
garlic
    Aïoli, 22, 243
    Brown Butter, 242
    Caramelized Garlic, 129
    Garlic Mayonnaise, 190
    Pistou (pesto), 128
    XO Sauce by Beichuan, 245
garlic, wild. *See* wild garlic
geoducks, 176
Goat Liver, Cured, 88
Gonzales, Cyril, 7, 118
grains
    Fried Fermented Walleye, 65
    Rice Dredge, 79
    Rye Berries with Red Wine, 48
grapes
    Concord Grape Jelly, 44–45
    Dehydrated Grapes, 165
    Grapes and Tarragon, 165
    Roasted Grapes, 165
    Schiacciata, 164
Greenling with Seaweed Butter, 196
Green Sauce, 106
Grilled Pepperoni and Sweet Pickles, 108
Grouse, Roast, 44–45
Guacamole, 217

H

halibut, 207
    Bouillabaisse, 28–29
    Fish and Chips, 218–19
    Halibut with Sauce Messine, 207
ham
    Asparagus à la Berlinoise, 131
    Boudin Blanc with Sauerkraut and Ham Hock, 80–81
    Ham Hocks, 80
    Humboldt Squid and Smoked Ham Beurre Blanc, 209
    Jambon Blanc, 113
    Smoked Ham Beurre Blanc, 209
    Swiss Chard Gratin, 121
    Wild Pheasant with Immature Juniper, Speck and Pine
        Mushrooms, 46

    XO Sauce by Beichuan, 245
    See also pork
Hardie, Norman, 176, 179
Hare Ravioli, 49
Head Cheese Torchon, 109
heart, moose, 55
Heidi's Spring Asparagus and Sorrel Soup, 169
Herb Rub, 110
Hollandaise, 131
honey
    artisanal varieties, 36, 59
    Honey Marshmallows, 59
Humboldt Squid and Smoked Ham Beurre Blanc, 209

I

Italian Buttercream, 172–73

J

Jackson, John, 100, 146
Jambon Blanc, 113
Jamones de Juviles (Spain), 100
Johansen, Steve, 183, 185–86, 200, 206, 207
juniper berries
    Juniper Salt, 46
    Pancetta (Phill Viens), 110–11
    Pickled Blueberries, 95
    Smoked Caribou Carpaccio, 95
    Wild Pheasant with Immature Juniper, Speck and Pine
        Mushrooms, 46

K

Keitsch, Frank, 183, 185–86, 200, 206, 207
kelp (bull kelp). *See* seaweed
Ketchup, 120
Khan, Farah, xiii
kombu. *See* seaweed

L

Labrador tea, 92
    Pickled Blueberries, 95
    Smoked Caribou Carpaccio, 95
Lake Fish Quenelles, 69–70

lamb
    lamb farming, 115, 117
    BBQ Lamb Shoulder, 83
    Devilled Venison Pluck, 53
    Well-Done Lamb Chops with Charmoula, 85
    Wild Boar and Rosemary Ragù, 41
lamb bones
    Basic Stock, 238
    Soupe au Pistou, 128
lamb brains
    Lamb Brain Profiteroles with Tartar Sauce, 91
lamb liver
    Lovage Maccheroni alla Chitarra with Cured Goat Liver
      and Pangritata, 88–90
Lardo and Strawberries, 105
Leboe, Justin, 146
Lee, Stephen, 7
leeks
    Bouillabaisse, 28–29
    Smoked Leek Crumble, 137
lemons
    Fish and Chips, 218–19
    Lemon Jam, 206
    Lemon Oil, 240
    Lemon Vinaigrette, 240
lentils du Puy
    Rye Berries with Red Wine, 48
Lepage, Ségué, 100
lettuce
    Taco Kit, 217
    Wedge Salad, 125
limes and lime juice
    A-pear-itif, 162
    Guacamole, 217
    Salt and Pepper Squid, 8
ling cod
    Fish and Chips, 218–19
    Greenling with Seaweed Butter, 196
lobster, 176, 179
    to cook, 9
    Almost-Raw and Cooked Lobster with Butter and
      Mayonnaise, 9
    Crab and Carrageen Mousse, 194
    Devilled Spot Prawns, 200
Lovage Maccheroni alla Chitarra with Cured Goat Liver and
    Pangritata, 88–90

M

Maître d'hôtel butter, 149
Mallard Cottage (St. John's), 3
maple syrup, 36, 118, 133
    Apple Vinegar, 163
    BBQ Glaze, 83
    Foie Gras and Maple Syrup, 142–43
    Maple Mustard, 55
    Pancakes and Bacon, 229
    Salmon Candy, 197
Marinated Foie Gras, 145
Marmite Mayonnaise, 189
Marshmallow, 155
Marshmallows, Honey, 59
Mascarpone Cheese, 241
Mashed Potatoes, 203
Mayonnaise, 120, 236
    to rescue, 236
    Garlic Mayonnaise, 190
    Marmite Mayonnaise, 189
McKay, Dale, 146
Model Milk (Calgary), 146
Moose Tongue Smoked Meat, 55
Mortadella, Seal, 96
Mortadella-Stuffed Squid, 20
mushrooms
    chanterelles, 4, 151
    to clean and tear, 51
    morels, 36, 160, 169
    pine mushrooms, 36, 46
    porcini, 36
    wild varieties, 4, 36, 50–51
    Chanterelle Pasties, 151
    Duxelles, 189
    Fish Fumet, 11
    Mushroom Pappardelle, 50–51
    Mushroom Ragù, 50–51
    Steak Rub, 149
    Wild Pheasant with Immature Juniper, Speck and Pine
      Mushrooms, 46
mussels, 179
    Bouillabaisse, 28–29
    Mussels with Peas and Brown Scones, 203
    Whelks in Escabèche, 16

R

rabbit
  to prepare and smoke, 43
  Braised Hare, 49
  Fried Smoked Rabbit, 43
  Hare Ravioli, 49
radishes
  Watercress, Radishes and Pickerel Bottarga, 71
Ragù, Mushroom, 50–51
Ragù, Wild Boar and Rosemary, 41
raisins
  Caponata, 129
  Salt Cod Gratin, 24–25
Ravioli, Hare, 49
Ravioli al Sole with the Best Parts of the Duck, 135–36
Raw Sockeye Salmon and Tomatoes, 198
Raymonds Restaurant (St. John's), 4
Red Beer Batter, 123
Red Fife Brioche, 145
Remonte-Pente maple syrup, 118, 133
Reynolds, Elliot, 176
Rice Dredge, 79
Roasted and Fried Potatoes, 23
Roasted Grapes, 165
Roast Grouse, 44–45
root cellars, 3
Roots, Rants and Roars Festival (Elliston, Newfoundland),
  1, 3, 24
Rouille, 28–29
Rye Berries with Red Wine, 48

S

Sablé Breton, 172
salad dressings. *See* vinaigrettes and salad dressings
salads
  Caponata, 129
  Celery Root Salad, 19
  Coleslaw, 224
  Parsley Salad garnish, 153
  Tomato Salad, 150
  Wedge Salad, 125
  See also vegetable dishes
salami, 103
  Duck and Foie Gras Salami, 112
  Phoque Jésus, 99

salmon
  varieties, 197, 198
  Devilled Spot Prawns, 200
  Heidi's Spring Asparagus and Sorrel Soup, 169
  Raw Sockeye Salmon and Tomatoes, 198
  Salmon Candy, 197
  Smoked Salmon, 208
Salsa Verde, 216, 235
Salt and Pepper Squid, 8
Salt Cod Gratin, 24–25
Sardines, Pickled, and 'Nduja, 205
sauces, savoury
  Aïoli, 22, 243
  Apricot Mustard, 144
  Béarnaise, 131
  Béchamel, 14, 24
  Black Pepper Gravy, 224
  Bread Sauce, 45
  Chicken Jus, 237
  Duck Jus, 135
  Green Sauce, 106
  Hollandaise, 131
  Ketchup, 120
  Mayonnaise, 236
  Mornay Sauce, 121
  Pistou (pesto), 128
  Salsa Verde, 235
  Sauce Messine, 207
  Sauce Paloise, 131
  Sweet and Sour Sauce, 79
  Tartar Sauce, 91
  Wild Garlic Purée, 40
  XO Sauce by Beichuan, 245
  See also mayonnaise; vinaigrettes and salad dressings
Sauerkraut, 80
sausages
  Boudin Blanc with Sauerkraut and Ham Hock, 80–81
  Duck and Foie Gras Salami, 112
  Grilled Pepperoni and Sweet Pickles, 108
  Phoque Jésus, 99
  Pork and Clams, 22–23
  Sausage and Peppers, 222
  Seal Mortadella, 96
  Summer Sausage and Green Sauce, 106
scallops, 179
  XO Sauce by Beichuan, 245

Schiacciata, 164

Scones, Brown, 203

sea bass

    Bouillabaisse, 28–29

seafood. *See* fish and seafood

seal, 92

    Phoque Jésus, 99

    Seal Mortadella, 96

sea urchins, 176

    sea urchin bottarga, 7

seaweed (carrageen, kelp, kombu, sea lettuce)

    Baked Oysters with Marmite, 189

    Crab and Carrageen Mousse, 194

    Greenling with Seaweed Butter, 196

Semmelhaack, Richard, 103, 115, 117–18, 133, 154

Shore Crab Bisque, 195

Slow-Roasted Shoulder of Pig, 77

smelts

    "Boquerónes" and "Anchovies" on Toast, 18

Smoked Butter, 242

Smoked Caribou Carpaccio, 95

Smoked Cheddar, 137

Smoked Ham Beurre Blanc, 209

Smoked Leek Crumble, 137

Smoked Oysters, Pop's, 210

Smoked Pork Fat Condiment, 154

Smoked Salmon, 208

snapper

    Bouillabaisse, 28–29

Snow Crab Toast, 13

Sofrito, 222

sorrel

    Heidi's Spring Asparagus and Sorrel Soup, 169

Soupe au Pistou, 128

soups and chowders

    Clam Chowder, 14–15

    Heidi's Spring Asparagus and Sorrel Soup, 169

    Shore Crab Bisque, 195

    Soupe au Pistou, 128

Sour Cherry Crumble, 171

Spain and Spanish cuisine, 16, 18, 100, 206

speck. *See* ham

spice and herb mixtures

    Charmoula, 85

    Devil Spice Paste, 53

    Devil Spice Rub, 53

    Four-Spice Blend, 170

    Herb Rub, 110

    Pain d'épices, 142

    Quatre Épices, 80

    Steak Rub, 149

    Taco Seasoning, 216

Spicy Pickles, 230

Spot Prawn Festival, 185

spot prawns, 179, 183, 185–86

    Crab and Carrageen Mousse, 194

    Devilled Spot Prawns, 200

    Spot Prawn Garum, 200

squab

    Roast Grouse, 44–45

squid

    to clean, 20

    to cook, 209

    Humboldt Squid and Smoked Ham Beurre Blanc, 209

    Mortadella-Stuffed Squid, 20

    Salt and Pepper Squid, 8

Steak for Two, 149

Steak Rub, 149

stocks, jus and fumet

    feet and bones for, 237, 238

    ham stock, 80

    Basic Stock, 238

    Court Bouillon, 64

    Duck Jus, 135

    Fish Fumet, 11

    Grouse Jus, 44

    Pike Fumet, 69

strawberries

    Lardo and Strawberries, 105

Streusel, 142

Sucre à la Crème Pot de Crème, 56

Summer Fruit Tart, 172–73

Summerland Research Station (BC), 159

Summer Sausage and Green Sauce, 106

Sweet and Sour Sauce, 79

sweetbreads

    Devilled Venison Pluck, 53

    Sweet-and-Sour Sweetbreads, 79

Sweet Pickles, 108

Swiss chard

    Bagna Cauda with Winter Vegetables, 127

    Swiss Chard Gratin, 121

Swordfish Bresaola and Celery Root Salad, 19

T

Taco Kit, 216–17

tarragon, fresh
Béarnaise, 131
Cod à la Nage, 11
Grapes and Tarragon, 165
Hollandaise, 131
Shore Crab Bisque, 195

Tartar Sauce, 91

Tkaczuk, Michael, 100

toasts
"Boquerónes" and "Anchovies" on Toast, 18
Pickled Sardines and 'Nduja, 205
Snow Crab Toast, 13
Welsh Rarebit, 226–27
See also breads, yeast

tomatillos
Salsa Verde, 216

tomatoes
Bouillabaisse, 28–29
Caponata, 129
Curry Fries, 227
Devilled Spot Prawns, 200
Ketchup, 120
Mortadella-Stuffed Squid, 20
Oven-Dried Tomatoes, 234
Pico de Gallo, 216
Pork and Clams, 22–23
Raw Sockeye Salmon and Tomatoes, 198
Shore Crab Bisque, 195
Sofrito, 222
Soupe au Pistou, 128
Tomato Salad, 150
Tomato Water and Tomato Vinaigrette, 198
Wedge Salad, 125

tongue
Blood Cake, 226
Moose Tongue Smoked Meat, 55

tortillas
Taco Kit, 216–17

Trigaux, Thierry, 36, 59

trout, 62
Smoked Salmon, 208
Trout Amandine, 67
Trout au Bleu, 64

truffles, black
Lake Fish Quenelles, 69–70
Smoked Pork Fat Condiment, 154
Truffle Purrée, 69

tuna
Albacore Mojama, 206
tuna hearts, 88
Pork and Tuna, 86
Tuna Mayonnaise, 86

V

veal bones
Basic Stock, 238
Bone Marrow and Anchovies, 153

veal liver
Lovage Maccheroni alla Chitarra with Cured Goat Liver and Pangritata, 88–90

veal sweetbreads
Sweet-and-Sour Sweetbreads, 79

veal tongue
Moose Tongue Smoked Meat, 55

vegetable dishes
Asparagus à la Berlinoise, 131
Bagna Cauda with Winter Vegetables, 127
Beer-Battered Beans, 123
Potato Croquettes, 120
Swiss Chard Gratin, 121
See also salads

venison
Devilled Venison Pluck, 53
Swordfish Bresaola and Celery Root Salad, 19
Wild Boar and Rosemary Ragù, 41

Viens, Phill, 103, 131
Asparagus à la Berlinoise, 131
Bacon, 239
Pancetta, 110–11

vinaigrettes and salad dressings
Apple Vinaigrette, 240
for Bagna Cauda, 127
Bleu d'Élizabeth Dressing, 125
Lemon Vinaigrette, 240
for Tomato Salad, 150

Vinegar, Apple, 163

W

walleye
    Fried Fermented Walleye, 65
    Lake Fish Quenelles, 69–70
watercress
    Roast Grouse, 45
    Watercress, Radishes and Pickerel Bottarga, 71
Wedge Salad, 125
Well-Done Lamb Chops with Charmoula, 85
Welsh Rarebit, 226–27
Whelks in Escabèche, 16
Whippets, 155
Wild Boar and Rosemary Ragù, 41
wild game. *See* game and hunting
wild garlic
    Mussels with Peas and Brown Scones, 203
    Wild Garlic Pasta, 39
    Wild Garlic Purée, 40
wild hare. *See under* rabbit
Wild Pheasant with Immature Juniper, Speck and Pine
        Mushrooms, 46
wild rice
    Fried Fermented Walleye, 65

X

XO Sauce by Beichuan, 245

Z

Zambri, Peter, and Zambri's restautant (Victoria), xiii, 20, 100
zucchini
    Soupe au Pistou, 128